THE TEMPLE SLEEP
OF THE RICH YOUNG RULER

THE TEMPLE SLEEP
OF THE RICH YOUNG RULER

How Lazarus Became the Evangelist John

EDWARD REAUGH SMITH

SteinerBooks

2011

STEINERBOOKS
Anthroposophic Press

610 Main Street
Great Barrington, Massachusetts 01230
www.steinerbooks.org

The quotation of Morton Smith's translation of the *Letter to Theodore* that appears on
pp. 11–15 is reprinted by permission of the publisher from *Clement of Alexandria and
a Secret Gospel of Mark* by Morton Smith, pp. 446-47, Cambridge, Mass.: Harvard
University Press, Copyright © 1973 the President and Fellows of Harvard College.

LIBRARY OF CONGRESS CATALOGING-IN-PUBLICATION DATA

Smith, Edward Reaugh, 1932-
 The temple sleep of the Rich Young Ruler : how Lazarus became the Evangelist
John / Edward Reaugh Smith.
     p. cm.
Includes bibliographical references and indexes.
ISBN 978-0-88010-732-7
1. John, the Apostle, Saint. 2. Lazarus, of Bethany, Saint. 3. Rich young man
(Biblical figure) 4. Secret Gospel according to Mark. 5. Anthroposophy. I. Title.
BS2455.S55 2011
229'.8–dc23
                                   2011030706

Contents

BOOK THREE

ACKNOWLEDGMENTS

Paul V. O'Leary
for priceless encouragement and advice

AND

Scott   G. Brown
for scholarly publications on Secret Mark

LIST OF ABBREVIATIONS

BAR	*Biblical Archaeology Review*
CMF	*Christianity as Mystical Fact* (by Rudolf Steiner)
CW	Collected Works (of Steiner)
GA	*Gesamtausgabe* (the collected works of Steiner in German)
JTS	Jewish Theological Seminary (in New York City)
MS, MSS	manuscript, manuscripts
NDE	near death experience
NHL	Nag Hammadi Library
RSAM	Relevant Substance of the Ancient Mysteries (contained in Book Three)
SBL	Society of Biblical Literature
UTS	Union Theological Seminary

Mar Saba Monastery

BOOK ONE

Introduction

It was the summer of 1958. After a month of cataloging manuscripts, Columbia University professor Morton Smith emerged from
the Mar Saba monastery in the Judean desert with photographs of a
manuscript describing what Smith named the Secret Gospel of Mark.
Written in an eighteenth-century style of Greek handwriting, the
manuscript purports to be a copy of an otherwise unattested letter
from the late second-century Clement of Alexandria (ca. 150–ca.
215) to one Theodore answering the latter's questions about a suspect
version of Mark's Gospel. Evidently some followers of the Alexandrian
heretic Carpocrates were using a different version of the Gospel of
Mark to justify their libertine doctrine, and Theodore had written
to Clement to find out whether Mark really wrote the stories that
these "Carpocratians" were quoting. Clement's reply, now commonly
termed the *Letter to Theodore*, explains that Mark indeed added
passages to his gospel when he came to Alexandria, in order to make it
more useful to Christians who were well advanced in knowledge, but
Carpocrates stole a copy of this gospel and falsified it with his own
blasphemous additions. To prove this point, Clement quotes verbatim
a passage that Theodore had asked about, showing him that it does
not contain the words "'naked (man) with naked (man)' and the other
things about which you wrote."

This passage turns out to be a very different version of the raising
of Lazarus, written in Mark's style and lacking all dialogue save the
sister's request for help. In this concise account, situated, says Clement, just before James and John's request for the positions of greatest
honor (after Mark 10:34), the dead brother is an unidentified rich

young man who responds to his raising by becoming a disciple; they retire to his house, and after six days the man wraps himself in a linen sheet and Jesus privately teaches him the mystery of the kingdom of God. A little bit later in the narrative, when Jesus comes to Jericho, he refuses to welcome the young man's sister, his mother, and Salome.

Like the earlier, more extensive discoveries in the 1940s of the Nag Hammadi codices and Dead Sea Scrolls, scholarly assessment of this letter has taken decades. Yet unlike those earlier discoveries, its appearance has not been widely hailed, and its authenticity as an ancient writing has been doubted by many.

Indeed two recent books have argued that the letter is a forgery by Smith himself. The first of these two, *The Gospel Hoax*, which appeared at the 2005 annual convention of the Society of Biblical Literature (SBL) in Philadelphia, garnered immediate acclaim and intensified the scholarly debate.[1] The second appeared in 2007 and based its challenge on different grounds from the first.[2]

That state of affairs constituted a unique opportunity for the present undertaking. Secret Mark, as Smith's find is sometimes called, is the key that opens the door to a new perspective on the rich young ruler who went away sorrowful when told by Jesus that if he would attain what he sought he must sell his possessions and give all to the poor (Mark 10:17–22; Matt 19:16–22; Luke 18:18–23). Until now, tradition has assumed that the youth, by going away sorrowful, failed in his personal quest for "eternal life." But given the verbal ties between this rich man and the man whom Jesus raises in the Secret Gospel, it may actually be the case that his story does not end here. This book proposes that this rich young man is none other than Lazarus from John's Gospel, and that Lazarus is both the anonymous "disciple whom Jesus loved" in John's Gospel and the author, later known as John and "the Elder," who wrote that gospel.

---

[1] Stephen C. Carlson, *The Gospel Hoax: Morton Smith's Invention of Secret Mark* (Waco, Tex.: Baylor University Press, 2005).

[2] Peter Jeffery, *The Secret Gospel of Mark Unveiled: Imagined Rituals of Sex, Death, and Madness in a Biblical Forgery* (New Haven: Yale University Press, 2007).

To make this case I turn in Book Two to three hitherto discrete domains of study and argue that they mutually corroborate each other and coalesce to support this thesis. The uniqueness of the opportunity has to do with the fact that the first and, to a lesser extent, the second of such domains are based not upon ancient texts or historical documents, which are the primary focus in biblical scholarship, but upon the intuitions of the late seer Rudolf Steiner (1861–1925).

The first domain, chapter one in Book Two, comprises the substantive content, the spiritual insight, that guided humanity in prehistorical times, which Steiner called the *ancient mysteries*. Since these guiding influences are primarily prehistorical and thus not subject to documentary research, their contents, as intuited by Steiner, cannot be verified through normal historical inquiry. We will consider, however, how existing Christian texts, both canonical and non-canonical, as in the case of the Nag Hammadi codices, can be seen to comport with significant elements of what Steiner intuited about these ancient mysteries.

The second domain, chapter two in Book Two, deals with John's Gospel with particular focus upon the nature of the raising of Lazarus. Steiner taught that this incident was a form of initiation into the ancient mysteries, a process which had become dangerous by the time of Christ, whereby the candidate for initiation actually died under the guidance of a hierophant (priest) for a period of three and a half days before the higher components of his being were brought back into his physical body. Jesus thus initiated Lazarus, as in the ancient mysteries, allowing him to experience the spiritual realms in a direct way, which gave Lazarus a more profound grasp of spiritual realities than was available to the twelve disciples. To someone unfamiliar with Steiner, this idea might seem far-fetched. Yet I imagine such a person might still be intrigued to learn that Steiner referred to this knowledge of the spiritual realms as the mystery (or mysteries) of the kingdom of heaven, and this mystery is precisely what Jesus is depicted teaching the young man (Lazarus) in the Secret Gospel of Mark. Despite the many differences between the accounts of this incident in Secret Mark and John 11, Smith's discovery corroborates Steiner's interpretation of this miracle and its connection to the mystery of the kingdom of God as well as Steiner's intuitions that Lazarus was the beloved disciple and that the special knowledge Lazarus attained through this initiation allowed him to become the author of this spiritual gospel.

The third domain, chapter three in Book Two, looks at the meaning of Mark's mysterious fleeing youth (Mark 14:51–52) and its relationship to Secret Mark and the raising of Lazarus.

Book Three comprises two major subjects relevant to Book Two. Consideration of them is deferred to avoid major disruption to the telling of the central story in Book Two.

The present undertaking attempts to bring together the work of researchers whose methods and worldviews are in a significant amount of tension. On the one hand we have academically trained biblical scholars, who try to think within the confines of the scientific worldview. On another hand we have those theologians who take revelation seriously. Then we have researchers who attempt to do both. These latter consist of both traditional religious scholars, who adhere to existing revelation, and less traditional religious researchers, who are also open to their own spiritual intuitions and insights.

These different approaches to investigation spawn disagreements about what constitutes a legitimate interpretation of an ancient text. Biblical scholars in general rely chiefly on the literary and historical contexts of the texts they are studying to help them determine what the texts are communicating—what is called exegesis. Scholars try to be objective in their exegeses by letting the texts, rather than any external authorities, speak for themselves. Once they determine what the texts mean, the scholars who are also believers accept that meaning as religious truth, or they at least try to work that meaning into their existing conception of religious truth. But the theological part of what they do is kept separate from the exegesis itself. The point of exegesis is evident in its etymology, "to lead out," and refers to systematic approaches to interpretation that are designed to allow texts to communicate on their own terms, that is, approaches that counter the natural tendency to read into a text what one thinks it should say. The religious and non-religious scholars share this premise, but many religious scholars believe that the texts themselves were inspired by God and that therefore their meaning, as determined objectively by exegesis, establishes truth. Researchers who are more open to their own spiritual intuitions, while not ignoring the literal level of meaning, may, however, feel less beholden to the strictures of exegesis and may privilege another more spiritual level of meaning.

Through much of its history the church accepted the legitimacy of a higher, allegorical level of meaning to scripture, which was not so deeply rooted in the literal meaning but was nevertheless considered to be real and legitimate. With the rise of secular exegesis during the Enlightenment, the allegorical approach to interpretation fell into disfavor, due to the impossibility of demonstrating that the authors intended these higher meanings and that any such meaning is objectively correct. These are legitimate concerns, but the problems that interpreters have defending allegorical readings do not actually establish that these readings are illegitimate. The authors of the New Testament themselves employed allegory, finding higher Christian meanings in, for example, the Old Testament stories of the patriarchs, meanings that are not always fully compatible with the stories' meaning on the literal level. Mark depicts Jesus himself teaching his disciples to interpret his own words and actions this way (4:10–20), and the *Letter to Theodore* describes Mark's Secret Gospel as a "mystic" and "more spiritual gospel," meaning a gospel that was supposed to be read allegorically. Clement believed that Jesus taught the truer allegorical meanings of all scriptures to the apostles, who passed them on to their own disciples as secret oral traditions. Gnostics claimed to have learned these oral traditions from their own teachers, and actively contributed their own insights to the chain of transmission. The orthodox were no less willing to learn and elaborate allegorical interpretations, but subjected them to a standard of correctness known as the canon of the church. The allegorical approach to scripture is therefore at least as old as the New Testament itself; arguably, one cannot do full justice to the message of the Bible without reading it allegorically. But if that is the case, then one must also be open to the possibility that some allegorical interpreters, whether Steiner, the gnostics, or the church fathers, were capable of intuiting this higher meaning.

While scholars rely chiefly on the literary and historical context of the texts they are studying to help them determine what the texts are communicating, theologians also rely on doctrine and revelation, usually as a check on the meaning (they don't let exegesis produce meanings that are contradicted by dogma). My approach is similar to what theologians do, but also appeals to an external authority to justify allegorical meanings that cannot be grounded in conventional exegesis. This external source is the intuitions of Steiner. But it was only where Steiner's teachings gave meaning to the canon itself, deeper meaning in my perception, that they have become the basis for the generally unique interpretations in this book. The possibility of new meaning to many of the old passages should be obvious to the reader.

Scholarship means different things to different people. Steiner's works, which are vast, are available as texts. Their comprehension requires extensive study. One can thus be a scholar of Steiner's works. My own profession was in the practice of law. But, retired from that, for the last twenty-three years I have been a scholar of, and writer on, Steiner's works. Although Steiner often wrote about biblical meaning, his interpretations have not been the subject of academic biblical scholarship, the domain of the scholars described above, probably because his interpretations are based largely upon his own intuitions. From the perspective of academic biblical scholarship, his works fall within the category of theology.

The Beginning

Few writings have impressed me more than Teilhard de Chardin's *The Phenomenon of Man*: "In the world, nothing could ever burst forth as final across the different thresholds successively traversed by evolution ... which has not already existed in an obscure and primordial way.... Nothing is so delicate and fugitive by its very nature as a beginning.... What, then, will be the effect of time on this area of weakness? Inevitably to destroy all vestiges of it. Beginnings have an irritating but essential fragility...."[3] For all who are attracted to the

---

[3] Pierre Teilhard de Chardin, *The Phenomenon of Man* (2d ed.; New York: Harper Colophon, 1975), 71, 120–1.

idea that all things come into being for a purpose, the ability of the spiritual eye of Steiner to see back to beginnings, to the genesis of things, and to project those beginnings into their far distant fulfillment is perhaps his most unique gift to humanity.

As I approach this book's Lazarus motif and its connection to Morton Smith's 1958 discovery of the *Letter to Theodore* and the so-called Secret Gospel of Mark that it contained, I look back to where my own interest in this subject matter had its genesis.

A significant portion of the *Letter to Theodore* was copied in the notorious and errant *Holy Blood, Holy Grail* by Michael Baigent et al., which was first published in 1982.[4] The letter's deep significance escaped me when I read that book in the mid-1980s. A few years later, in 1988, when I was fifty-six years of age, with a history of study and teaching of scripture, the works of Steiner first came to my attention. It was at a time in my life when I was able to devote almost full time to the intensive study of his works. At a point in 1994 when I had completed the intensive study of well over one hundred titles of Steiner's work in English translation, I began to work on the manuscript for *The Burning Bush*.[5] Toward the end of that reading period I read Andrew J. Welburn's *The Beginnings of Christianity*.[6] That is where, toward the end of my six-year study period before beginning the manuscript, I first came across a reference to Secret Mark at a time when I could appreciate its immense significance.

Then at a point when I was well along with the manuscript I had the timely good fortune to meet René Querido. When I told him of my project and that I was working at the time on the account of the raising of Lazarus, he told me of the relevant studies of Karl König, a Steiner devotee. Eventually I was able to secure, through the graces of the trustees of the König archives near Aberdeen, Scotland (in Newton Dee, Aberdeenshire), a typescript copy of König's essay

---

[4] Michael Baigent, Richard Leigh, and Henry Lincoln, *Holy Blood, Holy Grail* (New York: Dell Publishing, 1982), 316–59, esp. 318–22, 335–36, 339–40.
[5] Edward Reaugh Smith, *The Burning Bush* (vol. 1 of *Rudolf Steiner, Anthroposophy, and the Holy Scriptures*; rev. ed.; Great Barrington, Mass.: Anthroposophic Press, 2001).
[6] Andrew J. Welburn, *The Beginnings of Christianity: Essene Mystery, Gnostic Revelation and the Christian Vision* (Edinburgh: Floris Books, 1991).

"The Two Disciples John," based on a study written Easter 1962. On May 15, 2001, I received from Christof-Andreas Lindenberg, one of the trustees, a copy of the new book entitled *The Mystery of John and the Cycle of the Year*, published in Scotland the previous year.[7] When I thanked him for the book, he said that my instigations were a significant inducement to their preparation of the manuscript for publication. The core of the book comprises twelve lectures all delivered in the season of St. John's Day (summer solstice) interspersed through the years from 1941 to 1965 plus the essay "The Two Disciples John." This essay is the subsequently edited typescript I had received in 1995, but lectures four and five (which were not available to me when I wrote *The Burning Bush*), delivered June 30 and July 2, 1961, respectively, on the three Johns are also closely related to the subject matter of the essay.

While the *Letter to Theodore* that embodied Secret Mark was discovered by Smith in 1958, its disclosure was limited to a closed circle of scholars until Smith published it in 1973.[8] There is no indication that König was aware of it at the time of either his lectures in 1961 or his essay in 1962. It is hard to imagine that he would have omitted mentioning such a relevant discovery had he known of its existence. Yet it was in that essay that he posited that the rich young ruler in the tenth chapter of Mark was Lazarus. Secret Mark supports this identification in the way that it borrows elements from the story of the rich man's question in its account of Jesus' raising of the young man (= Lazarus): in both places the men are unnamed; they are described

---

[7] Karl König, *The Mystery of John and the Cycle of the Year* (n.p.: Camphill Books, 2000). On the publication page the British Library CIP Data states, "A catalogue record of this book is available from the British Library" (ISBN 1 89789 16 2), the copyright being in the name of the Trustees of the Karl König Archive.

[8] Smith names them and tells of sharing with them in *The Secret Gospel: The Discovery and Interpretation of the Secret Gospel according to Mark* (New York: Harper & Row, 1973; repr., Clearlake, Calif.: Dawn Horse, 1982), ch. 4. Based upon the dialogue between Smith and these scholars, he disclosed his discovery, late in 1960, to the program committee of the SBL, which devoted an evening session in the 1960 fall convention to Smith's report on the text and another report on it by Professor Pierson Parker of the General Theological Seminary (see *Secret Gospel*, 30). On December 30 and 31, 1960, the New York Times reported on Smith's presentation at the 1960 SBL meeting.

as rich in sentences that share the same structure ("for he had many possessions"; "for he was rich"); and the phrase "looking upon him loved him" occurs. In the story of the rich man's question, it is Jesus who looks upon the rich man and loves him (Mark 10:21). In the raising narrative, it is the young man who looks upon Jesus and loves him. Is he now returning Jesus' love, in gratitude for being rescued from the grave? The clearest hint that the young man Jesus raised is the same rich man occurs in Secret Mark, where the young man is described as "the young man whom Jesus loved" (*Letter to Theodore* III.15). What young man did Jesus love? A reader who looks back through Mark's narrative will find only the rich man of Mark 10. Hence Secret Mark strongly hints that Lazarus is the rich man of Mark 10, just as König concluded in developing Steiner's identification of Lazarus as "the disciple whom Jesus loved," an identification also supported by the Secret Gospel, which applies this phrasing to "the young man whom Jesus loved."

König's reasons for identifying the rich man with Lazarus, the author of the John Gospel at the time when he had become known as Elder John in Ephesus, have to do with the role that Lazarus needed to fill—the "John role" of being an announcing messenger of the Lord.[9] Luke's Gospel had stressed the significance of that name for John the Baptist at his birth. As König pointed out in his lecture five, this role was related to the announcing of Egohood, that is, the *I Am*, a characterization that will be explained later. After the death of John the Baptist one might expect this role to be taken over by one of the three closest disciples: Peter, James, and John. Yet such a role requires a person of superior spiritual comprehension, and König noted three failings, reproved by Jesus, that included the Zebedee brothers; namely, they disputed about who was the greatest among them (Mark 9:34–35); they forbade others to cast out demons in Jesus' name, contrary to Jesus' wishes (9:38–40); and they improperly requested to sit at Jesus' right hand and his left in his glory (10:35–45). Peter is party to their folly in 9:34–35 and 10:41, where the self-preoccupation of the twelve as a whole is underscored (Peter's most complete

---

[9] König, *Mystery of John*, 138–40.

disqualification occurs later when he thrice denies Christ). At this point in Mark 10, therefore, the most obvious candidates for the role of the announcing of Egohood had excluded themselves from contention. Enter here, in König's account, "the rich youth" (10:17–31; he is called a youth in Matthew's version of this story).

So around 1961 König proposed that the rich ruler of Mark 10 is Lazarus, the one who through his raising/initiation was qualified to take over the John role, and at about this time Smith discovered an ancient letter that described a longer version of the Gospel of Mark that strongly implies that the rich man of Mark 10 is both Lazarus and the beloved disciple who wrote John's Gospel. The placement of the raising of the rich young man within the Secret Gospel makes the coincidence even more notable. We can infer from König's reasoning that he would have located John's story of the raising of Lazarus within the Markan chronology in the space between Mark 10:45 and 46, for it is the story in Mark 10:35–45 that displays the third and most significant failure on the part of the brothers James and John. The *Letter to Theodore*, on the other hand, places the raising narrative immediately before this pericope, between Mark 10:34 and 35 (*Letter to Theodore* II.21–III.11), that is, one pericope earlier within the chronological framework. Although the placement is not identical, the story in Secret Mark occurs very close to where König implies that it should. Interestingly, the fact that this raising story and its resumption in Jericho occur immediately before and immediately after the request of James and John for positions of honor effects a literary contrast between the young man, who behaves in an exemplary way as a disciple, and James and John and the ten, who behave very inappropriately. So the reason for this slightly different placement actually underscores König's impression that the rich man/Lazarus took over the role for which the other disciples had disqualified themselves. Later in the narrative, Mark presents this contrast between these closest three disciples and the rich youth even more powerfully. The poignant rejection of Christ by these three in 14:26–42 is set almost immediately before the mysterious fleeing youth passage in 14:51–52, the significance of which can be seen in Chapter Three—Mark's Fleeing Youth, below.

I have dwelled at some length upon this König work because it uniquely begged for, and thus suggested the validity of, such a twentieth-century discovery as Secret Mark long before the latter became a matter of general scholarly knowledge, let alone public awareness if such exists even at this late date.[10]

The Discovery

After years of struggling to interpret what he had found, in 1973 Smith published two books on Secret Mark. One was intensely scholarly and beyond the capacity of most non-academics to benefit from.[11] The other, *The Secret Gospel*, was a popular and most readable volume. While I have inspected a library copy of the former, my copy is the Harper & Row version of the latter, and it is generally from this that I work. The letter's contents are as follows (Secret Mark in bold print):[12]

I.1 From the letters of the most holy Clement, author of the *Stromateis*. To Theodore:

I.2 You did well in silencing the unspeakable teachings of the Carpocratians.

I.3 For these are the "wandering stars" referred to in the prophecy, who wander from the

I.4 narrow road of the commandments into a boundless abyss of the carnal and bodily sins.

I.5 For, priding themselves in knowledge, as they say, "of the deep things of Satan," they do not know that they are casting themselves away into

---

[10] For a more complete description of the applicability of König's work in identifying the beloved disciple as Lazarus, the rich young ruler, see Smith, *Burning Bush*, 492–500, 536–38.

[11] Morton Smith, *Clement of Alexandria and a Secret Gospel of Mark* (Cambridge, Mass.: Harvard University Press, 1973).

[12] The English translation is that of Smith, *Clement*, 448–52, as modified by Scott G. Brown in *Mark's Other Gospel* (Waterloo, Ont.: Wilfrid Laurier University Press, 2005), xvii–xxii (Brown's changes appear in brackets). The roman numerals refer to pages of the letter, the arabic numerals to the lines on the page.

I.6   "the nether world of the darkness" of falsity, and, boasting

I.7   that they are free, they have become slaves of servile desires. Such men

I.8   are to be opposed in all ways and altogether. For, even if they should say something true, one who

I.9   loves the truth should not, even so, agree with them. For not all true things are the truth, nor

I.10   should that truth which merely seems true according to human opinions be preferred to the

I.11   true truth, that according to the faith. Now of the things they keep saying about the divinely inspired

I.12   Gospel according to Mark, some are altogether falsifications, and others, even if they do contain some true

I.13   elements, nevertheless are not reported truly. For the true things, being mixed

I.14   with inventions, are falsified, so that, as the saying goes, even the

I.15   salt loses its savor. As for Mark, then, during Peter's stay in Rome

I.16   he wrote an account of the Lord's doings, not, however, declaring all of them, nor yet hinting at the

I.17   [mystic] ones, but selecting what he thought most useful for increasing the

I.18   faith of those who were being instructed. But when Peter died a martyr, Mark came

I.19   over to Alexandria, bringing both his own notes and those of Peter,

I.20   from which he transferred to his former book the things suitable to those studies which make for[13] progress

I.21   toward knowledge. Thus he composed a more spiritual

I.22   Gospel for the use of those who were being perfected. Nevertheless, he yet did not divulge the things not to be uttered,

---

[13] Smith's translation has "to whatever makes for progress toward knowledge." Brown replaced that phrase with the rendition Smith gave in *Clement*, 91.

I.23   nor did he write down the hierophantic teaching of

I.24   the Lord, but to the stories already written he added yet others and, moreover,

I.25   brought in certain [traditions] of which he knew the interpretation would, as a mystagogue, lead the hearers into the

I.26   innermost sanctuary of that truth hidden by seven veils. Thus, in sum,

I.27   he prepared matters, neither grudgingly nor incautiously, in my opinion, and,

I.28   dying, he left his composition to the church

II.1   in Alexandria, where it even yet is [kept with utmost discretion[14]], being read

II.2   only to those who are being initiated into the great mysteries. But since the

II.3   foul demons are always devising destruction for the race of men,

II.4   Carpocrates, instructed by them and using deceitful arts, so enslaved

II.5   a certain presbyter of the church in Alexandria

II.6   that he got from him a copy of the [mystic] Gospel, which he

II.7   both interpreted according to his blasphemous and carnal doctrine and,

II.8   moreover, polluted, mixing with the spotless and holy words utterly shameless

II.9   lies. From this mixture is drawn off the teaching of the Carpocratians.

II.10   To them, therefore, as I said above, one must never give way;

II.11   nor, when they put forward their falsifications, should one concede that [it is Mark's

II.12   mystic Gospel], but should even deny it on oath. For, "Not all

II.13   true things are to be said to all men." For this reason the

---

[14] Smith has "most carefully guarded." Brown's revision follows Jeff Jay, "A New Look at the Epistolary Framework of the *Secret Gospel of Mark*," *Journal of Early Christian Studies* 16 (2008): 592–93.

Wisdom of God, through Solomon,

II.14   advises, "Answer the fool from his folly," teaching that

II.15   the light of the truth should be hidden from those who are mentally blind. Again

II.16   it says, "From him who has not shall be taken away," and, "Let the fool walk in darkness." But we

II.17   are "children of light," having been illuminated by "the dayspring" of the Spirit

II.18   of the Lord "from on high," and "Where the Spirit of the Lord is," it says, "there is liberty," for "All

II.19   things are pure to the pure." To you, therefore, I shall not hesitate to answer the questions you have asked,

II.20   refuting the falsifications by the very words of the Gospel.

II.21   For example, after "And they were in the road going up to Jerusalem," and what

II.22   follows, until "After three days he shall arise," the [text] brings the following material word for word:

II.23   **"And they come into Bethany. And a certain woman, whose brother**

II.24   **had died, was there. And, coming, she prostrated herself before Jesus and says to him, 'Son**

II.25   **of David, have mercy on me.' But the disciples rebuked her. And Jesus, being angered,**

II.26   **went off with her into the garden where the tomb was, and**

III.1   **straightway a great cry was heard from the tomb. And going near Jesus**

III.2   **rolled away the stone from the door of the tomb. And straightway going in where**

III.3   **the youth was, he stretched forth his hand and raised him, seizing**

III.4   **his hand. But the youth, looking upon him, loved him and**

III.5   **began to beseech him that he might be with him. And going out of**

III.6   **the tomb they came into the house of the youth, for he was rich. And after**

III.7   **six days Jesus told him what to do and in the evening the**

III.8   youth comes to him, wearing a linen cloth over his naked body. And

III.9   he remained with him that night, for Jesus taught him

III.10 the mystery of the kingdom of God. And thence, arising,

III.11 he returned to the other side of the Jordan." After these words follows the text, "And

III.12 James and John come to him," and all that

III.13 section. But "naked man with naked man," and the other things about which you wrote, are not

III.14 found. And after the words, "And he comes into Jericho," the [text] adds only, **"And**

III.15 **the sister of the youth whom Jesus loved and**

III.16 **his mother and Salome were there, and Jesus did not receive them."**

III.17 But the many other things about which you wrote both seem to be and are falsifications.

III.18 Now the true explanation and that which accords with the true philosophy ...

At this point, Smith says, "the text broke off, in the middle of a page."

Stalemate

Move ahead three decades from Smith's publication of the document to 2003. Its ship seemed stalled, becalmed in scholarly doldrums, its authenticity generally accepted but only provisionally. Early nagging suspicions of forgery—a forgery perhaps even perpetrated by Smith—as well as the absence of both the document itself and any serious, systematic textual study, left it in authoritative limbo. In apparent frustration with this state of drift, Charles W. Hedrick wrote the catalytic article "The Secret Gospel of Mark: Stalemate in the Academy." The article paved the way for Scott G. Brown's book soon to follow in 2005, and it headlined a scholarly triptych in which Guy G. Stroumsa supported Hedrick's view that Smith did not forge the document and Bart D. Ehrman, though not claiming forgery, walked the fence, concluding finally that we will never know unless and until the document itself is found.[15]

Stroumsa himself had gone to Mar Saba in 1976 with two other scholars, who are now deceased, and a young Greek Orthodox monk, Father Meliton, who was Archimandrite from the Greek Patriarchate in Jerusalem. There they found the document. "It was obvious to all of us," wrote Stroumsa, "that the precious book should not be left in place, but rather be deposited in the library of the Patriarchate. So we took the book back to Jerusalem, and Father Meliton brought it to the library. We hoped to analyze the manuscript seriously and contemplated an ink analysis. At the National and University Library, however, we were told that only at the police headquarters were people equipped with the necessary knowledge and tools for such an analysis. Father Meliton made it quite clear that he had no intention of putting the Vossius book in the hands of Israeli police."[16]

A detailed account of what happened to the book and manuscript is given by Brown.[17] The librarian in Jerusalem made photographs of the manuscript as soon as Father Meliton delivered it to the library. Quentin Quesnell is said, in the early 1980s, to have seen enlarged photographs of the manuscript and then not long after that to have seen the manuscript himself and been granted "permission from the Patriarchate to have color photographs made of the folios by a firm in Jerusalem."[18]

Between 1990 and 2000 several scholars, including Hedrick, made efforts to locate the book to no avail, but the librarian did provide Hedrick and his companion Nikolaos Olympiou copies of

---

[15] Charles W. Hedrick, "The Secret Gospel of Mark: Stalemate in the Academy," *Journal of Early Christian Studies* 11 (2003): 133–45. Guy G. Stroumsa, "Comments on Charles Hedrick's Article: A Testimony," ibid., 147–53. Bart D. Ehrman, "Response to Charles Hedrick's Stalemate," ibid., 155–63.

[16] Stroumsa, "Comments," 147–48.

[17] Brown, *Mark's Other Gospel*, 25–26.

[18] Adela Yarbro Collins, *Mark: A Commentary* (Minneapolis: Fortress, 2007), 491. Timo S. Paananen provides additional information on the blog Salainen evankelista (http://salainenevankelista.blogspot.com/2009/11/more-on-quentin-quesnells-encounter.html).

the color photographs that an earlier librarian had made when he removed the manuscript from the back of the book. These additional photographs were published by Hedrick and Olympiou in 2000.[19]

Ehrman faults Smith for his failure to return to Israel and have the document examined, and some members of the pro-forgery group seem to imply that Smith's failure to do this is part and parcel of his fraud. All parties to the issue wish that such an examination had been done and live in the hope that it might still someday be possible. Not all parties, however, fault Smith for this failure considering that he worked under conditions that would have greatly complicated such task, and the facts make it clear beyond question that Smith had no control over or right to remove the book and made no effort to prevent other scholars from examining the document itself. The Patriarchate library, not Smith, is responsible for its becoming unavailable therefor. Ehrman found it appropriate to mention Smith's many vitriolic responses to critics. He also thought that it was appropriate that the debate included Smith's interpretation, particularly Smith's tentative speculation that Jesus' initiation of the young man involved physical symbolism of spiritual union.

Ehrman disclaimed basing his conclusions on these elements, but doubtless they played a significant part in his unwillingness to abide by the preponderance of circumstantial evidence without the production of the original document for expert examination, a condition that is now seemingly and indefinitely beyond the hands of scholars in the Western world. The net effect of such a position would be to leave the matter in stalemate with forgery remaining in the picture indefinitely, which is probably the best that Smith's critics can hope to perpetuate.

Hedrick's article in *Journal of Early Christian Studies* seems to have been the watershed that opened the gates to an intensification of focus upon the authenticity of Secret Mark, with the controversy swirling primarily around whether or not it was a forgery by

---

[19] Charles W. Hedrick and Nikolaos Olympiou, "Secret Mark: New Photographs, New Witnesses," *The Fourth R* 13, no. 5 (September/October 2000): 3–16.

Smith.[20] The time was ripe for Hedrick to thrust his gauntlet. That it triggered the frontal assaults on Smith's veracity by both Stephen C. Carlson and Peter Jeffery is abundantly clear. Carlson cites it as the third and last event of 2003 that ignited his prior suspicions into action, the first being the James Ossuary controversy and the second being the U.S. Supreme Court's decision in Lawrence v. Texas, "legalizing," Carlson says, "private, consensual homosexual activity."[21] Jeffery had already written, but never published, a critical comment about Smith's discovery, but his surprise from Hedrick's article at "how seriously this other Marcan gospel was being taken in some quarters" sparked his own attack.[22]

The Three Books—Brown, Carlson, Jeffery

In the current state of the matter, it is the books of Brown, Carlson, and Jeffery around which scholars have focused their primary attention in the debate over the authenticity of Secret Mark.[23] The first, *Mark's Other Gospel*, by Brown (2005), supports its authenticity, while the last two, *The Gospel Hoax*, by Carlson (2005), and *The Secret Gospel of Mark Unveiled*, by Jeffery (2007), challenge it. It appears that a majority of scholars who have thus far considered the matter have accepted the authenticity of the *Letter to Theodore*, as against the charge that Morton Smith forged it, but many of these have done so conditionally, subject to expert analysis of the original document if it becomes available in the future. That majority would also include others who, while rejecting the modern forgery charge,

---

[20] Actually, two significant books on Secret Mark were essentially contemporaneous with Hedrick's article, both published the same year and presumably for that reason not cited by Hedrick or either of his respondents. Both supported the authenticity of Smith's discovery: Marvin W. Meyer, *Secret Gospels: Essays on Thomas and the Secret Gospel of Mark* (Harrisburg: Trinity Press International, 2003); John Dart, *Decoding Mark* (Harrisburg: Trinity Press International, 2003).

[21] Carlson, *Gospel Hoax*, xv–xvii, 69–70.

[22] Jeffery, *Unveiled*, ix.

[23] When I speak of the "authenticity" of Secret Mark herein, I refer to the critical issue of whether or not Morton Smith forged the document and not to the authenticity of Smith's interpretation of the document.

have reservations about whether Clement of Alexandria wrote the letter or whether Mark wrote the Secret Mark passages within it. It is fairly safe to assume that the thesis presented in this book has not yet been considered by the scholars. Based upon that assumption, I will present my thesis first and defer responding to the cases made by Jeffery and Carlson until Book Three herein.

But before we get to the argument in Book Two, we need first to address Morton Smith the man, particularly those aspects that have attracted criticism or even hostility, and then look at how Smith interpreted his own discovery.

Morton Smith the Man

Brown's no-nonsense adaptation of his doctoral dissertation into *Mark's Other Gospel*, while doubtless done with some realization that Smith's perceived character influenced some scholarly opposition to the authenticity of Secret Mark, did not focus upon that matter as relevant to the basic issues of whether the letter was a work of Clement and the gospel quotations of Mark himself. In this respect, he was blindsided when, just after his own book was published, Carlson announced that his forthcoming book would prove Smith to be the real author. Upon publication, Carlson's book created a firestorm, welcomed and acclaimed as it was by so many, especially among the more religiously conservative, who generally liked Smith even less than they like the gospels that were not included in the canon. Brown proceeded to meticulously address each of Carlson's points, as well as those of Jeffery, in a series of responses in scholarly publications, as we shall see. But at this point it is well to set out a snippet or so of what it was about Smith that made it easy for some people to believe that he was capable of forgery.

Smith often reacted caustically, even venomously, to his critics, understandably stimulating offense and dislike. He was a brilliant man who did not suffer fools gladly, as the saying goes. In all of this Smith laid a firm basis for a skeptical assessment and reception of his work as well as of his own moral character. He was ordained an Episcopal priest in the 1940s, serving in Baltimore and Boston. But he was widely considered to have later become an atheist. Many of his detractors have said that he was defrocked, and most have suspected him of being gay. Any alleged discovery by a gay atheist of a document that added to or detracted from Holy Scripture would understandably tend to be looked upon with distrust by those of certain philosophical leanings.

A year or two before his death Smith empowered Shaye J. D. Cohen to publish a collection of Smith's articles containing whichever Cohen "thought worthy." The result was the posthumous two-volume *Studies in the Cult of Yahweh*.[24] Fittingly, at the end of the second volume Cohen offers a seven-page "In Memoriam Morton Smith." The first sentence reads, "Morton Smith (1915–1991) was a great scholar, blessed with extraordinary acuity, mordant wit, and expansive range."

Not to be pedantic, but the noun "mordant" denotes a chemical, the derivative adjective of which Merriam-Webster's defines as "biting and caustic in thought, manner, or style." The inclusion of that characteristic as the middle of only three is suggestive of a factor that figures into the reception of Smith's discovery, and many who have interacted critically with Smith in regard to that discovery would doubtless consider the use of the term "wit" a euphemistic adaptation.

After giving a brief résumé of Smith, Cohen gives an assessment of the former's contribution to four fields of academic endeavor, namely, ancient Israel, New Testament and early Christianity, ancient Judaism, and ancient magic. He then elaborates five "general themes and concerns" Smith had as he dealt with these four fields. He highlights the first of these five as "a determination to destroy boundaries."[25] Perhaps that alone suggests an appetite for iconoclasm or irreverence. But it is the fifth one that seems the most relevant for our purposes and bears repeating in full:

Fifth, scorn for pseudo-scholarship, that is, pronouncements and opinions born of religious faith and confessional conviction

---

[24] Morton Smith, *Studies in the Cult of Yahweh* (ed. Shaye J. D. Cohen; 2 vols.; Leiden: Brill, 1996).

[25] Shaye J. D. Cohen, "In Memoriam Morton Smith," in *New Testament, Early Christianity, and Magic* (vol. 2 of *Studies in the Cult of Yahweh*; ed. Shaye J. D. Cohen; Leiden: Brill, 1996), 283.

but masquerading as "objective scholarship." Smith argued that "the Bible" is a theological category inherited from Judaism and Christianity, and as such is an obstacle to a proper understanding of ancient Judaism and Christianity. Smith had only scorn for those who believed that any truth might somehow be lurking in the New Testament miracle stories (except insofar as the cures allegedly effected by Jesus might have been psycho-somatically induced cures of psycho-somatically induced illnesses). Smith had only scorn too for those who saw any truth in the prophetic experiences of either the Old Testament or the New Testament, as if God or any god would ever or did ever communicate in such a way with humans. For Smith the ideal of scholarly objectivity could be met only through atheism or Epicureanism, that is, the assumption that if the gods exist, they intervene not at all in human affairs.... (Whether Smith actually was an atheist or an Epicurean, I do not know.)

Smith never tired of discomfiting the faithful. An ordained Episcopalian priest who left the church (but was never defrocked), Smith well knew that his portrait of Jesus the Magician,[26] and his picture of a Christianity dominated by magic, heavenly ascents, and spiritual possession, was far from the respectable, rational, middle-class Christianity of most of his readers. Smith well knew that his picture of a syncretistic Judaism living on from biblical to rabbinic times would discomfit many of his Jewish readers. Smith reveled in this. But in private life Smith was hardly the wild-eyed radical or the strident orator. On the contrary. In person he was staid and somewhat stiff, always well dressed, perfectly mannered, and an impeccable gentleman.[27]

If I may be permitted an observation on Smith's persona, it is that he represents an example of how the intense academic study of scripture and religious writings in general often leads to a distancing of the scholar from the subject matter. The scholar's thinking about religion

---

[26] Morton Smith, *Jesus the Magician* (San Francisco: Harper & Row, 1978; repr., New York: Barnes & Noble, 1993).
[27] Cohen, "In Memoriam," 285.

becomes agnostic if not atheistic, at least in general appearance. Among those who hail from conservative or fundamentalist backgrounds, the transition often constitutes a withdrawal from a life of blind faith in confessional doctrine. Knowledge of this phenomenon is spreading.[28] A notable doubter of Secret Mark's authenticity is Ehrman, a renowned biblical scholar of considerable press in recent years, who says "I lost my fundamentalist faith because of my scholarship" and who does not appear to have adopted any other religious belief system in its place.[29] So also Elaine Pagels, author of the popular *The Gnostic Gospels*, implies in the first chapter of her *Beyond Belief* that as "a historian of religion" she had drifted away from her fundamentalist faith by the time in her life when she was faced with the crushing personal realization that her infant son would not live.[30] These two are not at all unique in such respect. A study cited in a sidebar in the *Biblical Archaeology Review* article containing Ehrman's statement strongly substantiates the fact that among college or university professors, the higher one climbs in institutional rank the more one tends to become either atheistic or agnostic. Smith appears to represent the vanguard in that tendency.

Smith's Own Interpretation of Secret Mark

Still, if one carefully considers what Smith said about his efforts to interpret the meaning of what he found, it is hard to conclude that he wasn't intensely serious in his search. If such was the case it disintegrates any thought that he had conjured up a forgery. Smith meticulously analyzed the text over the course of eight years, and

---

[28] Charles W. Hedrick, ed., *When Faith Meets Reason: Religion Scholars Reflect on Their Spiritual Journeys* (Santa Rosa, Calif.: Polebridge, 2008). Thirteen accomplished biblical scholars, honest enough to express their own convictions, share the experience of their own paths and resulting beliefs. Richard Holloway, Bishop of Edinburgh and Primus of the Scottish Episcopal Church retired, says of the book, on its back cover, "This book could lead to a dangerous epidemic of honesty among religious thinkers."

[29] Bart D. Ehrman, as quoted in Hershel Shanks, "Losing Faith: How Scholarship Affects Scholars," *Biblical Archaeology Review* 33, no. 2 (March/April 2007): 50–57.

[30] Elaine H. Pagels, *The Gnostic Gospels* (New York: Random House, 1981); *Beyond Belief: The Secret Gospel of Thomas* (New York: Random House, 2003).

throughout the rest of his life he continued to refine and defend his interpretation. Ironically, the very interpretation he worked so hard to develop seems to have spawned most of the attacks against his sincerity. But what was Smith's interpretation of his discovery? That the story quoted in the *Letter to Theodore* was the synoptic counterpart to the raising of Lazarus, Smith recognized. For him it answered the otherwise puzzling question why an event so major as the raising of a man who was buried for four days, as reported by John, could have been completely omitted in the synoptic tradition. Smith's conclusion: it wasn't omitted. Secret Mark was known to the evangelist who gave us the earliest of the Synoptic Gospels.[31] Smith, contrary to the position herein, concluded that on the basis of form criticism "the story in the secret Gospel is older than the story in John."[32] However, that conclusion was still an intermediary one, for his study led him further to something of an epiphany in the spring of 1963 that he describes as a "blaze of invisible light" that "was probably the high point of my life." He realized that "the resurrection story of the secret Gospel" was even earlier than canonical Mark and "had been in the source both Mark and John had used."[33]

One who reads Smith's *The Secret Gospel* up through chapter eight will probably wonder what all the fuss is about. Everything seems straightforward, plausible, hardly offensive to any open-minded reader. The conclusions Smith reached in chapters nine ("The Secret Tradition: Introduction") and ten ("The Mystery and the Kingdom") laid the groundwork for the transition thereafter from the acceptable to the offensive. It was in these chapters that he focused upon the initiatory teaching that followed six days after the resuscitation, but he struggled to determine the nature of the initiation. Concluding that it was a baptism, he struggled further with the question of why it was secret. In chapter nine he says: "All the above—secrecy in general, in the teaching of Jesus, and in the New Testament, Jesus' relation to the kingdom of God and to the Baptist, Pauline baptism and the

---

[31] Smith, *Secret Gospel*, 46.
[32] Smith, *Secret Gospel*, 52.
[33] Smith, *Secret Gospel*, 60–62.

magical background of its peculiarities, the libertine tradition and the Carpocratians—all these subjects, I could see, were directly relevant to my problem." Still struggling with why a baptismal rite should be secret, in chapter ten he says, "The first problem was to find out the secret." He searches the traditions with which he was so familiar in the ancient Middle East, including those within Judaism. He touches upon a promising aspect when he says, "Particularly important for our purpose is the presence of the kingdom in God's rule of the heavens, which were thought to be a number of spherical bodies, concentric with the earth and surrounding it, one outside another."[34] Although inadvertent, such language accords with some of the cosmogonic aspects of the ancient mysteries set out in the first chapter of Book Two, including its analysis of the *Apocryphon of John*, but the similarity quickly fades out of Smith's picture.

Smith's slide into troubling conclusions seems to have started with chapter eleven. Having wrestled earlier with the question of why any baptism would be secret, he nevertheless here concluded that "Jesus probably admitted his chosen followers to the kingdom by some sort of baptism ... *the mystery rite by which the kingdom was entered.*"[35] Smith inferred the nature of this baptism from five aspects he sees in Paul's baptism: union with Jesus, the work of the spirit, magic, ascent into the heavens, and liberation from the law.[36] Chapter twelve concludes with the following paragraph (emphasis added):

> Thus from the differences between Paul's baptism and that of the Baptist, and from the scattered indications in the canonical Gospels and the secret Gospel of Mark, we can put together a picture of Jesus' baptism, "the mystery of the kingdom of God." It was a water baptism administered by Jesus to chosen disciples, singly and by night. The costume, for the disciple, was a linen cloth worn over the naked body. This cloth was probably removed for the baptism proper, the immersion in water, which was now reduced to

---

[34] Smith, *Secret Gospel*, 75, 81, 87.
[35] Smith, *Secret Gospel*, 96 (italics original).
[36] Smith, *Secret Gospel*, 101–14.

a preparatory purification. After that, by unknown ceremonies,[37] the disciple was possessed by Jesus' spirit and so united with Jesus. One with him, he participated by hallucination in Jesus' ascent into the heavens, he entered the kingdom of God, and was thereby set free from the laws ordained for and in the lower world. *Freedom from the law may have resulted in completion of the spiritual union by physical union.* This certainly occurred in many forms of gnostic Christianity; how early it began there is no telling.[38]

In the penultimate chapter thirteen, he suggests that libertine aspects were widespread in early Christianity, concluding, "The libertine interpretation went back to Jesus himself and preserved and developed elements of his esoteric teaching," and further, "This libertine tradition, its strength, its diffusion, its unanimity, and its evident age, is explicable only by our understanding of Jesus' teaching about the mystery of the kingdom." A bit later he says, "The relation between the primitive secret tradition and gnosticism can be seen clearly in the case of Carpocrates, the founder of the sect attacked by Clement's letter."[39]

In the final chapter, entitled "The History of the Document," he poses the question why the letter disappeared from view from the time of Clement till his own discovery of it at Mar Saba. He proposes an explanation which he admits is conjectural but fits the facts as he has presented them, including the libertine nature of the rites involved in the Secret Gospel.[40]

According to Smith's account Jesus felt himself possessed of a spirit at the time of his baptism by John. He was thereby enabled to become an exorcist, to self-hypnotize and also hypnotize others, enabling him to attract a following. He felt he had ascended into the heavens, entering

---

[37] The footnote here reads: "To judge from the hekalot [*sic*] and Qumran texts, the magical papyri and the Byzantine liturgy, these will have been mainly the recitation of repetitive, hypnotic prayers and hymns. The magical tradition also prescribes, in some instances, interference with breathing. *Manipulation, too, was probably involved; the stories of Jesus' miracles give a very large place to the use of his hands*" (italics added).

[38] Smith, *Secret Gospel*, 113–14.

[39] Smith, *Secret Gospel*, 131, 134.

[40] Smith, *Secret Gospel*, 139–48.

the kingdom of God and being freed from the Mosaic law. Moreover, Smith writes (emphasis added):

> A peculiar feature of the ancient techniques for "ascent" was that they provided for the initiation of others—the magician could take a pupil along on his "trip." Jesus therefore developed the Baptist's rite by adding to it an ascent into the kingdom, which gave his followers supernatural powers like his own and freed them, too, from the law. Finally, he added another rite, derived from ancient erotic magic, by which his followers were enabled, they believed, to eat his body and drink his blood and be joined with him, not only because possessed by his spirit, *but also in physical union.*
>
> By use of these rites Jesus made himself the center of a libertine circle.[41]

Smith's reference to physical union in this context probably refers to the physical symbolism of spiritual union with Jesus that is involved in the rite of "ingesting" his body and blood (the bread and wine). But not everyone recognized this distinction, and Smith's probably erroneous suggestion that the communion sacrament "derived from ancient erotic magic" did not help him ward off the arrows of criticism.

In Smith's reconstruction, the libertine tradition developed into different movements. The trajectory that Smith traces through Paul, whose gospel of freedom from the Torah occupies a mediating and comparatively conservative position, developed into something of a center group that was willing to compromise, giving rise by the middle of the third century to a clear majority that claimed to be orthodox. Nevertheless, "the libertine wing gave rise to many of the gnostic heresies, but also persisted in esoteric groups, like that of Clement, within the 'orthodox' communities."[42]

It is fair to ask what Smith meant by the term "libertine" as used in the above quote. Smith traces the origin of libertine practices back

---

[41] Smith, *Secret Gospel*, 140.
[42] Smith, *Secret Gospel*, 141–42.

not only to Paul's gospel of Christian freedom from the law, but also to Christ himself, yet to neither figure does he anywhere attribute immoral practices, unless they can be inferred from the limited passages quoted above.[43] Smith would have been bold indeed, and to suggest that he did so one should, in good conscience, present clear and convincing evidence. This is hardly the case.[44] What is clear is that Smith was indiscreet in his language in *The Secret Gospel*, as he later recognized and attempted to correct.[45]

Whatever other causes might eventually have derailed him, Smith's conclusion that the initiation ceremony in Secret Mark was a baptismal rite led to his tortured analysis. That the account was presumed baptismal, with its assumed, but never stated, nakedness, opened the door for his conjectures of physical union. These were unfortunate, whatever his perceptions behind them might have been, for they also opened the door for scholars who suppose that Secret Mark promotes homosexuality to suggest that he contrived the story himself. The substance of the first two chapters of Book Two show that the raising of Lazarus, and thus the related incident in Secret Mark, was not a baptismal rite but something far above that in the spiritual sense. Smith's baptismal reading of the Secret Gospel version made possible the interpretations that he then developed, which his critics have deemed so prurient.

Referring to the "young man wearing a linen cloth over his naked body" in Mark 14:51, Smith writes, "Through seventeen hundred years of New Testament scholarship, nobody has ever been able to explain what that young man was doing alone with Jesus in such a place, at such a time, and in such a costume."[46] I submit that Steiner's insights, which occurred within that time, do justice to this puzzle. Much has been made of the language of nakedness without taking into account the use of that term within scripture itself. We

---

[43] Smith, *Secret Gospel*, 113–14, 130–31.

[44] See Scott G. Brown, "The Question of Motive in the Case against Morton Smith," *Journal of Biblical Literature* 125 (2006): 353–73, esp. 354–65.

[45] Brown, "Question of Motive," 357–65.

[46] Smith, *Secret Gospel*, 80–81.

misapprehend how the term is used in scripture when we apply our common understanding to the term.[47]

That offense was taken by so many is not terribly surprising. Smith's 1973 publications do contain these disturbing conjectures, but in the course of the often vitriolic dialogue that followed, as well as in his subsequent publications, he showed no interest in defending those conjectures. It seems that Smith was not trying to "discomfit the faithful" but was rather trying to develop a theory that he thought best accounted for the evidence. As it has turned out, in doing so, language that was not central to his thesis has stirred his doubters to presume unworthy motives, leading to suspicion that he forged the document. That his motives were neither to offend nor to dupe, but rather to understand and explain, is elsewhere extensively shown.[48]

Especially do I find Smith's integrity on this matter more appealing when the powerful synergies of the relationship between this discovery and the first two chapters of Book Two are taken into account. This should be seen as especially true if the points put forward by Smith's leading complainants, Carlson and Jeffery, can be decisively rebutted. We shall examine in Book Three whether or not they have been.

---

[47] We will consider the scriptural meaning of "naked" and "nakedness" in ch. 3 of Book Two, on Mark's fleeing youth (Mark 14:51–52).

[48] Brown, "Question of Motive."

BOOK TWO

CHAPTER ONE—THE ANCIENT MYSTERIES

The Hidden Ones

This book's linchpin is the content and significance of the ancient mysteries. Knowledge of their content is essential to comprehension of their significance.

Yet from all extant texts relating to the mysteries it is clear that their essential kernel was not to be found in any writing, at least not in a way that was apparent to most. Initiates into these mysteries were prohibited from divulging what had been revealed to them in their initiation. Consequently, as Marvin W. Meyer notes in the introduction to his anthology of the most significant texts, "we possess little information about the central features of the mysteries" and "the secret ceremonies of the mystery religions ... remain largely hidden from us." He further recognizes the "great antiquity" of many of the mysteries, "their origins [being] hidden in the mists of prehistory" and thus not reduced to writing.[49]

To the extent the mysteries retained into the age of writing any of their more ancient gnosis, any initiate who reduced them to writing was obliged to do so in a manner such that their essential truths would be veiled to common understanding, recognizable only by those who through like disciplines and preparation, even initiation,

---

[49] Marvin W. Meyer, *The Ancient Mysteries: A Sourcebook: Sacred Texts of the Mystery Religions of the Ancient Mediterranean World* (New York: HarperCollins, 1987; repr., Philadelphia: University of Pennsylvania Press, 1999), 4, 10, 5.

would perceive their meaning. In other words, in their revelatory character such writings were occult, esoteric, hidden, but only from those insufficiently prepared. Christ's admonition in the Sermon on the Mount against giving dogs what is holy or throwing pearls before swine could be seen by initiates or those otherwise so prepared as still reflecting this ancient enjoinder.[50]

A certain consciousness of this nature of the ancient mysteries carried over into the early Christian era. Because of the incompatibility of this esotericism with the necessity of a wider evangelization, and of the establishment of a Christendom based on *faith* rather than *gnosis*, the formulation of dogma was the best that could be attained in that age of deep darkness to which Isaiah had alluded (Isa 9:2; see also Matt 4:16; Isa 6). All that could be described as gnostic had to be suppressed. Until the twentieth century, all that could be known about the character of gnosticism came from its orthodox enemies, most notably Irenaeus. Only with the emergence of the Nag Hammadi codices has the esoteric nature of second-century Christendom come increasingly into our awareness. Yet of those gnostic writings, and of their limitations, too little can even yet be appreciated, as we shall see later when we consider what is now known as the Nag Hammadi Library (NHL).[51]

While Meyer indicates that most *mystai* (initiates) observed their pledge of secrecy, resulting in little information about the central features of the mysteries, he goes on to say that "Christian converts who once had been initiated into the mystery religions sometimes felt no hesitation about betraying the mysteries and readily unveiled what they believed to be godless and shameless secrets."[52] By the Christian era there was much in what then remained of the mysteries that had become decadent and deserved condemnation. But the

---

[50] Thus, those so prepared would be described in Matt 7:13–14, their enjoinder being in 7:6.

[51] I will be referring to the translation in James M. Robinson, ed., *The Nag Hammadi Library in English* (3d rev. ed.; San Francisco: HarperCollins, 1990).

[52] Meyer, *Ancient Mysteries*, 4. Clement of Alexandria himself appears to have retained deep respect for the ancient mysteries themselves but didn't hesitate to condemn what had become godless and shameless within them; see his *Exhortations to the Heathen*.

pre-dogma Christianity revealed by the twentieth-century discoveries demonstrated that the whole picture was not available in the writings of the heresy hunters of orthodoxy. The most significant of these were the numerous Coptic codices, mostly gnostic, discovered near a place called Nag Hammadi in Egypt in 1945, now largely translated and published in the NHL. Their content is far greater in both depth and range than what can be garnered from the writings of Irenaeus and the church fathers. But that content presents a far different face than what is in the Christian canon or the early apocryphal writings, so that a new era of interpretation is only now in its early stages, and we are still asking very basic questions. In the light of the new materials, Helmut Koester, for instance, has written: "We know too little about 'gnostic hermeneutics.' What are the rules and criteria of interpretation, and how have they been applied in the process of transmission and exegesis of traditional materials?"[53]

Though traditionally minded scholars have relentlessly resisted the conclusion, my position in this book is that the ancient mysteries were part of the fabric out of which Christianity emerged in its earliest days.[54] In the first evangelization stages mystery references surface over and over in the letters of Paul, whose initiation on the Damascus

---

[53] Helmut Koester, "Gnostic Sayings and Controversy Traditions in John 8:12–59," in *Nag Hammadi, Gnosticism, and Early Christianity* (ed. C. W. Hedrick and R. Hodgson Jr.; Peabody, Mass.: Hendrickson, 1986; repr., Eugene, Oreg.: Wipf & Stock, 2005), 110.

[54] Jonathan Z. Smith, *Drudgery Divine: On the Comparison of Early Christianities and the Religions of Late Antiquity* (Chicago: University of Chicago Press, 1990), traces the history of a debate on the question of whether or not the "mystery" of Christianity was *sui generis*, a totally new phenomenon, or whether its roots extended back into the mystery religions of the past. As against the railings of Joseph Priestley (26 n. 43) and some others, Smith presented the work of Charles Francois Dupuis, *Abrégé de l'Origine de tous les cultes* (1798), as containing "some rudimentary sense of depth" (33). Dupuis concluded, according to Smith, that it was "the Persian system [*mysterion*] which forms the 'basis' for all the developed religions of the west" (30), and that "while their ultimate origins are lost in obscurity, the Egyptians had 'the most ancient' mysteries, and that 'it was from them that they passed to the rest of the world'" (31). The position of Dupuis is nearer to the position adopted here, which sees the Christ event as the fulfillment of, and thus necessarily related to, the ancient mysteries which go back to the time of Atlantis, far beyond ancient Egypt, as presented by the Relevant Substance of the Ancient Mysteries (RSAM) in Book Three.

road and in the period of special preparation that followed revealed great spiritual heights and depths to him.[55] He spoke of "the *mystery* which was kept *secret* for long ages but is now disclosed and through the prophetic writings is made known to all nations ..." (Rom 16:25–26);[56] and of "how the *mystery* was made known to me by revelation ... to make all men see what is the plan of the *mystery hidden* for ages" (Eph 3:3, 9; cf. also 1:9–10); and again "the *mystery hidden* for ages and generations but now made manifest to his saints" (Col 1:26).[57] We may infer from Paul's own Damascus road experience and the fourteen years or so he spent in Arabia, presumably in spiritual preparation, that he was himself initiated into the mysteries to which he often later referred. That they were very real to him seems apparent. But his letters, for the most part, addressed ad hoc situations in the churches he founded. Was it because these concerns left little opportunity to elaborate on the substance of these mysteries that he gave so little of it? Or was it rather because as an initiate he honored the ancient principle that such substance was to be revealed only to those adequately prepared—as had almost certainly been the case with him? Perhaps it was some of both.

As we shall see, it is suggested in this work that the faded and thus largely decadent remnants of those mysteries constituted the content of so much of gnostic Christianity in the early centuries. There seems to be a presumption within orthodoxy that what finally prevailed and crystallized as orthodox in its battles with the gnostic Christians of the second century is itself "the mystery hidden for ages" that Paul spoke of.

Three Relevant Twentieth-Century Events

This book undertakes to demonstrate not only the plausibility but also the high probability that the rich young ruler of Mark

---

[55] See Smith, *Burning Bush*, 328–65.

[56] Except where indicated, all biblical quotations are from the Revised Standard Version.

[57] Whether or not Paul himself wrote Ephesians and Colossians, their statements here ring true to the content of his undisputed letters, esp. Romans, 1 and 2 Corinthians, and Galatians.

10:17–22[58] is Lazarus as well as *the disciple whom Jesus loved* in John's Gospel and the one who gave us that gospel.

Three developments of the twentieth century make it possible not only to penetrate the mystery that has surrounded so much in John's Gospel but also at the same time to see how powerfully the evidence points to this rich young ruler who went away sorrowful as the one who gave us the "spiritual" gospel, John. First came the appearance at the start of the twentieth century of a man proclaiming supersensible perception including the long-hidden content of the ancient mysteries. Second was the discovery in 1945 of the Nag Hammadi codices and their subsequent translation. Third was Morton Smith's controversial discovery in 1958 of the *Letter to Theodore* containing what he called the Secret Gospel of Mark.

A special synergy, relating to our undertaking, arises from the interrelationship of these three phenomena. It is as though they appeared on the scene in logical sequence. To see what they collectively reveal, we must start with that one who appeared on the scene early in the twentieth century giving us what he termed *anthroposophy*. He indicated that the content of anthroposophy and the ancient mysteries are essentially the same and are the key to understanding the raising of Lazarus. It took most of the rest of the twentieth century for the content of the 1945 discovery to be widely available to scholars, for whom many difficult questions of translation and interpretation yet remain even now. Its assimilation into a wider public awareness and understanding is only in the earliest stages, if that. Still, those texts are now inexpensively available to all who wish to study them. I suggest that those texts contain significant vestiges, however faded or decadent, of what Steiner presented as

---

[58] I will be citing Mark's version of this incident rather than the parallels from Matthew (19:16–22) or Luke (18:18–23) for the dual reasons that Mark is the gospel that describes the youth as being *loved* by Jesus and that, being in the earliest gospel, it is generally presumed to be the source of the parallel accounts in Matthew and Luke. The "rich young ruler" designation is conflated from all three accounts. All three describe the man as rich (or wealthy). Only Matthew describes him as still young, the other two saying he had observed the law *since* his youth. Only Luke describes him as a ruler, though perhaps Matthew and Mark presuppose the idea simply because ruling and riches often coexist.

ancient mystery knowledge.[59] Such vestiges lend a degree of credibility to what Steiner said about the content of those earlier mysteries. Moreover, it is from that content that a different and highly meaningful understanding of the nature of the raising of Lazarus can be seen. At this point the discovery in 1958 enters the picture. Like the 1945 discovery at Nag Hammadi it took several decades for the great significance of the 1958 discovery to come fully into focus. The notable similarity in many particulars of the Johannine account of the raising of Lazarus and Secret Mark's account of the raising of the youth has been widely observed from the outset. The writer sees these three phenomena to be powerfully and meaningfully related. I suggest that their triangular relationship provides mutual corroboration for the verity of each of them. The implications are extensive.

Because Smith's 1958 discovery of the putative letter of Clement has raised such a storm of controversy, I suggest that these new insights have a direct bearing on the issue of the authenticity of this discovery.

Steiner and Anthroposophy

Some groundwork had been laid in the nineteenth century for what Steiner introduced early in the twentieth. Such groundwork was not, however, the spiritualism that worked its way through American life in the nineteenth century and was within the focus of Steiner's critical lecture cycle in Dornach, Switzerland, in October 1915.[60] Rather, that groundwork came from Helena P. Blavatsky and the Theosophical Society that rose from her magnum opus *The Secret Doctrine*.[61]

---

[59] The decadence of which Steiner spoke had to do more with diminishment of true perceptiveness in the spiritual realm for both hierophant and candidate than with self-indulgence or dissoluteness, though some of the latter appears to have existed in some gnostic sects. An indication of his meaning might be had by comparing the RSAM in Book Three with what is available in the NHL. The NHL points back to an earlier day much like the remains of earlier civilizations or creatures give evidence of their prior existence. We shall see that later herein.

[60] Rudolf Steiner, *The Occult Movement in the Nineteenth Century and Its Relation to Modern Culture* (London: Rudolf Steiner Press, 1973) (CW 254).

[61] Helena P. Blavatsky, *The Secret Doctrine: The Synthesis of Science, Religion, and Philosophy* (London: Theosophical, 1888; repr., Pasadena: Theosophical University Press, 1977).

In the academy it is as though Steiner and anthroposophy have no existence independent of Blavatsky and theosophy. Catherine Albanese, in her monumental work on American metaphysical religion, gives considerable coverage to Blavatsky and theosophy. No mention is made of anthroposophy.[62] Steiner is named once in a sentence quoted from a popular book by Barbara Ann Brennan, his name following Blavatsky's in regard to healing, an aspect of his work quite minor in relation to the whole. Similarly he is never mentioned by Albanese in her introductory article on metaphysical religion in the *Journal of the American Academy of Religion* or by any of the other three writers in that issue who wrote on that theme.[63]

Because he needed a receptive audience, Steiner affiliated himself with the Theosophical Society early in 1902, becoming the general secretary of its German Section. He did so on condition that he be allowed free rein to reveal the results of his own spiritual intuition. But in spite of many cosmological and ontological aspects of *The Secret Doctrine* he confirmed, he felt it contained many errors, and the Eastern orientation of the Society conflicted more and more with his insistence upon the Mystery of Golgotha as the central event in human evolution. Eventually by early 1913 the differences resulted in his being expelled from that society, whereupon members who left with him founded the Anthroposophical Society.

Steiner's immense oeuvre comprises no less than 373 volumes (in German) in his archives at the international headquarters of the Anthroposophical Society in Dornach.[64] Over the years a substantial portion has been selectively translated into English and exists in some printed or other written form in various and often inconsistent titles.

---

[62] Catherine L. Albanese, *A Republic of Mind and Spirit: A Cultural History of American Metaphysical Religion* (New Haven: Yale University Press, 2007).

[63] Catherine L. Albanese, "Introduction: Awash in a Sea of Metaphysics," *Journal of the American Academy of Religion* 75 (2007): 582–88.

[64] The number of the last such volume is actually 354. However, taking into account volumes that bear the same number with distinguishing letter (i.e., "a," "b," etc.), volumes that bear more than one number, skips between numbers, and the fact that CW 42 is now contained in nos. 264–266, the number is increased by nineteen to 373. This count is made from the listing of titles in the new Collected Works series discussed in the text that follows above.

Those titles bore no systematic relationship to the archive volumes from which they were derived. These publishing efforts were always under the constraint of severely limited resources. In recent years the Anthroposophic Press, Inc. (SteinerBooks), of New York City and Great Barrington, Massachusetts, has undertaken the ambitious goal of publishing the entire archive in English translation. The German archive is known as *Gesamtausgabe*, and its volumes are identified by the initials GA. The volumes in English translation bear an appropriately similar name and substantive content as their German counterpart but are called Collected Works and are identified by the initials CW. The first such volume was published in 2006 as CW 211,[65] and several more volumes have been published since then. The publishers hope that this project will at last make Steiner's works more widely accessible within the academy and among others seeking to benefit from the profound insights therein.

What can be given here from this vast body of work is in the highest sense skeletal. The following summary of anthroposophy is prefaced by the admonition that it will often seem bizarre according to the mode of thinking of our time in history. Most who have delved diligently and persistently into the body of Steiner's work have little doubt that it emanated from one who was both an intellectual and a spiritual genius. In this materialistic age, patience has been hard to come by for revelation admittedly derived from intuition, even when joined to the power of logical demonstration. The demand in both science and religion has been for that which can be tested by observation in the sensate world. And even when what is given can be observed in phenomena, it is typically given short shrift if associated in its demonstration with any reference to the supersensible world.

In the present effort it can only be hoped that the reader's judgment will be held in abeyance throughout the laying of necessary predicate and then be rendered upon a consideration of the meaning that is brought to obscure passages of scripture or to difficult life questions.

---

[65] Rudolf Steiner, *The Sun Mystery and the Mystery of Death and Resurrection: Exoteric and Esoteric Christianity* (trans. Catherine E. Creeger; CW 211; Great Barrington, Mass.: SteinerBooks, 2006).

In his *Autobiography* and the numerous other biographies available, one can see how powerfully Steiner was prepared for the mission that was his destiny.[66] Grounded in the sciences, mathematics, and philosophy a soul was emerging steeped in the power of observation in both the world of matter and the world of spirit. As the turn of the century approached he wondered how long he must remain silent on things of the spirit that he deemed of great urgency. In 1899, as he would later write in his unfinished deathbed autobiography, an epiphany-like catalyst occurred that culminated in his standing in the spiritual presence of the Mystery of Golgotha in a "deep and solemn celebration of knowledge."[67] This was his call to action, a summons much like the call of Isaiah and other ancient prophets. He began to lecture in the year 1900, and in 1902 published the work that clearly identified him with what anthroposophists refer to as the Christ impulse, an impulse that he believed was entering human evolution in a special way in his own life and times. Recognizing that his *Christianity as Mystical Fact (CMF)* was written before his readers or hearers were yet fully prepared for the things he had to say, in later lecture cycles he explained its thesis. It was to show that the Christ event was the enactment "once for all" of the substance of the ancient mysteries on the stage of world history for all to see, even though humanity was not in that era yet ready to comprehend its immense significance.[68]

---

[66] Rudolf Steiner, *Autobiography: Chapters in the Course of My Life, 1861–1907* (trans. Rita Stebbing; CW 28; Great Barrington, Mass.: SteinerBooks, 2006). Other biographies, listed in the order of their original publishing dates, include A. P. Shepherd, *Rudolf Steiner: Scientist of the Invisible* (Rochester, Vt.: Inner Traditions, 1983); repr. of *A Scientist of the Invisible: An Introduction to the Life and Work of Rudolf Steiner* (London: Hodder & Stoughton, 1954); Johannes Hemleben, *Rudolf Steiner: An Illustrated Biography* (trans. Leo Twyman; London: Sophia Books, 2000); Stewart C. Easton, *Rudolf Steiner: Herald of a New Epoch* (Hudson, N.Y.: Anthroposophic Press, 1980); Rudi Lissau, *Rudolf Steiner: Life, Work, Inner Path and Social Initiatives* (Stroud, UK: Hawthorn, 1987).

[67] Steiner, *Autobiography*, 188, xx.

[68] Rudolf Steiner, *Christianity as Mystical Fact and the Mysteries of Antiquity* (trans. Andrew J. Welburn; CW 8; Great Barrington, Mass: SteinerBooks, 2006), ch. 7. See also idem, *According to Matthew: The Gospel of Christ's Humanity* (trans. Catherine E. Creeger; Great Barrington, Mass.: SteinerBooks, 2003), 144–45 (CW 123, lect. 9); *From Jesus to Christ* (trans. H. Collison and C. Davy; London: Rudolf Steiner Press, 1973), 73 (CW 131, lect. 4), 102–5 (lect. 6).

I suggest that Paul's references to the mysteries and to the mystery of Christ could also have encompassed this understanding.

It was in *CMF* that Steiner disclosed the nature of the raising of Lazarus as an initiation in the tradition of the ancient mysteries, but it remained for him later in the decade to flesh out the more detailed aspects of how such an initiation could occur between a candidate and his hierophant, Christ in this case, which in turn allowed for the identification of Lazarus as the one who eventually came to be known as evangelist John. This Steiner did most especially in 1908 in his lecture cycle on John.[69] Later, as appropriate, we shall look more fully at what he said in that cycle. Over the intervening years, biblical scholars have increasingly come to identify Lazarus, rather than John son of Zebedee, as the person behind the mysterious designation "the disciple whom Jesus loved," which the Gospel of John uses to describe its author. We shall see this in the later section on John. But Steiner was essentially the first to make that identification, and he did so unequivocally and cogently. While most of the points he made have been pointed to by later writers, almost always without any recognition of Steiner, the most potent of all his points has not been mentioned by them, namely, the nature of the raising of Lazarus and its connection with the ancient mysteries.

In chapter ten of *CMF* Steiner made observations that anticipate the ancient works that were to be discovered later in the century, the Nag Hammadi codices and Secret Mark. He there spoke of the transition from the ancient mysteries to Christianity and of the struggles of the second century and of the gnostics "as thinkers steeped in the ancient mysteriosophy and striving to comprehend Christianity from the viewpoint of the Mysteries."[70] And in the middle of elaborating this transition he quoted Clement of Alexandria (*Stromateis* I.1.13):

> Thus the Lord did not hinder from doing good on the sabbath, but allowed us to communicate those divine Mysteries and that holy

---

[69] Rudolf Steiner, *The Gospel of St. John* (rev. ed.; New York: Anthroposophic Press, 1962) (CW 103).

[70] Steiner, *Christianity as Mystical Fact*, 148.

light to those who are able to receive them. He certainly did not disclose to the many what did not belong to the many, but to the few to whom he knew that they belonged, and who were capable of receiving and being molded according to them. But secret things are entrusted to speech, not to writing, as is the case with God....

I said that Steiner was "essentially" the first to identify Lazarus as the beloved disciple because it is possible he was not the first. In terms of publication dates, the first was one Johannes Kreyenbühl (1846–1929), whose work was published in 1900.[71] Like all of those who later have identified Lazarus as the evangelist, Kreyenbühl did not give the rationale that Steiner gave in *CMF* and its later elaboration that spoke of the nature of the raising of Lazarus and its relationship to the ancient mysteries. To comprehend that connection, it is necessary to here explore, at least in a skeletal form, the content of the ancient mysteries.

Anthroposophy and the Ancient Mysteries

Much like Christ's statement in John 14:6, "No one comes to the Father but by me," Steiner's identification of the content of the ancient mysteries might seem presumptuous if not arrogant to those who either are not yet exposed to that content or reject the possibility of such intuitions.

What was experienced and taught in the mysteries was, he said in 1909, "to a great extent ... the same as what we have come to know today as anthroposophy. It differed only in that it was adapted to the customs of that time and imparted according to strict rules."[72] It is

---

[71] See "Der Verfasser des Evangeliums" in Johannes Kreyenbühl, *Das Evangelium der Wahrheit: Neue Lösung der Johanneischen Frage* (2 vols.; Berlin; C. A. Schwetschke und Sohn, 1900, 1905), 1:146–369, esp. 151–52, 156–62. Although I have not been able to determine whether Steiner read this work, it is clear that Steiner knew earlier works by Kreyenbühl. The Johannes Kreyenbühl Academy is in Dornach, the same suburb of Basel, Switzerland, as is the international headquarters of the Anthroposophical Society.

[72] Rudolf Steiner, *The Gospel of St. John and Its Relation to the Other Gospels* (trans. Samuel Lockwood and Loni Lockwood; 2d ed.; Spring Valley, N.Y.: Anthroposophic Press, 1982) (CW 112).

immediately apparent that if this is true then in his systematic laying down of the esoteric substance of anthroposophy he was violating that sacred principle of the mysteries that bound the candidate on severe penalty not to reveal the innermost nature and content of their experienced revelation. He recognized this, but by virtue of the very nature of the evolution of human consciousness, and especially of the relationship of that evolution to an increasing comprehension of the effect of the Christ event in human history, he explained that the time had come for the spiritual realities of human evolution and the Christ event to be shared more openly with those prepared to receive them.[73]

In light of the vast breadth of his anthroposophical oeuvre, which commented on the long sweep of human evolution, one may rightly feel that compass to be maddeningly broad. We shall here pull from his writings only enough to give meaning to the subject matter at hand. If even that seems quite much, it is from necessity.

While the ancient mysteries can be seen as relevant in the study of most of the Bible, we can deal here only with a limited portion. Nevertheless, in order to elucidate this very limited portion of that canon it is necessary to place it in the context of the larger biblical setting.

The larger biblical setting, as it is understood in anthroposophy, is that of the soul's long journey, which is also the title of the last book in my trilogy attempting to bring anthroposophical insight into biblical understanding. In this perspective the Bible's greatest relevance from beginning to end is that it portrays "not only humanity but every human soul as being engaged in a very long journey through the ages, from long ago until ages hereafter."[74] It is a story of the long journey of human consciousness. This is a journey not only for humanity, or the human "kingdom," but also for the three lower "kingdoms," animal, plant, and mineral, all of which are embodied and encompassed within

---

[73] Steiner, *Autobiography*, 253–55.

[74] Edward Reaugh Smith, *The Soul's Long Journey: How the Bible Reveals Reincarnation* (vol. 3 of *Rudolf Steiner, Anthroposophy, and the Holy Scriptures*; Great Barrington, Mass.: SteinerBooks, 2003), vii.

the human kingdom and will be redeemed by the human kingdom
(cf. Rom 8:19–23; Eph 1:9–10).

Overview of the Relevant Substance of the Ancient Mysteries

At this point in the narrative a monstrous dilemma confronts
us. At the outset of Book Two I said, "This book's linchpin is the
content and significance of the ancient mysteries." In order to lay the
groundwork for an understanding of the scope of this human journey, and how the Bible can be seen to reflect it, and thus, as here
presented, to comprehend the nature of the raising of Lazarus, I deem
it essential at the outset to present an overview of that journey. It
comprises substantive content from the ancient mysteries necessary
to comprehend not only the raising of Lazarus but also the esoteric
nature of many other aspects of the canon. Here we face a dilemma.
One horn of our dilemma is the fact that without understanding that
content one cannot adequately understand everything that follows it.
The other horn is that such content is sufficiently extensive that its
presentation at this point totally disrupts the flow of the narrative.
Which comes first, the chicken or the egg? You the reader must be
engaged in that decision. In order to let the narrative flow on, the
larger body of content is moved to an appendix, letting each reader
decide when to address that material. Though extensive, it contains
only what is deemed relevant for our present purposes. It is called
Relevant Substance of the Ancient Mysteries and is herein referred to
by its acronym RSAM.

For the reader who chooses, with considerable justification, to go
on through the narrative at least once before getting to the RSAM, a
certain minimal perspective regarding the human being is essential.
According to that perspective, the human being can be considered
to be of a multitiered nature, either threefold, fourfold, sevenfold, or
ninefold—actually all of them. Most essential at this point are the first
two, the threefold and the fourfold. The threefold is that of which
Paul spoke—body, soul, and spirit (1 Thess 5:23). Each of these is
itself threefold in the ninefold nature, as later shown. The fourfold
nature comprises three bodies and an Ego, or "I Am." As a practical

matter, the "I Am" stands in for both soul and spirit though these two are distinct in the more complete human nature as the fuller content shows. Over the long journey of the human being the "I Am" must perfect (i.e., spiritualize) the lower three aspects, the three bodies. In the process the human being will have also redeemed the lower three kingdoms, animal, plant, and mineral, as Paul envisioned, thus completing the long human journey. The human being came first into spiritual existence but last into earthly materialization. Each of the three lower kingdoms represent elements of the original spiritual element that failed to progress at successive stages and fell into the lower realm, thus providing the elements upon which human earthly life could exist. Seen this way, the lower kingdoms evolved from the human and not the human from the lower kingdoms.

The three bodies are the physical, etheric, and astral. In its earliest state before descent from the highest spiritual realm each body was invisible.[75] It is to this highest realm that humanity (and with it creation) must return in its long journey to the realm from which it "fell." This deep spiritual reality is reflected in that otherwise obscure parable in Matt 13:33, "The kingdom of heaven is like leaven which a woman took and hid in three measures of flour, till it was all leavened." Here "heaven" is creation's eventual destination. The "leaven" is the human Ego or "I Am," that part of the human that is in the "image" of the Christ (Gen 1:26–27), the true "I Am" (the descending "Lord" that spoke to Moses on Mount Sinai). The "woman" is the Virgin Sophia, the eternal feminine that is the mother of the earthly Christ in the great mystery of the incarnation. The "three measures of flour" are the three bodies and the three lower kingdoms that are found in them.[76] The parable symbolizes that heaven will be attained only when the human Ego (leaven) has redeemed its lower three bodies, and thereby its three lower kingdoms, from the material state that resulted from its fall.

---

[75] Visibility, in the sense of what we could have seen with our earthly eyes had we been present then, did not commence, biblically speaking, until Gen 2:4b, everything up till then being still suspended in what can be called the astral and higher supersensible realms. See Smith, *Soul's Long Journey*, 86–99.

[76] The three bodies are extensively reflected in the canon metaphorically and allegorically. See Smith, *Burning Bush*, x, 411–73.

It can be said that the *physical body* is the force field or spiritual structure, so to speak, the pattern upon which matter emerges during the mineralization stage of Earth evolution, a stage that represents the depth of descent from the spiritual world. The *etheric body* is also known as the *life body*, for it is the seat of life. The *astral body* is also known as the *sense body*, and is the seat of consciousness, passions, and desires. It manifests in the nervous system. The Ego or "I Am" is the lasting or eternal individuality. In regard to each human being we speak of the *personality* as that portion of the karmic being that is addressed during any one incarnation of that being, while we use the term *individuality* for the more lasting and eternal being. The "I Am" is the non-material image of the Christ in which we were formed (by the elohim), and in the language of Revelation it is the name "which no one knows except him who receives it" (2:17 et al.), for as Steiner pointed out, "I" is the only name that no one can speak of anyone else but self.[77] It is the "burning bush" that first appeared to Moses on Mount Sinai (Exod 3:14, "I Am the I Am"),[78] the eternal human being that must pass through a purifying fire between incarnations but never dies on its long road to perfection.

The three younger and finer elements of the fourfold human being, the etheric, astral, and Ego in that order, have only gradually entered into the older physical body. Only those portions of these three finer elements that had not yet entered the physical were capable of perception in the supersensible realms, for entry into the mineral-physical body veiled those worlds from human perception. The entry of

---

[77] Rudolf Steiner, *The Apocalypse of St. John* (4th ed.; London: Rudolf Steiner Press, 1977), 21 (CW 104, introductory lect., June 17, 1908); idem, "The Gospel of St. John" (typescript at Rudolf Steiner Library, Ghent, N.Y.), 11–12 (CW 100, lect. 2, November 17, 1907); idem, *At the Gates of Spiritual Science* (trans. E. H. Goddard and C. Davy; 2d ed.; London: Rudolf Steiner Press, 1986), 14 (CW 95, lect. 1); idem, *Deeper Secrets of Human History in the Light of the Gospel of St. Matthew* (trans. D. S. Osmond and A. P. Shepherd; rev. ed.; London: Rudolf Steiner Press, 1957), 46 (CW 117, lect. 3, November 23, 1909); idem, *The Book of Revelation and the Work of the Priest* (trans. J. Collis; London: Rudolf Steiner Press, 1998), 139 (CW 346, lect. 10).

[78] Steiner, *Gospel of St. John*, 107–8 (lect. 6); idem, *The Principle of Spiritual Economy* (trans. Peter Mollenhauer; Hudson, N.Y.: Anthroposophic Press, 1986), 93 (CW 109/111, lect. 7, April 10, 1909).

the finer elements was very gradual over the ages but was generally complete by the time of Christ. Only the physical body is present within the mineral during earthly existence. Both the physical and etheric (life) bodies exist with the plant, while all three bodies exist within the animal. Only the human kingdom carries its "I Am" within its earthly body, where it dwells within the blood. But all three lower kingdoms have one or more of the three bodies within their earthly existence. Each of the four "kingdoms" observable by the human being's physical senses is itself a fourfold being, the difference between them being the locus of their respective "bodies":[79]

	Human Being	Animal	Plant	Mineral
Upper Devachan[80]	—	—	—	Ego
Lower Devachan	—	—	Ego	Astral
Astral Plane	—	Ego	Astral	Etheric
Physical Plane	Ego	Astral	Etheric	Physical
	Astral Body	Etheric	Physical	
	Etheric Body	Physical		
	Physical Body			

This is the barest statement of the human structure, inadequate in the final analysis but perhaps serving to add meaning to a first reading without the more lengthy interruption.

The Relationship of Sleep and Death

Anyone knows the difference between sleep and death, or so it is generally supposed. In outward result or medical observation that is so, but in the sense that was understood by those initiated into the ancient mysteries and thus, I suggest, for understanding the deeper meaning of many passages of scripture it is not so obvious but is actually quite obscure.

---

[79] The schematic is taken from chart I–11 in Smith, *Burning Bush*, based on Steiner's works cited there.
[80] Devachan means "spiritual world."

Without all the subtleties that Steiner gave in his books dealing with the matter, the relationship between sleep and death can be fairly simply stated, at least as it applies to our present stage in the long journey of human evolution, which, he believed, is not identical with the time when John baptized, two millennia earlier, which had also changed from still earlier times. To comprehend the difference between sleep and death one must return to the fourfold nature of the human being, the three bodies (physical, etheric or life, and astral or sense) and the Ego (the "I Am"). We recall that the human being has all three of the lower kingdoms within itself, but is distinguished from them in that the Ego or "I Am" dwells within the three bodies during earthly life. At night, when one sleeps, the two higher (younger and less perfected) elements, the astral body and Ego, withdraw to be spiritually refreshed by hierarchical beings in the higher worlds, the supersensible realms. Science knows that the human being cannot go indefinitely without sleep but does not fully understand why merely resting cannot accomplish the necessary refreshing that is inexorably demanded. Since the astral body (the conscious part of the nervous system) is not present during sleep there is no consciousness or sense perception. But life, the domain of the etheric or life body, remains largely within the physical, and thus death does not result. Death results only when the etheric body also leaves the physical body. When that happens the physical body begins to return to its purely mineral elements (it decays).

Some twenty-five years before discovering the works of Steiner, at about thirty years of age, I underwent a near death experience (NDE), one with the light that is so often described. But until comprehending the differences between sleep and death as above explained I never could understand why some who had undergone clinical death but returned to life had different experiences during their lifeless period. In those cases they reported hovering above their bodies while being able to see and hear those around their physical bodies. After studying anthroposophy, I concluded that it had to do with the distinction that in the latter phenomenon, that of clinical death, the etheric body left the physical body and joined the astral body and Ego in the supersensible realm where, hovering nearby, they could experience happenings near the physical body. Anthroposophy maintains that for a period of approximately three days the etheric body of a deceased person remains in the vicinity of the physical body before dissolving into the general etheric realm of the earth when the two higher elements separate from it and move on into the next stage of their journey. But in the former phenomenon, the light-experience type of NDE, the etheric body remains sufficiently within the physical body that clinical death never quite results, although one is so near death that the etheric body reaches out beyond the physical, producing what can be described as an astral or light experience. I have never heard any other rational explanation for the difference between these two types of reported experience.

It is essential to be able to understand the difference between sleep and death in this light in order to understand the raising of Lazarus. We shall look at both of these reported biblical phenomena in the light of this distinction.

Baptism

While Morton Smith's conclusion that the youth in Secret Mark was involved in a form of baptism is not one compatible with the position taken herein, it does make the subject of baptism to some extent relevant. Our purpose here is not to stimulate heated debate over whether baptism is essential to salvation. Certainly there are New Testament passages that, standing alone and in the common understanding, suggest that it is, while there are others that may be interpreted otherwise. One may wonder why, if baptism is thus so essential, neither Jesus nor Paul made a practice of baptizing, or why John the Baptist distinguished his baptism by water from that of Jesus by fire.[81] There are passages suggesting that the requisite baptism is something other than a ceremonial baptism by water. Steiner explains it, though, as an initiation process requiring something more exalted

---

[81] The indications are that neither Jesus nor Paul conducted baptisms themselves, those being conducted by their disciples (as to Jesus, see John 4:1–2; cf. 3:26; regarding Paul, see 1 Cor 1:10–17).

that he calls the "water trial" and the "air trial."[82] I have elsewhere, in considering Christ's statement "I came to cast fire upon the earth" (Luke 12:49), looked at the biblical meaning of *fire* and suggest that the baptism that is really requisite is that and that alone.[83]

Quite aside from these theological positions, I have yet to see or hear any explanation of how the mere ceremonial contact with regular water can have any inherently salvific effect *in modern times*. Regular water is matter in the same nature as flesh, yet in the very next verse after Christ says that birth by water and Spirit are necessary he distinguishes the fleshly (i.e., regular water) nature from the spiritual that is involved in the requisite birth (John 3:5–7). Anthroposophy postulates that the etheric realm, the realm related to the classical element of water, exists between the realm of earth and the spiritual realms. One descending into incarnation comes through both. One can see this in the RSAM, and for those initiated into the ancient mysteries these words had different meaning from the way they are now commonly understood. Christ was here speaking to Nicodemus in a most profound spiritual way.

But let us move beyond this aspect for now in order to look particularly at the baptism of John and its uniqueness in the long journey of human evolution. To comprehend the significance of John's baptism it is necessary to place it in the context of the long human journey portrayed in the RSAM and the development and relationship of the components of the fourfold human being as they existed at that turning point of time, the Christ event, or what Steiner calls the Mystery of Golgotha. An understanding of that baptism is an essential building block for understanding the raising of Lazarus and the significance

---

82 Rudolf Steiner, *How to Know Higher Worlds: A Modern Path of Initiation* (trans. Christopher Bamford; Hudson, N.Y.: Anthroposophic Press, 1994), 69–82 (CW 10, ch. 3). It is of some significance that Christ's "born of water and spirit" is explaining his statement to Nicodemus that one must be "born anew" or "born again." Cf. Smith, *Soul's Long Journey*, 227–38. Those attaining such initiation experience the kingdom long before the rest of humanity, so that the phrase "born again" can apply to experiencing the kingdom either through initiation or through the course of subsequent earthly lives.

83 See Edward Reaugh Smith, *David's Question: "What Is Man?" (Psalm 8)* (vol. 2 of *Rudolf Steiner, Anthroposophy, and the Holy Scriptures*; Great Barrington, Mass.: Anthroposophic Press, 2001), 116–204.

of the putative Secret Gospel of Mark. The New Testament's clear indication that the Christ event had occurred at the "right time," or when "the time had been fulfilled," fits precisely, indeed seems clearly to imply, a providential understanding that humanity, even creation itself (cf. Rom 8:19–23), had reached a point when the creative God, the Word, had to become flesh. In anthroposophy, the purpose of Christ's incarnation was to reverse humanity's parabolic descent into matter. The younger and more spiritual bodies of the human being, the astral and etheric, were approaching their maximum entry into the mineral-physical body. The veil of the temple was being pulled shut. If the blood of Christ were not to enter into the etheric (life) realm of the earth, all elements of the human being, meaning creation, would pass irredeemably into the abyss, hardened beyond redemption.

By the time of John's baptism, it had become increasingly difficult to cause the etheric body to be loosened and pulled outside the physical so that some perception of the spiritual realms could be experienced once again as they had been before God had "hidden his face" in the evolutionary descent that was the removal from the garden or tree of (etheric) life. The critical aspect of John's baptism was the effect the lowering and holding of a candidate underwater had upon the candidate's etheric body. That effect, Steiner explains, was to bring about a loosening and a temporary extension of the etheric body beyond the physical where it could perceive things in the supersensible realms not otherwise to be experienced in the physical:

> The candidate was submerged under water for a certain length of time, varying according to circumstances. What this signified we shall now learn by delving into the mystery of the being of man.
>
> Recall to mind that the human being consists of physical body, etheric body, astral body, and ego. In the waking state during the daytime, these four principles are firmly knit together, but in sleep the physical and etheric bodies remain in bed, while the astral body and the ego are outside. In death, on the other hand, the physical body remains as a corpse: the etheric body withdraws, and for a short time, the ego, the astral body and the etheric body remain united. To those of you who have heard even a few of my lectures

it must be clear that in this moment a quite definite experience appears first: the deceased sees his past life spread out before him like a magnificent tableau. Side by side, in space, all the situations of his life surround him. That is because one of the functions of the etheric body is that of memory bearer, and even during life only the physical body prevents all this from appearing before him. After death, with the physical body laid aside, everything man has experienced during his lifetime can enter his consciousness.

Now, I have mentioned as well that such a review of life also results from being in peril of death, or from any severe fright or shock. You know, of course, from reports that when a man is in danger of drowning or falling from a mountain height, he experiences his whole past life as in a great tableau, provided he does not lose consciousness. Well, what a man thus experiences as the result of some danger, such as drowning, was experienced by nearly all who were baptized by John. The baptism consisted in keeping a person under water until he had experienced his past life. But what was experienced in this way was, of course, experienced as a spiritual picture ... so that after being lifted out of the water again, after the baptism by John, a man knew: There is a spiritual world![84]

This experience prepared the way for the candidates' reception of the message of Christ, the one John knew was to come. According to Steiner, not all candidates were able to experience that effect, for etheric bodies were generally well entrenched by then within the mineral-physical body. However, enough were able to have the experience and report it to others, so that what they reported came to be known as the baptism of John. The expectations it created paved the way for the Christ.

Noticeably absent from the above description of John's baptism is the concept of remorse for past sins. While that may have come about as a result of the insights gained, the real meaning of the term

---

[84] Steiner, *Gospel of St. John and Its Relation to the Other Gospels*, 110–11 (lect. 6). Steiner gave this explanation in Kassel on June 29, 1909.

repentance according to Steiner, and a more appropriate translation of the Greek (*metanoia*), is "change your way of thinking." It was not a matter of personal remorse for past sins as much as a recognition of what was now happening, namely, that a God, none other than the "I Am" that appeared to Moses on Mount Sinai, was entering bodily into human form. According to Steiner, the experience of undergoing John's baptism revealed to a Palestinian Jew the reality of his or her own "I Am," that person's own past lives and spiritual being, which was no longer to be condemned to dwell in Sheol.[85] In the larger perspective of humanity and the passage of two millennia, anthroposophy sees the entry of the higher "I Am" into earthly flesh as a divine necessity in order that his blood might carry his very being into the etheric (life) element of the earth for the salvation of what was otherwise in a process of death. Of course, personal sin was involved in that ongoing process of death, and for that sin remorse was appropriate, but the issue was far larger than that. What was really being addressed was what we call "original sin," that which brought about the fall (Genesis 3). But as the RSAM explains, the Luciferic infection that brought about such fall occurred before the Ego, the "I Am," had even entered into the physical body—indeed, all that was described in Genesis 3 preceded the descent of the first Adam into materiality, who as described in the RSAM first appeared in Gen 4:25. Steiner pointed out that the fact that humanity was burdened with sin before it had any consciousness or moral responsibility for sin (not having yet, while in the garden, an indwelling Ego or soul) was counterbalanced by a divine grace that was not earned but freely given for the ultimate redemption of all.

The reader who encounters these concepts for the first time may find them puzzling at best, or perhaps repugnant at worst, but the

---

[85] See Steiner, *Gospel of St. John and Its Relation to the Other Gospels*, chs. 6 and 7; idem, *Background to the Gospel of St. Mark* (trans. E. H. Goddard and D. S. Osmond; Hudson, N.Y.: Anthroposophic Press, 1985), 66 (CW 124, lect. 4). Knowledge of past lives points to a recognition of reincarnation, as suggested by questions about the Baptist being the reincarnated Elijah or questions about whose sin caused the affliction of the man born blind (John 9). But the expectation of an early return of Christ, with the consummation that his return was expected to bring, would render future reincarnation irrelevant to those who wrote the New Testament.

more one examines the full scope of the biblical picture the more one finds that these concepts appear compatible with, if not demanded by, it.

In any event, the nature of the baptism of John was important to consider at this juncture because it moves us one step closer to an examination of the phenomenon involved in the raising of Lazarus, where the matter of the stage of human evolution and the imprisonment of the etheric body within the physical are both key ingredients, as is also the relationship between sleep and death.

The Ancient Temple Sleep

The farther back in human evolution one moves from Christ, the turning point of time, the less of the finer bodies, etheric and astral, had entered into the confines of the mineral-physical body. To the extent they dwelled outside of it, they were in the supersensible realm; their consciousness was there, perceiving other beings in those realms. But to the extent they dwelled in those realms, they did not have at their disposal what the mineral-physical body could provide. In addition to perception of spiritual beings, memory was virtually without limit. But intellect as we know it did not exist, for there was no adequately developed physical brain to provide it. Over the course of time, as the gods "hid their face" and memory waned, intellect correspondingly increased. Before there was intellect, human beings were led by spiritual beings in an instinct-like existence.

The complexity of the human being is obvious. Anthroposophy has an explanation not only for how each of the four human components came into being but also for how they interact. In simplest terms, intellect is a product of all four components working cooperatively within an embodied person. The physical brain is an essential element, being part of the nervous system, which is the earthly home of the astral body. For each part of the physical body there is an etheric counterpart, and it is that counterpart that creates and maintains the physical. The human brain has evolved over the ages as the etheric brain has drawn within the physical. The etheric body is also the seat of memory. Today the etheric and astral bodies are almost

entirely within the physical body. To the extent the etheric body
drew more and more into the physical body, it perfected the brain,
and intellect increased. The increase came at the expense of memory,
which was now limited by the confines of the physical body. In like
manner perception in the spiritual realm became increasingly veiled.
Anthroposophy sees the more profound meaning of the piercing of
the temple veil to be the effect of the blood of Christ having entered
into the etheric realm of the earth in order to provide the spiritual
power in the human being for its return journey to the spiritual home
that it left long ago.

Gradually, as perception in and leadership from higher realms
faded, humans were obliged to rely for leadership upon those who
retained the greater spiritual connection, those who came to be the
ancient priests or masters of the mysteries. But the process we are
talking about involved thousands of years, and by the time of the
Christ event, perception in the spiritual world was largely obscured,
and prophecy diminished in those final centuries. What remained of
the ancient mysteries had become largely decadent, though there were
those who looked back to them with a longing for what they had
previously given. So completely had the etheric body entered into
the mineral-physical body that any effort to remove it for spiritual
purposes became increasingly dangerous to earthly life itself.[86]

We may assume that perhaps some such danger may have existed
for those who submitted themselves to John's baptism. But for those
who, by that time, were candidates for initiation in what is known as
the *temple sleep*, Steiner has indicated that the danger was very much
present. From a lecture at Dornach, Switzerland, on December 22,
1923, we read these words:

> Whoever really understands the Mystery of Golgotha—and no one
> of course understands it simply by knowing the historical records
> which relate about it—anyone who really understands the Mystery
> of Golgotha understands at the same time all the Mysteries which
> preceded it.

---

[86] Steiner, *Gospel of St. John and Its Relation to the Other Gospels*, 105–8 (lect. 6).

These Mysteries which preceded the Mystery of Golgotha and found their culmination point therein, all had one peculiarity in reference to their effect on the life of feeling. There was much of tragedy in them, and any man who sought initiation into these Mysteries had to undergo pain and sorrow. I have often described that to you; but speaking quite generally, one can say that right up to the time of the Mystery of Golgotha anyone who was to experience initiation, and was told that he would have to undergo much self-denial, pain and suffering, and to experience many tragic things, would nevertheless say: "I will go through all the fire of the world, for that will lead me finally into the Light-region of the spirit, in which one beholds what otherwise with the ordinary consciousness of man on the earth one can only dimly divine at a definite epoch of time."[87]

In the light of this it is not surprising that we read, "Now a certain man was ill, Lazarus of Bethany..." (John 11:1). According to Steiner the illness had to do with the fact that all Lazarus had been, up to that point, and all the Mosaic heritage and culture that was his, was in effect coming to an end. We are told that candidates for initiation had to undergo much disciplined preparation, and we can gather that it was not without pain and suffering in one or many forms. The position taken here is that Lazarus is the "rich young ruler" of the synoptic tradition, the one who went away sorrowful when told that the one thing he lacked was relinquishing all his wealth to the poor.[88] While there are differences, scholars recognize many similarities between Secret Mark and the Lazarus account. But the only two men in any gospel who, as individuals, Jesus is said to have loved are Lazarus in John's Gospel and this rich man who went away sorrowful in Mark's Gospel. In this work the two men are considered to be one and the same. To the extent that Lazarus was the "rich young ruler" of

---

[87] Quoted from Rudolf Steiner, *Mystery Centers* (Blauvelt, N.Y.: Garber Communications, 1989), lect. 13 (CW 232).
[88] Mark 10:17–22; Matt 19:16–22; Luke 18:18–23. On the conflation "rich young ruler," see n. 58.

a synoptic-gospel conflation, perhaps his need to sacrifice all that he had was also an element of his illness.

According to Mark (and Matthew) he went away sorrowful; Luke merely indicates that he became sad. These accounts suggest that perhaps he did not immediately dispose of his wealth as prescribed. That he ultimately followed in some manner the advice Jesus gave, perhaps at least in part by placing portions of his wealth at the disposal of the needs of the disciples, must be assumed according to the position taken herein. It is interesting that Clement of Alexandria, in his *Who Is the Rich Man That Shall Be Saved?*, interprets Mark's passage about the rich youth whom Jesus loved (10:17–31) to indicate that one does not need to abandon all of one's property so long as its importance is abandoned within the soul and the money is used for doing good. Within the context of Mark 10:21 (cf. Matt 19:21 and Luke 18:22–27), however, it would seem that Lazarus must surely have given his wealth away, though the idea expressed that he may have been the owner of the "upper room" (an idea considered in the John chapter) and perhaps other facilities similarly provided would suggest that he made at least part of it available to Christ and his followers. By the end of the second century, when Clement of Alexandria was active, knowledge of the identity of "the disciple whom Jesus loved," at least as presented here, had largely disappeared in favor of the apostle John, the son of Zebedee.

As previously indicated, as early as 1902 in *CMF* Steiner disclosed that the raising of Lazarus was an initiation in the tradition of the ancient mysteries, but he did so knowing that he was entering a massive subject matter for which his audiences were not fully prepared. We might say that over the next few years he was laying groundwork for the period between 1908 and 1914 when it is fair to say that the primary focus of his lectures and writings was an eye-opening portrayal of the biblical message. Many lecture cycles were specifically biblical, but virtually his entire production during those years was in some meaningful way connected with his exposition of biblical meaning. But it was in 1907 when he returned specifically to the Gospel of John and to the Lazarus story as though it was the essential prelude to what was then just ahead.

In a lecture in Munich on March 17, 1907, he gave an early explanation of the ancient temple sleep initiation (footnote added):

In pre-Christian ages, pupils were first prepared for initiation with all that esoteric science can impart up to the point when they had gained familiarity with all the concepts and images, all the habits and feelings that are needed in order to live and perceive in higher worlds. Then came what was called the awakening, which lasted for three and a half days and nights. This consisted in the human being's being placed artificially, by the art of the temple priest, in a sleep state similar to death for three and a half days. While the physical and etheric bodies usually remain together during sleep, during the time of initiation the etheric body of the one being initiated was lifted out of the physical body by the initiating priest so that only a loose connection continued to exist between the physical body and the other bodies. It was a deep trance. During this time the human I-being lived in higher worlds. Because the pupils were given a knowledge of higher worlds, they knew their way around there. They were guided by priests. The priest had first to free the etheric body from the lethargic physical body in order to guide the pupil out into the spiritual worlds. In a fully conscious condition, the human being could never have ascended into those higher worlds, but had to be lifted out of this condition.

Even though what the initiates experienced there in the higher worlds was very majestic and powerful, nevertheless, they were entirely in the hands of the priest.[89] Another person ruled over

---

89 This function of the priest might be seen as reflected in the Secret Gospel passages in Clement's *Letter to Theodore*. Clement portrays Jesus functioning as a hierophant in Secret Mark. This seems consistent with Clement's allegorical interpretation of Leviticus 16, the high priest's preparations to enter the holy of holies on the Day of Atonement (*Stromateis* V.6). For Clement, the high priest symbolizes the Christian who has attained gnosis, and the holy of holies symbolizes the noetic world that this Christian can perceive. See Judith L. Kovacs, "Concealment and Gnostic Exegesis: Clement of Alexandria's Interpretation of the Tabernacle," in *Studia Patristica: Papers Presented at the Twelfth International Conference on Patristic Studies Held in Oxford, 1995* (Studia patristica 31; ed. Elizabeth A. Livingstone; Leuven: Peeters, 1997), 414–37. While Clement does not speak of the high priest as hierophant, the requisite advanced spiritual status is proclaimed.

them; they were able to penetrate into higher worlds only at this price. You can imagine what these people were like after initiation, if you consider that they had experienced their eternal essence. They had been freed of that part of their mortality that they had no use for so that they were able to move about in higher worlds. Such people emerged as human beings who were "knowers," who, out of their own experience, were able to bear witness to the victory of life over death. The etheric body had to be lifted out of the physical body in order for the human being to experience Christ. These initiates could say, "I myself have experienced that there is an eternal part in the human being that survives through all incarnations. I know it. I have experienced this eternal essence myself." But the price they had to pay for this was passage through three days in a total trance.[90]

In November 1907 Steiner gave an eight-lecture cycle in Basel on John's Gospel.[91] But it was his twelve-lecture cycle on that gospel delivered in Hamburg between May 18 and 31, 1908, that should probably be deemed the time when he made the biblical message his primary focus. In this cycle of lectures he presented many of the cogent points later taken up by those several scholars who have identified Lazarus as evangelist John. But the critical element that he and he alone provided, namely, an understanding of the raising of Lazarus, was his unique contribution on the issue to this day and is probably the most powerful of all insights into the authorship of that gospel. Yet within the academy and among academic theological writers, few have mentioned Steiner as accredited to write or speak

---

[90] Rudolf Steiner, "Earlier Initiation and Esoteric Christianity," in *The Christian Mystery* (trans. James H. Hindes et al.; Hudson, N.Y.: Anthroposophic Press, 1998), 187–88 (CW 97). On various occasions Steiner touched further on this temple sleep phenomenon, often with some nuance that added understanding of the process. See, for instance, Rudolf Steiner, "Easter: The Mystery of the Future," in *The Festivals and Their Meaning* (trans. M. Cotterell; 2d ed.; London: Rudolf Steiner Press, 1992), 204–5 (CW 102, April 13, 1908). I have reproduced the pertinent portion of the lecture in Appendix Two.

[91] Steiner, "Gospel of St. John."

on the matter.[92] This element more than any other gives meaning to Morton Smith's alleged discovery, the Secret Gospel of Mark, and does so independently of any argument Smith or any other (non-anthroposophical) scholar to my knowledge has advanced in support of the authenticity of that highly controversial writing.

Because of the importance of Steiner's explanation of the eleventh chapter of John's Gospel and its relevance to all that is in this volume, it is given here:

One who knows how to read this Gospel will understand that a mystery lies hidden within this chapter. The mystery concealed therein is, in truth, concerned with the actual identity of the man who says all that we find written there. In order to understand this, we must turn our attention to what in the ancient Mysteries is called "initiation." How did these initiations in the ancient Mysteries take place?

A man who was initiated could himself have experiences and personal knowledge of the spiritual worlds and thus he could bear witness of them. Those who were found sufficiently developed for initiation were led into the Mysteries. Everywhere—in Greece, among the Chaldeans, among the Egyptians and the Indians— these Mysteries existed. There the neophytes were instructed for a long time in approximately the same things which we now learn in [anthroposophy]. Then when they were sufficiently instructed, there followed that part of the training which opened up to them the way to a perception of the spiritual world. However, in ancient times this could only be brought about by putting the neophyte into a very extraordinary condition in respect of his four principles— his physical, ether and astral bodies and his ego. The next thing that occurred to the neophyte was that he was put into a death-like sleep by the initiator or hierophant who understood the matter and there he remained for three and a half days. Why this occurred can be seen if we consider that in the present cycle of evolution,

---

[92] Even James H. Charlesworth, in his *The Beloved Disciple: Whose Witness Validates the Gospel of John?* (Valley Forge: Trinity Press International, 1995), makes no mention of Steiner, despite listing many individuals who identified Lazarus as the beloved disciple, including Kreyenbühl.

when the human being sleeps in the ordinary sense of the word, his physical and ether bodies lie in bed and his astral body and ego are withdrawn. In that condition he cannot observe any of the spiritual events taking place about him, because his astral body has not yet developed the spiritual sense-organs for a perception of the world in which he then finds himself. Only when his astral body and ego have slipped back into his physical and ether bodies, and he once more makes use of his eyes and ears, does he again perceive the physical world, that is, he perceives a world about him. Through what he had learned, the neophyte was capable of developing spiritual organs of perception in his astral body and when he was sufficiently evolved for the astral body to have formed these organs, then all that the astral body had received into itself had to be impressed upon the ether body just as the design on a seal is impressed upon the sealing-wax. This is the important thing. All preparations for initiation depended upon the surrender of the man himself to the inner processes which reorganized his astral body.

The human being at one time did not have eyes and ears in his physical body as he has today, but undeveloped organs instead— just as animals who have never been exposed to the light have no eyes. The light forms the eye, sound fashions the ear. What the neophyte practiced through meditation and concentration and what he experienced inwardly through them, acted like light upon the eye and sound upon the ear. In this way the astral body was transformed and organs of perception for seeing in the astral or higher world were evolved. But these organs are not yet firmly enough fixed in the ether body. They will become so when what has been formed in the astral body will have been stamped upon the ether body. However, as long as the ether body remains bound to the physical, it is not possible for all that has been accomplished by means of spiritual exercises to be really impressed upon it. Before this can happen, the ether body must be drawn out of the physical. Therefore when the ether body was drawn out of the physical body during the three and a half day death-like sleep, all that had been prepared in the astral body was stamped upon the ether body. The neophyte then experienced the spiritual world. Then when he was called back into the physical body by the Priest-Initiator, he bore witness through his own experience of what takes place in the spiritual worlds. This procedure has now become unnecessary through the experience of Christ-Jesus. This three and a half day death-like sleep can now be replaced by the force proceeding from the Christ. For we shall soon see that in the Gospel of St. John strong forces are present which render it possible for the present astral body, even though the ether body is still within the physical, to have the power to stamp upon the etheric what had previously been prepared within it. But for this to take place, Christ-Jesus must first be present. Up to this time without the above-characterized procedure, humanity was not far enough advanced for the astral body to be able to imprint upon the ether body what had been prepared within it through meditation and concentration. This was a process which often took place within the Mysteries; a neophyte was brought into a death-like sleep by the Priest-Initiator and was guided through the higher worlds. He was then again called back into his physical body by the Priest-Initiator and thus became a witness of the spiritual world through his own experience.

This took place always in the greatest secrecy and the outer world knew nothing of the occurrences within these ancient Mysteries. Through Christ-Jesus a new initiation had to arise to replace the old, an initiation produced by means of forces of which we have yet to speak. The old form of initiation must end, but a transition had to be made from the old to the new age and to make this transition, someone had once more to be initiated in the old way, but initiated into Christian Esotericism. This only Christ-Jesus Himself could perform and the neophyte was the one who is called Lazarus. "This sickness is not unto death," means here that it is the three and a half day death-like sleep. This is clearly indicated.

You will see that the presentation is of a very veiled character, but for one who is able to decipher a presentation of this kind it represents initiation. The individuality Lazarus had to be initiated in such a way that he could be a witness of the spiritual worlds. An expression is used, a very significant expression in the language of the Mysteries, "that the Lord loved Lazarus." What does "to love" mean in the language of the Mysteries? It expresses the relationship of the pupil to the teacher. "He whom the Lord loved" is the most intimate, the most deeply initiated pupil.[93]

When one comes to understand the raising of Lazarus as an initiation in the manner of the ancient temple sleep just described, quite a number of biblical passages begin to make sense in a way that could not previously have been recognized. For instance, in keeping with the ancient goal of having one's name reflect one's true character, we can readily accept the fact that upon the experience Lazarus had been through his name should reflect his new spiritual reality, so he became known as John, just as the Baptist had so pointedly been given that name.[94] There was not only a similarity in their mission, but also an actual spiritual relationship between them. It was described by Steiner during his last illness in response to a question asked by his physician, Dr. Ludwig Noll:

> At the awakening of Lazarus, the spiritual Being, John the Baptist, who since his death had been the overshadowing Spirit of the disciples, penetrated from above into Lazarus as far as the Consciousness Soul; the Being of Lazarus himself, from below, intermingled with the spiritual Being of John the Baptist from above. After the awakening of Lazarus, this Being is Lazarus-John, the disciple whom the Lord loved.[95]

From the schematic of the ninefold human given early in the RSAM, it can be seen that this penetration or indwelling of the Baptist was in the highest level of Lazarus-John's soul being. It was this that made it possible for Lazarus-John to give testimony of John the Baptist about events at which he himself may not have been present. Steiner points out that from John 1:19 ("And this is the testimony of John...") up to John 10:41 ("And many came to him; and they said, 'John did no

---

[93] Steiner, *Gospel of St. John*, 62–64 (lect. 4).

[94] See Appendix One (The Giving of a Name).

[95] According to Alfred Heidenreich's preface to Steiner's *The Last Address* (trans. George Adams; London: Rudolf Steiner Press, 1967), 9, (CW 238), the authenticated statement in the text was quoted in "the postscript printed in the most recent German edition of the 'Last Address.'" Hopefully it will also appear in the CW series.

sign, but everything that John said about this man was true'") were the words of John the Baptist coming through the consciousness soul of Lazarus-John.[96] From 10:41 on, the testimony is that of Lazarus-John himself, beginning with the central chapter 11, his own raising.[97]

What has been said in this section about the nature of the raising of Lazarus from the dead should not be taken as applying to other reported instances of raising the dead or resuscitation. Steiner himself indicated that the young man of Nain (Luke 7:11–15) was dead in the normal sense. However, one might surmise that in those instances, canonical or otherwise, where a person is brought back to life, the etheric body has remained intact near the physical body rather than having dissipated back into the earth's ether. The situation is akin to the clinical death cases discussed earlier in the section comparing sleep and death, but aside from instances where the resuscitation is spontaneous it would seem that, in addition to the Christ, some human beings have had sufficient spiritual power to assist in the return to life.

The earlier discussion of the distinction between sleep and death mentioned the anthroposophical teaching that the etheric body remained near the physical body for three days before dissipating back into the general ether of the earth. This would appear to comport with Jewish belief of the time. Herman C. Waetjen, in his *The Gospel of*

---

[96] Steiner, *Gospel of St. John*, 60–61, 64–65. I share with Richard Bauckham and some other scholars the view that the disciple whom Jesus loved is the one anonymous disciple of the Baptist who was with Jesus very soon after the latter's baptism and who, along with Andrew, appears to have spent the evening with Jesus at that time (John 1:35–40). Thus, according to John's Gospel, though not one of the twelve, he was one of the first two disciples, preceding even Peter. His discipleship seems based in Judea, however. Steiner expressly rejected the suggestion that Lazarus was the unnamed "other disciple" in John 1:35–40, saying that the beloved disciple did not enter the story until John 11 (*Gospel of St. John*, 79; *Gospel of St. John and Its Relation to the Other Gospels*, 133–34), though in *Gospel of St. John* it appears that his position was influenced by the "ancient exoteric tradition" that the apostle John was the author of the gospel, which view, he said, "is supported by Matthew IV 21" ("And going on from there he saw two other brothers, James the son of Zebedee and John his brother ..."). Steiner's vigorous opposition to the then widely accepted authorship by John son of Zebedee probably influenced his position on a point that may not then have seemed of great significance. On this matter, I must reluctantly differ with Steiner.

[97] For one of Steiner's more stimulating insights into the power of John's Gospel, see Appendix Three.

the Beloved Disciple, tells of a rabbinic tradition that "testimony about the identity of a corpse is given only during a period of three days after death" because by the fourth day decomposition begins to make the face of the corpse no longer recognizable. "The soul, which has remained close to the corpse, no longer recognizes the body to which it belonged and therefore abandons it and 'goes its own way.'"[98] Citing this popular Jewish belief, Desmond Stewart suggested that Martha's remark "Lord, by this time there will be an odor, for he [Lazarus] has been dead four days" concerned not odor per se but corruption, or the state of being "completely dead."[99]

It would seem that the ancient temple sleep, by lasting three and a half days, went right to the point that dissolution of the etheric body commenced. This period of time seems to be reflected in Rev 11:11, "But after the three and a half days a breath of life from God entered them, and they stood up on their feet, and great fear fell on those who saw them." Obviously any period of three and a half days would occupy a part of at least four days, justifying Martha's reference.

Was Lazarus Dead or Just Sleeping?

Because Jesus refers to Lazarus both as sleeping ("Our friend Lazarus has fallen asleep, but I go to awake him out of sleep"; John 11:11) and as dead ("Lazarus is dead"; 11:14), and because in the Synoptic Gospels Jesus refers to one person as sleeping who he had been told was dead ("The child is not dead but sleeping"; Mark 5:39; Matt 9:23; Luke 8:52), it is well that we be clear as to the status of Lazarus in the few days before he was raised. Was he dead or sleeping?

Lazarus was dead. A person is dead when the etheric body (life body) departs the physical. In those instances where the etheric body returns again into the physical, the person is again alive. In modern times, the clinical deaths which resuscitate, with or without assistance, are manifestations of this phenomenon. The individuals are actually

---

[98] Herman C. Waetjen, *The Gospel of the Beloved Disciple: A Work in Two Editions* (New York: T&T Clark, 2005), 276.
[99] Desmond Stewart, *The Foreigner* (London: Hamish Hamilton, 1981), 108.

dead for a period. In the case of Lazarus, whose death, as we shall see, was not brought about in the normal temple sleep mode, Jesus was nevertheless able to serve as hierophant in bringing the etheric body of Lazarus back. More will be said later about the period he was dead. It is sufficient for now to state that he was dead.

Jesus would not have been contradicting himself by speaking of Lazarus as both sleeping and dead in the light of the ancient initiatory practice of the temple sleep. That sleep involved a period of time during which the candidate was actually dead, but under the monitoring auspices of a priest or hierophant.

Abram's Deep Sleep?

We can now reflect with more informed understanding on the meaning of the "deep sleep" of Abram (Gen 15:12), for we may surmise that he was still in the presence of Melchizedek, the priest of the God Most High (Gen 14:18), who like the Christ Spirit, having neither an earthly father nor a mother (Heb 7:1–3),[100] was supremely able to serve as the priestly hierophant, and in due course thereafter Abram was given his new name, Abraham (Gen 17:5). We should not make too much of the twenty-four years that can be identified between the encounter with Melchizedek and the giving of the new name.[101] The encounter with Melchizedek commenced a process of initiation the description of which is spread over at least five chapters (14–18), which are laced through with much symbolism, including that of his being "under the tree" (18:4, 8).[102] Philo recognizes Abraham as having had his eyes opened from his "deep slumber" to see "a certain governor and director of the world" (*On Abraham* 70) and as having been able "to behold the secret mysteries of God" (*Allegorical Interpretations* 2.15–16; trans. C. D. Yonge). These facts suggest to

---

[100] For the similarity of Melchizedek to Christ in having neither mother nor father nor beginning nor end of life, see Smith, *Soul's Long Journey*, 142–54, as well as Appendix Three herein, n. 179.

[101] "Twenty-four years": ten years in Canaan (Gen 16:3), plus thirteen years between age eighty-six and ninety-nine (16:16–17:1), plus one year to age one hundred (17:17).

[102] "Under the tree": see "The Fig Tree Conundrum," below.

me that Abraham was initiated into the great mysteries through the experience of the temple sleep or its equivalent.

The Three Days' Journey

The *three days' journey* in those eight Old Testament passages that speak of it now takes on new meaning.[103] That it has reference to the ancient temple sleep initiation seems powerfully indicated, particularly in view of the involvement of the phrase in the account of Jonah's journey. That the Jonah account involved an initiation is but a small part of what is suggested here. It is hard to imagine any other book of the canon dislodging the modern reader from a literal interpretation more dynamically than this one with its story of the big fish. Nor has this little book been an easy read for scholars. I have in my personal library some works on Jonah by three scholars.[104] A brief word from each of these is informative before a brief anthroposophical analysis of Jonah is offered.

Jack M. Sasson writes, the "arguments [of Jonah] are highly nuanced and sophisticated and can accommodate many interpretations at the same time." Uriel Simon says, "Biblical narrative tends to prefer indirect expression over explicit ideological, ethical, or psychological statements. This tendency reaches its most radical manifestation in the Book of Jonah."[105] Phyllis Trible's *Rhetorical Criticism* obviously emphasizes the book's rhetoric, but not without noting for context "what other biblical disciplines say about Jonah." Of them she says, "Textual criticism finds no major problems in the book," its manuscripts having been well preserved. But, "By contrast, historical criticism struggles without resolution to determine author, date, setting,

---

[103] The first of these involves Laban and Jacob (Gen 30:36), the next six involve Moses and the Hebrew people (Exod 3:18; 5:3; 8:27; Num 10:33 [2 x]; 33:8), and the last Jonah (3:3).

[104] Jack M. Sasson, *Jonah: A New Translation with Introduction, Commentary, and Interpretations* (Anchor Bible 24B; New York: Doubleday, 1990). Phyllis Trible, *Rhetorical Criticism: Context, Method, and the Book of Jonah* (Minneapolis: Fortress, 1994); idem, "The Book of Jonah," *The New Interpreter's Bible* 7:463–529. Uriel Simon, *Jonah: The Traditional Hebrew Text with the New JPS Translation* (trans. Lenn J. Schramm; Philadelphia: Jewish Publication Society, 1999).

[105] Sasson, *Jonah*, xi. Simon, *Jonah*, vii.

and purpose. The major source critical problem centers on the psalm in chapter 2:3–10" (the big-fish account), which, if an insertion, brings up redaction criticism and how such insertion "shapes the theological framework." Canonical criticism seeks its theology, which calls up the question of its genre, as to which form criticism generates a profusion, "allegory, fable, fairy tale, folktale, legend, *Märchen, māšāl, midrash*, novel, parable, prophetic tale, saga, satire, sermon, short story and even tragedy." Not surprisingly, "Theologies of Jonah differ strikingly."[106]

As with the book of Job and many others, anthroposophy offers a strikingly different way to understand the book's message.[107] Following is a summary rendition.

To begin with, as with Job there is no need to redact or rearrange the account as it appears. The story is ordered right and can be seen to reveal great spiritual meaning. A good place to start is with a greatly simplified version of Steiner's explanation of the soul's long journey between death and rebirth.[108] The sequence experienced by the journeying soul (more accurately termed "spirit" at this stage) is portrayed in the left column below, reflected in its earthly form in the right column:

Soul's Long Journey in the Spiritland Region	*Form It Assumes on Earth*
Solid land	Physical
Oceans, rivers, or blood circulation	Life
Atmosphere	Sensation, raging tempest, battlefield
Warmth	Thought
Light	Wisdom

---

[106] Trible, *Rhetorical Criticism,* 107–8.

[107] For an anthroposophical understanding of Job, see Smith, *Soul's Long Journey,* 99–121.

[108] Many of Steiner's works give aspects of this journey. The best place to start is with his 1909 foundational book *An Outline of Esoteric Science* (trans. Catherine E. Creeger; Great Barrington, Mass.: Anthroposophic Press, 1997) (CW 13). Its ch. 3, "Sleep and Death," gives an account. A considerable exposition on it is also available in Smith, *Burning Bush,* 112–27 and chart I-33 (pp. 603–6).

The classical four elements—earth, water, air, and fire (solid, fluid, gas, warmth)—as well as the fourfold nature of the human being can be seen in this sequence. Upon observing that, it occurred to me that this sequence is precisely what is portrayed in so many of the biblical stories that involve storms or water launchings. Foremost among these is the book of Jonah, followed closely by the storm on the Sea of Galilee (Matt 8:18, 23–27; Mark 4:35–41; Luke 8:22–25) and Paul's last journey (Acts 27–28). Numerous others also portray the same progression: a stable situation like being on land; followed by movement, as on water; then turmoil, storm, or crisis; next resolution of the crisis; and finally insight.[109] The esoteric principle of "as above, so below," inherent in the biblical view that all things seen come from the unseen (Heb 11:3), can be observed in these instances.

But how is this reflected in the book of Jonah?

While she did not analyze the book in the light of anthroposophy, Trible did give a schematic that is useful to the latter approach. She presents a *ninefold* "External Design: A Study in Symmetry," in which she shows the remarkable repetition in chapters 3 and 4 of what first plays out in chapters 1 and 2.[110] An anthroposophist can see the first two chapters giving the water-launching sequence above, followed by the actual three-day initiation in the belly of the fish (Jonah's initiatory tomb or cave). This prepares the prophet in his journey through the spiritual world before incarnating to replay his destiny in earthly life. His earthly journey is a mirror image of that in the spiritual world, the initiation (*three-days' journey*) taking place prior to the start of his mission. Initiation does not relieve one of the trials of the world but prepares one to face them with a greater depth of understanding.

---

[109] These would include Noah and the flood (Genesis 6–8); Jacob's crossing of the Jabbok to meet Esau (Genesis 32–33); the birth of Moses (Exod 2:1–10); the crossing of the Red Sea (Exodus 14–15); more expansively the entire journey of Israel through the giving of the Ten Commandments (Exodus 1–20); the reprise of the Red Sea crossing in Joshua's crossing the Jordan at Gilgal (Joshua 4); Jesus walking on the Sea of Galilee (John 6:16–21); and the risen Jesus appearing to the fishermen (John 21). And the same sequence through land, water, air, and fire can be seen in the accounts of the progressive sequences of the seven trumpets and the seven bowls of wrath in John's Revelation (chs. 8–9 and 16).

[110] Trible, *Rhetorical Criticism*, 110–12.

A superficial reading of the earthly part misses many very esoteric symbols to be found in it. Jonah's anger over God's decision to spare Nineveh functionally parallels the prophets' feelings of inadequacy in response to their call (Exod 3:11 [Moses]; Isa 6:5; Jer 1:6). The making of a "booth" (Jonah 4:5) is the creation of one's own spiritual dwelling on earth, esoterically "building one's house" (or "one's hut" or "booth"). The plant that provided shade (4:6) functions as Jonah's *fig tree*, an ancient symbol of initiation as we shall shortly see, often expressed simply as "under the tree." Most intriguing is the *worm* (4:7), a term that I have pondered as meaning something like the eternal element in a person's being.[111] The worm in the Jonah account that attacked the plant, causing it to wither, is prophetic of Christ's cursing of the fig tree, his indication that the type of initiation represented by the ancient temple sleep, the three-days' journey, was to be replaced by the redemptive impulse to be planted in the etheric earth by the shedding of his blood. Initiation would thenceforth be through the power of that etheric force. Next we have the *east wind* (4:8). Whenever the word "east" appears one must look for some connection with the spiritual realm.[112] The conclusion of Jonah can leave one feeling suspended without a resolution, much like the ending in Mark's Gospel. That it ends with a reference to "a hundred and twenty thousand persons" in Nineveh, a multiple of the zodiacal twelve, suggests the many ages of the human journey. The reference to "much cattle" points to the spiritual reality that the human kingdom, through Christ, must redeem all creation (cf. Rom 8:19–23 and Eph 1:9–10, as well as the consummating realm of the twelves that concludes Revelation). This cryptic reference suggests that one who is initiated into the higher spiritual realms experiences Christ's footwashing (John 13:1–17) and thenceforth humbly serves all creation (cf. Mark 9:33–35).

Reading Jonah in this light puts it in a very different perspective and offers a new and different depth of meaning.

---

111 See, for instance, Smith, *Soul's Long Journey*, 188–94.
112 See Smith, *Soul's Long Journey*, 195–204.

The Two-Day Delay Conundrum

One of those things that have puzzled scholars is why, when Jesus learned that Lazarus whom he loved was ill, he stayed where he was for two more days instead of going immediately to minister to him (John 11:5–6). And not only so, but the Greek is properly translated to indicate that it was *because* Jesus loved Lazarus (and his sisters) that he stayed two more days. Most generally it is translated, "So when he heard that he was ill, he stayed two days longer in the place where he was," or sometimes the word "therefore" is used, or the word "yet." How can this seemingly callous disregard for the condition of his friend be explained? Jesus had just said that the illness was "so that the Son of God may be glorified by means of it" (v. 4). But Lazarus had been dead four days when Jesus got to his tomb. Had Jesus not delayed the two days, Lazarus would still have been dead upon his arrival. The two-day delay had some other purpose. Something else had to be working here. Surely it was to see the power of that final initiation according to the method that was to pass away with his own redemptive submission to, and resurrection from, crucifixion death.

When the two-day delay is seen in the context of the three and a half day temple sleep, in which Christ, from his distant place, served as the hierophant and Lazarus as the candidate for initiation, obscure from worldly sight as was the ancient custom, it is obvious that Christ would not have awakened Lazarus any earlier. Thus, it was better that he not be there in the family's presence until the necessary time had expired for him to call Lazarus forth.

Here we must understand that Christ did not cause Lazarus to go into the three and a half day temple sleep in the normal way but rather through a process of instruction that led him into it on his own, after which Christ served in the normal role of the hierophant in raising Lazarus and bringing him forth from the tomb.[113]

---

[113] Steiner, *Gospel of St. John and Its Relation to the Other Gospels*, 136–37 (lect. 8).

The Fig Tree Conundrum

The fig tree appears in the Old Testament and in John's Gospel, but the disconcerting appearances in the three Synoptic Gospels (Mark 11:11–14, 20–21; Matt 21:18–20; Luke 13:6–9) are the ones that have attracted the most attention. It is especially Christ's perplexing and seemingly uncharacteristic "cursing" of the fig tree in the first two gospels that has occasioned much interpretive, and often apologetic, writing.[114] The difficulties presented by this incident disappear when the content of the ancient mysteries as Steiner has revealed them is considered.

While as usual there is some variation in each of the three accounts, there is one theme that is common in all—the fig tree has had it! True, Luke gives it one more year, but the handwriting is on the wall, and one senses a futility in the extension. The pattern is clearest and most explicit in Mark:

Mark 11: [11]And he entered Jerusalem, and went into the temple; and when he had looked round at everything, as it was already late, he went out to Bethany with the twelve.

[12]On the following day, when they came from Bethany, he was hungry. [13]And seeing in the distance a fig tree in leaf, he went to see if he could find anything on it. When he came to it, he found nothing but leaves, for it was not the season for figs. [14]And he said to it, "May no one ever eat fruit from you again." And his disciples heard it.

---

[114] For surveys of scholarly opinions, see Collins, *Mark*, 522–26; Joel Marcus, *Mark 8–16: A New Translation with Introduction and Commentary* (Anchor Bible 27A; New Haven: Yale University Press, 2009), 789–90. A leading work in support of the prevalent view that the fig tree incident, entwined as it was with the temple-cleaning incident in Mark's Gospel, was a pronunciation of judgment upon the temple is William R. Telford, *The Barren Temple and the Withered Tree: A Redaction-Critical Analysis of the Cursing of the Fig-Tree in Mark's Gospel and Its Relation to the Cleansing of the Temple Tradition* (Sheffield: JSOT Press, 1980). See also Scott G. Brown, "Mark 11:1–12:12: A Triple Intercalation?" *Catholic Biblical Quarterly* 64 (2002): 78–89; J. Duncan M. Derrett, "Fig Trees in the New Testament," *Heythrop Journal* 14 (1973): 249–65.

[In vv. 15–19, they came into Jerusalem, Jesus cleared the temple, and they went again out of the city.]

[20] As they passed by in the morning, they saw the fig tree withered away to its roots. [21] And Peter remembered and said to him, "Master, look! The fig tree which you cursed has withered."

The story in Mark alternates between temple and fig tree. To begin with Jesus arrives at the temple and observes its operation. On the following day he is hungry, and upon seeing the fig tree empty he makes his condemning remark. On the morning of the next day his disciples take note that the fig tree has withered, after which they return to the temple and the priests question him about his actions in the temple on the previous day (11:27–33). Matthew's version (21:18–22) roughly follows the pattern of Mark, except for the timing of the fig tree's demise, which happens instantaneously rather than after the temple's clearing.

From the alternating pattern in which Mark narrates the clearing of the temple and the cursing of the fig tree, scholars have inferred that the cursing and withering of the tree prophetically symbolize the temple's doom, or alternately the demise of the temple leadership or even of the Jewish people.[115] But there is no such temple juxtaposition in Luke, which presents a parable about an unfruitful fig tree (13:6–9):

And he told this parable: "A man had a fig tree planted in his vineyard; and he came seeking fruit on it and found none. And he said to the vinedresser, 'Lo, these three years I have come seeking fruit on this fig tree, and I find none. Cut it down; why should it use up the ground?' And he answered him, 'Let it alone, sir, this year also, till I dig about it and put on manure. And if it bears fruit next year, well and good; but if not, you can cut it down.'"

---

[115] Philip F. Esler, "The Incident of the Withered Fig Tree in Mark 11: A New Source and Redactional Explanation," *Journal for the Study of the New Testament* 28 (2005): 48–49 and writers there cited.

There is no implied hostility toward the temple or the Jewish authorities or people in the simple parable in Luke.

But one theme is there in all of the accounts—the fig tree is a goner.

In each of the three Synoptic Gospels the fig tree appears again in a
later chapter (Mark 13:28; Matt 24:32; Luke 21:29–33). In each case it
is used to indicate that the coming of the kingdom can be anticipated by
signs of the times the same way that the arrival of summer is announced
by the blossoming of leaves on trees. Each of these passages is placed in
the gospel's so-called little apocalypse chapter dealing with end times,
and because in each instance it refers to the time when "these things"
can be seen to be happening, the reference has traditionally been interpreted to refer to the Parousia. This later fig tree reference in each of the
Synoptic Gospels is similar to the earlier only in the fact that each use is
one of timing, pointing to the end of a significant stage or to the occur-
rence of a transitional event in the human journey.

The temple inference stated above is reasonable. Its rationale is
supported by the *placement* of the fig tree incident in relation to the
temple incident in Mark and Matthew, particularly the former. Luke,
however, does not relate his fig tree parable to the temple.

We are fortunate in having three different versions relating to the fig
tree's demise, for indeed one can detect three different levels of meaning in that terminus. At the basic level, the demise relates prophetically
to the physical temple in Jerusalem, which was destroyed in 70 C.E.,
never to be rebuilt, which is meaningful only to the Jews. At the next
level, it pertains to the physical body of every human being in that the
destruction of the mineral-physical body marks the end only of a stage
in the long spiritual journey of that individuality (cf. the equation of
the temple with Jesus' body in John's account of the clearing of the
temple; 2:13–22); it also symbolizes the end of the ancient "fig tree"
mode of initiation, which was not limited to the Jews. At the highest
level, reflected by Luke's parable, the three years that the man came
seeking fruit can refer to the three years of Christ's earthly ministry,
during which, at least following the Nathanael experience (John 1:48),
no initiations of that more ancient nature appear to have occurred. The
delay in cutting the fig tree down could refer to the fact that it still had
one more application before the end, namely, the raising of Lazarus. If

we follow this line of interpretation, the parable implies that the initiation symbolized by the fig tree produced no fruit of its own thereafter. Nevertheless, this fig tree indirectly continues to produce lasting results through the raising of Lazarus, which continues to produce fruit through the gospel written by Lazarus-John. In that limited sense only, the fig tree lives on, while it was implicitly "cut down" as a prospective methodology.

Mark's Gospel is the only one clearly encompassing all three meanings. Matthew's Gospel can be taken as intermediary, encompassing all three but being less clear than Mark on the physical temple and certainly less clear than Luke on the one-year delay. It is the Secret Gospel of Mark that by incorporating the raising of Lazarus into the synoptic tradition brings that one-year delay into its broader scope also. Luke's version, being free of hostility toward the temple, relates most explicitly to the third meaning.

To be clear, the term temple sleep does not refer to sleep in the Jerusalem temple, but rather to the mode of initiation into the ancient mysteries whereby a priest or hierophant presided over the body of the candidate for initiation for three and a half days while the latter lay in a death-like state with her or his etheric (life) body removed but remaining under the priest's control.

Although the similarities between Secret Mark and the Lazarus incident in John's Gospel have been widely noted, the differences are obvious too. Inevitably the question arises whether they describe two totally unrelated incidents or a single one, and if the latter, whether one is more original or both derive from a common source.

In his study on the fig tree incident, Philip F. Esler suggests that all of Mark 11–16 is based upon an early Jerusalemite source. He cites the recent work by Gerd Theissen as providing "particular sustenance" for his proposal.[116] If Esler's conclusion were to be extrapolated by considering the fig tree incident in Mark 11 to be intimately related to the raising of Lazarus event and to the initiation described in Secret Mark, as suggested herein, it would seem to follow that the suggested early

---

[116] Gerd Theissen, *The Gospels in Context: Social and Political History in the Synoptic Tradition* (Minneapolis: Fortress, 1991), 166–99.

Jerusalemite source would have commenced in Mark 10:1 with Jesus' entry into Judea and the area beyond Jordan where John baptized.

Esler's stated main purpose is to "propose a new interpretation of the withered fig tree in Mark 11:12–14 and 20–25 whereby Mark has a source describing daily journeys by Jesus and his disciples between Jerusalem and Bethany that includes the incident of the fig tree over two such days and struggles in his redaction to make sense of so strange an event."[117] As he elaborates his theory, Esler's reasoning is intriguing, yet it leaves one feeling a bit up in the air for lack of a meaningful explanation of why Jesus would make such a remark about the fig tree in the first place. Esler concludes, wrongly in my estimation, that Mark didn't understand that either but because it was such a fully documented source he could not ignore it, so included it with a generalized explanation regarding faith—but what a strange way to illustrate faith, by the killing of a tree. More likely is it that Jesus was using the fig tree symbolically, for indeed the age of the initiation in the manner of the ancient mysteries, known esoterically as "under the fig tree," was coming to a close in the progress of the evolution of human consciousness. That Mark did know the deeper meaning is a better reason for him to include the incident than is his proposed inability to ignore it, plausible though that reasoning would be if a better one were not available.

Something significant was happening as a result of the imminent consummation of the Mystery of Golgotha, something that is reflected in the incident or parable of the fig tree. Recall the penultimate paragraph in the excerpt above from lecture four of Steiner's 1908 cycle in Hamburg, which is set out again below (emphasis added):

This [the ancient temple sleep initiation] took place always in the greatest secrecy and the outer world knew nothing of the occurrences within these ancient Mysteries. Through Christ-Jesus *a new initiation had to arise to replace the old*, an initiation produced by means of forces of which we have yet to speak. *The old form of initiation must end*, but a transition had to be made from the

---

[117] Esler, "Withered Fig Tree," 43.

old to the new age and to make this transition, someone had once more to be initiated in the old way, but initiated into Christian Esotericism. This only Christ-Jesus Himself could perform and the neophyte was the one who is called Lazarus. "This sickness is not unto death," means here that it is the three and a half day death-like sleep. This is clearly indicated.

With this, a new, and I suggest deeper, understanding of these troubling passages becomes possible. As we shall see, according to this new understanding, going all the way back to prehistoric times, the fig tree symbolized the gaining of insight into the true nature of things (cf. Gen 3:7), at first through direct perception of spiritual beings, and then, as humanity evolved down through the ages, progressively more and more through the ever-changing nature of initiation into these spiritual realities, which were called *mysteries*. Hence initiation into these realities was initiation into the ancient mysteries, or spiritual realities. Their buzz-word, to use modern colloquialism, was *the fig tree*, or *under the fig tree*, or simply *under the tree*.

This *under the tree* symbolism pervades the Old Testament.[118] In Deuteronomy, the Historical Books, and some of the writing Prophets the symbolism is used both positively and pejoratively, the latter as it applied to the practices of the pagans normally identified by the use of the term *green tree* as in Deut 12:2 ("under every green tree").[119]

Inasmuch as initiation by the ancient methods symbolized by the fig tree rubric was to pass by the way from the time of Christ forward, the symbol finds little application in the New Testament. Aside from its appearance in the fig tree incident and in two passages otherwise insignificant for our purposes (Jas 3:12 and Rev 6:13), it is found only in the Nathanael incident in the first chapter of John:

---

[118] References, doubtless with various meaning, include the following (those to fig trees are in italics): Gen 2:9, 17; 18:4, 8; Judg 4:5; 1 Sam 14:2; 22:6; 31:13; *1Kgs 4:25*; 19:4–5; Job 40:21–22; Song 8:5; Daniel 4; *Hos 9:10*; *Joel 1:12*; *2:22*; Jonah 4:6; *Mic 4:4*; *Hab 3:17–18*; *Hag 2:19*; *Zech 3:10*; *1 Macc 14:12*. Consider also Gen 21:33; 35:4; Exod 15:27; Deut 34:3; 1 Chr 10:11–12; 2 Chr 28:15; Ezekiel 31.

[119] Note the distinction in Ezek 17:22–24, and cf. 20:47. See also 1 Kgs 14:23; 2 Kgs 16:4; 17:10; 2 Chr 28:4; Isa 57:5; Jer 2:20; 3:6, 13; 17:2; Ezek 6:13.

Philip found Nathanael, and said to him, "We have found him of whom Moses in the law and also the prophets wrote, Jesus of Nazareth, the son of Joseph." Nathanael said to him, "Can anything good come out of Nazareth?" Philip said to him, "Come and see." Jesus saw Nathanael coming to him, and said of him, "Behold, an Israelite indeed, in whom is no guile!" Nathanael said to him, "How do you know me?" Jesus answered him, "Before Philip called you, when you were under the fig tree, I saw you." Nathanael answered him, "Rabbi, you are the Son of God! You are the King of Israel!" Jesus answered him, "Because I said to you, I saw you under the fig tree, do you believe? You shall see greater things than these." (John 1:45–50)

After noting, "The impression that Jesus' statement makes on Nathanael ... has led commentators to speculate about what Nathanael was doing under the tree," Raymond E. Brown, whose writings normally explore the available material in a balanced way, goes over those statements which presumably he finds worth noting, after which he denigrates all such commentary as speculation: "We are far from exhausting the suggestions, all of which are pure speculation."[120] As is usually the case in observations of this type, Steiner's work is not mentioned.

This is regrettable, for Steiner often delved deeply into the meaning of the fig tree symbol and of being under it.[121]

On May 23, 1908, in Hamburg, in lecture five of his cycle on John's Gospel, Steiner explained the Nathanael episode. He first explained

---

[120] Raymond E. Brown, *The Gospel according to John: Introduction, Translation, and Notes* (2 vols.; Anchor Bible 29–29A; Garden City, N.Y.: Doubleday, 1966), 1:83.

[121] The occasions would include at least the following, listed chronologically: Steiner, *Christianity as Mystical Fact*, ch. 7; *Foundations of Esotericism* (trans. Vera Compton-Burnett and Judith Compton-Burnett; London: Rudolf Steiner Press, 1983), lect. 12 (CW 93a); *Gospel of St. John*, lect. 5; *Gospel of St. John and Its Relation to the Other Gospels*, lect. 10; *Background to the Gospel of St. Mark*, lect. 5; *The Gospel of St. Mark* (ed. Stewart C. Easton; trans. C. Mainzer; Hudson, N.Y.: Anthroposophic Press, 1986), lect. 4 (CW 139); *The Bhagavad Gita and the West: The Esoteric Significance of the Bhagavad Gita and Its Relation to the Epistles of Paul* (trans. Doris Bugbey et al.; CW 142/146; Great Barrington, Mass.: SteinerBooks, 2009), 64–66.

the contextual meaning of the term "Israelite" ("Behold, an Israelite indeed, in whom is no guile!"). In the seven stages of initiation in the ancient Mithraic mysteries, the fifth stage was the "Persian."

The seven steps in that initiation are well known, being: 1. Raven, 2. Bridegroom (or according to Steiner, "Hidden"), 3. Warrior, 4. Lion, 5. Persian, 6. Sun-hero, 7. Father.[122] The fifth stage bore the name "Persian" in the Mithraic mysteries because those mysteries originated in Persia, but one initiated to that rank in Israel bore the name "Israelite." Steiner explained it thus:

> The human being of ancient times was especially a part of his community and therefore when he was conscious of his ego, he felt himself more as a member of a group-soul than as an individual. But the initiate of the fifth degree had made a certain sacrifice, had so far stripped off his own personality that he took the folk-soul into his own being. While other men felt their souls within the folk-soul, he took the folk-soul into his own being, and this was because all that belonged to his personality was of no importance to him but only the common folk-spirit. Therefore an initiate of this kind was called by the name of his particular folk.[123]

Speaking further of Nathanael, Steiner continues:

---

[122] As Steiner pointed out (see Smith, *Burning Bush*, 346), it can be seen in the book of Kings that Elijah was initiated into all seven of these stages: 1. He is fed by *ravens* (1 Kgs 17:4, 6); 2. He goes into hiding (*hidden one*) (17:3–5); 3. He confronts the prophets of Baal as a *Warrior* (18:19); 4. Fleeing, he takes refuge in a cave, from which he observes the wind, earthquake, and fire, and then the still small voice that emboldens him, and he goes out as a *Lion* (19:9–18); 5. He is taken up by the chariots of *Israel* and its horsemen, thus a *Persian* or *Israelite* in this case (2 Kgs 2:12); 6. He is a *Sun-hero*, or Sun-runner, represented by the chariots and horsemen carrying him upward (2:12); 7. He is a *Father* by the declaration of Elisha (2:12).

Whether one views Elijah to have reincarnated in John the Baptist (the anthroposophical position) or merely somehow to have indwelled him in spirit (Luke 1:17, if that can be different), there is warrant for this Elijah initiation to be reflected in John the Baptist (Mal 4:5–6; Mark 9:11–13; Matt 17:10–13) and thus, as previously explained in the text, for this consciousness to be present in Lazarus-John and to be reflected by him as the testimony of the Baptist.

[123] Steiner, *Gospel of St. John*, 80 (lect. 5).

He is not so highly developed that he is able to comprehend the Christ. The Christ is, of course, the Spirit of all-inclusive Knowledge which cannot be fathomed by a Nathanael, an initiate of the fifth degree. But the Christ could fathom Nathanael. This was shown by two facts. How did Christ designate him? "This man is a true Israelite!" Here we have the designation according to the name of the folk. Just as among the Persians, an initiate of the fifth degree is called a Persian, so among the Israelites, he is called an Israelite. Therefore Christ calls Nathanael an Israelite. He then says to him: "Even before Philip called thee, when thou wast under the fig-tree, I saw thee!" That is a symbolical designation of an initiate like the Buddha sitting under the Bodhi Tree.

The fig-tree is a symbol of Egyptian-Chaldean initiation. He meant with these words: I well know that thou art an initiate of a certain degree, and canst perceive certain things, for I saw thee! Then Nathanael recognized Him: "Rabbi, Thou art the Son of God; Thou art the King of Israel!" This word "King" signifies in this connection: Thou art one who is higher than I, otherwise thou couldst not say, "I saw thee when thou sattest under the fig-tree."[124]

The term "under the tree," or classically "under the fig tree," really goes back to the earliest stages of the descent of the human being into matter during the Earth Condition of Consciousness (Earth evolution). It goes back to the trees in the garden of Eden. The RSAM shows that the first human beings to be able to descend into and remain in solid matter were the Adam and "his wife" in Gen 4:25. Up to that point, all references to human beings had to do with their existence in the supersensible realm before descent.[125] It is in the highest sense misleading to think of the garden of Eden as ever having existed on the material earth. It is entirely in the spiritual or supersensible realm.[126]

---

[124] Steiner, *Gospel of St. John*, 80–81 (lect. 5).
[125] For a more complete account of this, see Smith, *Soul's Long Journey*, 86–99.
[126] See Smith, *Soul's Long Journey*, 195–204.

The "man" from which the woman was taken was an asexual[127] human etheric (life) body. The woman, as a sexual being, was first extracted and what was left was the male element, but both still in the etheric realm. This division of the sexes was during the "deep sleep" (Gen 2:21) between the Lemurian and Atlantean Epochs,[128] long, long ago.

We must understand the two trees in the garden, the trees of life and knowledge, to be the human etheric (life) and astral (conscious nervous system) bodies as they existed before they entered a material body on earth and before the incipient human Ego indwelled them, their consciousness thus being still animalistic in nature. These two bodies, etheric (life, or tree of life) and astral (sense, or tree of knowledge), were thus capable of conscious action, but without Ego control or guidance they were no more guilty of sinning than is an animal that acts out of basic instinct.

In a lecture in Munich on May 3, 1911, Steiner made the point that what is called the "original sin" in the garden took place in the supersensible world before the human bodies were invested with an Ego and thus capable of sin in the normal sense. Accordingly, human beings were sinless when they succumbed to that which caused their descent into the material world and brought about their earthly condition of death. Therefore, the Deed of Christ, the shedding of his blood as an act of grace rather than something earned by the human being, was the counterbalance. The human being, having been condemned to death by supersensible actions that were sinless, was saved by grace

---

[127] Phyllis Trible, *God and the Rhetoric of Sexuality* (Philadelphia: Fortress, 1978), 98, 141 n. 17. Consistent therewith, in a lecture at St. John's United Methodist Church in Lubbock, Texas, on January 18, 2001, Trible said that she had originally thought of the human being at this early stage as being *androgynous*, that is, of both sexes in one spiritual entity. However, it had become clear to her later that she was wrong in that understanding, for the nature of *man* at that time of its creation was *asexual*. While she recognizes a division into female and male in Gen 2:21–24, this is still consistent with the division at that point being only in the etheric realm, for the etheric body carries sexuality and is formative and sustaining of the physical body.

[128] I follow the practice herein of capitalizing the word "epoch" whenever it has direct or indirect reference to one or more of the major Epochs of Earth evolution, the five that have occurred to the present time being Polarian, Hyperborean, Lemurian, Atlantean, and Post-Atlantean.

that it did not earn. In Steiner's words, "Grace is the concept that is complementary to that of Original Sin."[129] The prophet Isaiah seems to have recognized a similar principle in telling his people, "For thus says the Lord: 'You were sold for nothing, and you shall be redeemed without money'" (52:3).

The account in Genesis 3 describes the period in human development when this original sin occurs. Steiner gives an account of this from the Bhagavad Gita as he relates Krishna's instruction of his pupil Arjuna, explaining to him "the nature of the *avayata* tree, the fig tree, saying that the roots of this tree grow upward and its branches downward."[130] Recall that only over long ages did the etheric body gradually enter the physical body, and at the time of Krishna the etheric body was partially within the physical but to a considerable extent still outside of it. Earlier, before it had begun to enter the physical body, such knowledge as the human had came only from supersensible realms through the etheric or life body (tree of life). Death did not exist in that supersensible realm, but there was an element entwined in that tree or etheric realm whereby the human awareness, such as it then was, looking down upon the creatures that existed in the mineral-physical realm, experienced a desire to experience what it could see in that lower realm. This element of awareness and desire was perceived as a serpent as it spoke from its place in that tree of life.

By the prehistoric, Post-Atlantean Epoch of human development when Krishna was instructing Arjuna, the desire to experience the world of matter had prevailed. The etheric body had considerably penetrated the physical body but had not yet done so nearly as completely as it had by the time of Christ, or today, when it is essentially completely veiled from supersensible perception within the confines of the mineral-physical body. By the time of Krishna's instruction, knowledge on earth came through that part of the etheric body that was within the physical.

---

[129] Rudolf Steiner, *The Concepts of Original Sin and Grace* (trans. D. S. Osmond; 2d ed.; London: Rudolf Steiner Press, 1973) (CW 127), http://wn.rsarchive.org/Lectures/Concpt_index.html.
[130] Steiner, *Bhagavad Gita and the West*, 64.

As Krishna explains the Bhagavad Gita to Arjuna, it is to show him that the higher human bodies, especially the astral body that materialized into the human nervous system, can be seen as a tree with its roots extending upward into the head and its branches downward into the body and limbs, accompanied as it is by the circulatory system (etheric body) extending into the bodily extremes along with the nerves. The tree is upside down. But if one were today able, through sufficient initiation, to perceive the matter, one would be able to look into the body and see this tree and in so doing would perceive oneself as the serpent in this tree.[131] Since one who so observes this tree does so from what would seem to be underneath this tree, the ancient phrase, as used by John (1:48), seems apt.

So this dialogue between Krishna and Arjuna illuminates the picture in Genesis of the two trees, one of life and one of knowledge. But the image of the serpent in the tree didn't jump straight from the Far East into Genesis 3. The imagery was more universally present in the evolution of human consciousness. John Armstrong shows the pervasive presence of the tree and serpent image in Sumerian and Greek myth and art. He reasons that "myths are the most accurate means that the human mind has devised of representing its own immeasurably complex structure and content" and suggests that "the first step towards understanding the tree and the snake *is to look at them*." Doing so, he proposes, reveals that the tree "is the most long-surviving and stable of living things" while "the snake is the most inconstant and unpredictable in formal outline of living things and approaches the verge of amorphousness."[132] But as Steiner presents Krishna and Arjuna, human passion for knowledge (rajas) was the serpent upon the tree and led to the descent described in Genesis 3 and the universal human characteristics described as Cain in Genesis 4. The Adam and his wife in Gen 4:25 were the first resulting material embodiment.[133]

---

[131] See Steiner, *Bhagavad Gita and the West*, 64–66.

[125] John Armstrong, *The Paradise Myth* (London: Oxford University Press, 1969), 7, 35; for discussion see 37–147.

[133] The great similarity of names between the generations in Genesis 4 and Genesis 5 is tabulated in Smith, *Soul's Long Journey*, 94, where it is also noted that those in Genesis 4 were not assigned ages in years as were those in Genesis 5.

It was the initiation symbolized by the fig tree that had to come to an end, hence the otherwise puzzling incident in all three of the Synoptic Gospels and their uniformity in this one and only aspect, the demise of that tree and its fruitfulness forever. In an earlier lecture that had also made this point about the fig tree, Steiner indicated that not all great spiritual leaders had been initiated in this way. Some were not, such as the ancient Zarathustra, the herald of Ahura Mazda during the Ancient Persian cultural age (roughly 5000 B.C.E.). Leaders such as this had not "risen through [their] own intrinsic merits" but were "chosen to be the bearer ... of a spiritual Being who cannot himself incarnate in the flesh, who can only send his illumination into and work within a human sheath."[134] In other cases, such as Solomon, wisdom is given without the necessity of initiation in the fig tree sense. And in still other cases, as with Melchizedek, an avatar, a spiritual being, has incarnated for the benefit of humanity without the incarnation having any benefit for himself as a spiritual being.[135] The highest of the avatars was the Christ Spirit, but it is the avatar nature of Melchizedek that causes the insightful author of Hebrews (Paul in my view, notwithstanding much contrary scholarly opinion) to ascribe the unique relationship between them.

The Relevance of Nag Hammadi

DISCOVERY AND SCHOLARLY EVALUATION

That a certain consciousness of the nature of the ancient mysteries was carried over into the early Christian era was noted early in this chapter. It was also noted, however, that only with the emergence of the Nag Hammadi codices has the multifaceted character of pre-Constantinian Christianity come increasingly into our awareness. With the advent of the Internet any reader has now at the fingertips information about this historic discovery and the ordeals that delayed its publication. These Coptic codices, to the extent they survived their initial use as kindling by their Arab finder and

---

[134] Steiner, *Background to the Gospel of St. Mark*, 86 (lect. 5, December 19, 1910).
[135] Steiner, *Principle of Spiritual Economy*, 45 (lect. 3, March 7, 1909).

the machinations of their intervening dealers and handlers, comprise the NHL. Continuing scholarly application has gradually enhanced awareness of Nag Hammadi's significance. The first big splash came in 1979 when Elaine Pagels' *The Gnostic Gospels* appeared garnering wide and well-deserved public acclaim. It was perhaps the first significant crack of the door so long tightly locked against all gnostics by Irenaeus and other early heresy hunters.

The first Nag Hammadi conference "to concentrate exclusively on the relationship between gnosticism and early Christianity" was held in Springfield, Missouri, in 1983, its thirteen papers being published under the title *Nag Hammadi, Gnosticism, and Early Christianity*.[136] Probably the single most comprehensive project covering Nag Hammadi is the one that commenced in the late 1940s and is now known as Nag Hammadi and Manichaean Studies (published by Brill).[137] Among its recent publications of interest to us are volumes 58 and 60 in the series, which we shall discuss shortly.

An important recent work is Karen L. King's *What Is Gnosticism?*[138] King, a professor at Harvard Divinity School, has here given us an extensively informative book that is readable by scholar and informed layperson alike. She offers an excellent historical background for consideration of the Nag Hammadi codices, an incisive analysis of their classification and typology, and a concluding evaluation of what fading future there is for the concept of gnosticism as it had been known during the Common Era prior to the discovery at Nag Hammadi and its assimilation into modern thinking.

By my count the NHL comprises some fifty-three titles. King observes that these were fourth-century papyrus codices "almost all [of which] were previously unknown."[139]

---

[136] Charles W. Hedrick and Robert Hodgson Jr., eds., *Nag Hammadi, Gnosticism, and Early Christianity* (Peabody, Mass.: Hendrickson, 1986; repr., Eugene, Oreg.: Wipf & Stock, 2005). The quoted words are from p. xi.

[137] Formerly Nag Hammadi Studies Series. See David M. Scholer, *Nag Hammadi Bibliography, 1948–1969* (Leiden: Brill, 1971); idem, *Nag Hammadi Bibliography, 1970–1994* (New York: Brill, 1997). Numerous scholarly publications have come out in this series since 1994.

[138] Karen L. King, *What Is Gnosticism?* (Cambridge, Mass.: Belknap, 2003).

[139] King, *What Is Gnosticism?* 149.

Based upon the work of numerous scholars, King differentiates two major classifications, Valentinian and Sethian, and four lesser ones. The bulk of the more significant treatises are classified either as Valentinian or Sethian. For the Sethian group, King lists eight identifying characteristics:

1. The Sethians understand themselves to be "the seed of Seth."
2. Seth is the Gnostic savior, or alternatively, Adam is the savior of his son Seth. Both may have a heavenly and/or an earthly aspect.
3. The heavenly place of rest for Adam, Seth, and the seed of Seth is the four aeons and illuminators of Autogenes: Harmozel, Oroiael, Deveithe, and Eleleth.
4. Autogenes is a member of the divine triad as the Son of the Father (often named the Invisible Spirit) and the Mother, Barbelo. This triad is itself specifically Sethian.
5. "Man" (Adam) in his primal form is connected with this heavenly triad.
6. Beneath the four lights is the realm of the Demiurge, Yaldabaoth.
7. The appearance of the divine Man is a result of the arrogance of Yaldabaoth and the punishment for his hubris.
8. Finally, Sethian mythology contains a distinctive periodization of history: the age of Adam, the age of Seth, the age of the original Sethians, and the present time.[140]

At the risk of oversimplifying the diversity of Valentinian and Sethian thought and mythology, King notes the following contrasts:[141]

VALENTINIAN	SETHIAN
More decidedly Christian	Less Christian in perspective
Primary savior is Christ	Several saviors, sometimes identified with Christ, though not as centrally

---

[140] King, *What Is Gnosticism?* 156–57.
[141] The following table is condensed from King, *What Is Gnosticism?* 159–62.

World creator viewed in partially favorable light	Sharply critical portrait of world creator
Human condition (fall, etc.) due to ignorance and error	Malevolence and evil caused human condition
Salvation through saving knowledge (gnosis)	Salvation through ascetic self-rule
Monistic view of world	Dualistic view of world
Tends to dissolve temporal divisions into timelessness of soul's worldly situation	Has room for salvation history from Adam & Seth down to the subject Sethians
Humanity is threefold: the spiritual and psychic, both of whom will be saved, and material persons, who will not	Humanity is twofold: those who will be saved and those who will not
Primal human condition was androgyny, separation causing death; Christ to reunite	Views female in more active and positive roles; sometimes criticizing illegitimate domination of women
Rituals (baptism, etc.) in context of bridal chamber	Rituals in context of ascent

For those not deeply involved in the study of the NHL or having considerable exposure to it in academic halls, what is given above should give some idea of the nature, extent, and immense variety of that part of early Christianity that did not survive the ascendance of orthodoxy. In spite of the great diversity reflected within the various tractates, certain common features stand out. Probably more than any other one aspect they can be said to deal with *protology*, the study of origins and first things. Typically they recognize a supreme, transcendent, ineffable, monadic God, above the fray so to speak. From this supreme God a series of aeons emanate long before any created world as we know it comes into existence, aeons populated by various hierarchies, archons, or other spiritual beings, until a "creator" god ("world creator" in the above listing) usually called the demiurge or Yaldabaoth comes into existence through a loss of the divine light. Creation as we know it, including the human kingdom, comes into being through the agency of this world creator, but something is bestowed upon the human being that comes from a higher level than the world creator. This higher level is an aeon (*epinoia* or thought), typically called Sophia. But this human being and the rest of creation all result from the loss of light and must in one way or another return to that state freed from imprisonment in materiality. Attaining a state of gnosis was an essential on the pathway of return.

Characteristic of the gnostic was an individualism that, considering the great diversity of approach, obviously could be seen to have impeded the spread of the "faith" of the early church. Some centralization of Christology was needed. Irenaeus and other early leaders doubtless sensed this and attacked aspects of the divergent philosophies. That approach finally triumphed at the First Ecumenical Council in Nicea in 325 C.E. under the impelling hand of Constantine.

References by Paul, Clement of Alexandria, and others to the existence of the mysteries, which must surely have been more than mere words, were all subsumed under the exigencies of a uniformity of faith. Church history thereafter is replete with accounts of the vigorous suppression of all who, or which, did not conform to the ecclesiastical dogma of Christendom.

At the outset and in the RSAM the largely decadent state of what remained of the ancient mysteries was mentioned. Nevertheless enough memory of some of their elements remains to corroborate what Steiner said of the protology and ontology and even cosmology of our being as summarized in the RSAM. In many places and ways he spoke of how the ancient clairvoyance was being dimmed as we approached the turning point of time, the Mystery of Golgotha.[142] Over and over again in *The Fifth Gospel* Steiner iterates, as in a refrain, what the soul of Jesus of Nazareth realized between his twelfth and thirtieth years, that the old wisdom was no longer perceived and that

---

[142] See, e.g., Steiner, *Gospel of St. John*, 104–5 (lect. 6); *Gospel of St. John and Its Relation to the Other Gospels*, 105–8 (lect. 6), 223–36 (lect. 12); *The Reappearance of Christ in the Etheric* (trans. Barbara Betteridge et al.; 2d ed.; Spring Valley, N.Y.: Anthroposophic Press, 1983), 71 (CW 118, lect. 5); *Background to the Gospel of St. Mark*, 203–4 (lect. 9); *From Jesus to Christ*, 157 (lect. 9); and *Christ and the Human Soul* (4th ed.; London: Rudolf Steiner Press, 1984), 19–24 (CW 155, lect. 1).

even if the prophets of old were to speak again there would be no one with ears to hear or the ability to understand.[143] The theme of the darkening of the consciousness that had existed in the ancient mysteries appeared again in *Philosophy, Cosmology, and Religion*, where he said, "The vestiges of the old initiation through which the initiates at the time of the Mystery of Golgotha, and even their successors, were able to speak correctly about the descent of the Christ and the path He took until His embodiment in the man Jesus—these vestiges continued until the fourth century A.D., though weakening increasingly in regard to the effectiveness they had for mankind. By that time, they had ceased to call forth in the human organization the kind of capacities that afforded reliable insights into the spiritual world."[144] The concomitant of this loss of touch with the spiritual world was a certain decadence, an obscuring or blurring of the understanding that had once existed within the ancient mysteries.

VESTIGE OF ANCIENT MYSTERY CONTENT

The highest rung of the classical ninefold hierarchical structure is that of the seraphim, five levels above the elohim.[145] Isaiah tells us that in the year 742 B.C.E., the year that King Uzziah died (Isa 6:1), these seraphim appeared to him, and after they had purified him by fire the Lord, the descending Christ Spirit according to the RSAM and John 12:41, spoke *with* him, not *about* or *of* him as John 12:41 is commonly translated.[146] The translations of Isa 6:10 have the Lord

---

[143] Rudolf Steiner, *The Fifth Gospel: From the Akashic Record* (trans. A. R. Meuss, C. Davy, and D. S. Osmond; 3d ed.; London: Rudolf Steiner Press, 1995), 45–48 (CW 148, lect. 4), 62–63, 65, 67, 77 (lect. 5), 193, 195, 197 (lect. 12), 215 (lect. 13); cf. Luke's rich man and Lazarus parable (16:19–31).

[144] Rudolf Steiner, *Philosophy, Cosmology, and Religion* (ed. Stewart C. Easton; trans. Lisa Monges and Doris Bugbey; Spring Valley, N.Y.: Anthroposophic Press, 1984), 103–7, quoting 105–6 (CW 25/215, lect. 7).

[145] For the hierarchical structure, see the documentation cited in n. 333 in the RSAM.

[146] The translations themselves of the Greek preposition *peri* are proper. That the communication in Isaiah 6 was *with* Christ was indicated by Steiner in *Gospel of St. John*, 143–44 (lect. 9). One must wonder if the preposition *peri* was a redaction by an early scribe who assumed that it was impossible for Isaiah to have talked *with* the Christ, who had not yet then incarnated. The passage is specifically referenced in Matt 13:13–15; John 12:38–40;

telling Isaiah to "make" it so that the people would not understandingly see and hear. The several New Testament passages that refer to the people's lack of ability to see, hear, and understand merely recognize this inability, whatever the cause or reason, without including this troubling imperative. In the RSAM we see how human consciousness, perceptivity in the supersensible, spiritual realm, was gradually lost from the time of the fall till the time of Christ. The canon itself bears witness to the gradual loss of prophecy, one of the manifestations of what was happening to human beings as the time of the Christ event approached. Since the days of the Enlightenment there is the tendency to look upon that darkness of human consciousness as having passed in spite of the long ages that Isa 6:11–13 suggest are still ahead. The extent to which Isaiah 6 has presented a hermeneutical challenge can be seen from the major commentaries, which identify the Lord in Isaiah 6 as Yahweh contrary to the position taken below. What is presented in this writing suggests that those long ages have not yet fully run their course. Indeed, one wonders if we are not more deeply enmeshed within the veil of materialism than ever before, though hopefully in this age of the consciousness soul some are beginning to at least be aware of this frightful spiritual fact.

But the focus here is upon the situation at the turning point of time and the early centuries following, when the tractates in the NHL were written. And our effort here is directed toward illustrating the extent to which, even in that darkened age, they carried forward elements of what had been perceived within the mysteries in more ancient times and the extent to which the evidence of those elements lends corroboration to what Steiner has related to us as summarized in the RSAM.

The Elohim and Yahweh

In the early modern age questions were beginning to arise about the Mosaic authorship of the Pentateuch. The eighteenth century's

---

and Acts 28:25–27, and the same theme of seeing but not perceiving and hearing but not comprehending is also found in Mark 4:11–12; Luke 8:10; and Rom 11:8–10.

Enlightenment intensified the questions and the search for the Pentateuch's sources. By the end of the nineteenth century the Four Document Hypothesis (JEDP, or Jahwist, Elohist, Deuteronomist, and Priestly, in chronological order), generally called the Wellhausen (or Graf-Wellhausen) Hypothesis, had become the orthodoxy on the matter in spite of resistance from more conservative quarters. In the excellent summary of the history of the Documentary Hypothesis in The New Interpreter's Bible, Joseph Blenkinsopp discusses the various twentieth-century sieves through which it has been pressed and says, "It is only in the last two decades or so that the Graf-Wellhausen construct can be said to be in serious and possibly terminal crisis."[147] Even now, however, it is not so terminal that its influence upon the interpretation of the first few chapters of Genesis can be ignored. The Documentary Hypothesis generally recognizes chapter 1 and at least the first three verses of chapter 2 of Genesis as being from the so-called Priestly, or P, source, and the rest of chapter 2, as well as chapter 3, as being from the Jahwist, or J, source. It has been reasoned that they are two different accounts that describe the same creation but in a different way, as though two witnesses were giving differing descriptions of the same event. Among other things, this theory would explain the different words used for the divinity in these narratives: elohim and Yahweh. I argue below, however, that the theory misconstrues the reason for the different names.

While this two-creation account interpretation still seems to be generally accepted by scholars, it is interesting to consider the creation accounts in the NHL treatises and whether they throw light upon the proper relationship of these two narratives to each other.

In his paper delivered at the SBL convention in San Diego in November 2007, Ben Dunning writes (emphasis mine): "Sophia's luminous human is at the first an androgyne. As indicated above, the figure of the primal androgyne looms large in Hellenistic Jewish and early Christian (i.e. platonizing) interpretations of Genesis 1–3.

---

[147] Joseph Blenkinsopp, "Introduction to the Pentateuch," The New Interpreter's Bible 1:305–18, quoting 312. In addition to this excellent review, see the Wikipedia entry Documentary Hypothesis.

Wayne Meeks and others have shown how early Christians followed a trend (seen clearly in Philo) to interpret Genesis 1 and 2 as two creation stories, *occurring consecutively*."[148] Dunning cites works by Daniel Boyarin, Wayne Meeks, Annewies van den Hoek, and Phyllis Trible, all prominent scholars, that indeed extensively support his statement, but do so without the consistency in the creative scenario set out in the RSAM, which clearly identifies the hierarchical status of the elohim, their sevenfold nature, and their relationship to their leader Yahweh (cf. Yaldabaoth).[149] In his analysis of the NHL's *On the Origin of the World*, Dunning refers to the elohim as sevenfold (Yaldabaoth and his six other archons) and as being so described in greater detail in the *Apocryphon of John*.[150]

Awareness of the sequential nature of the Genesis 1–3 creation story is clearly evident in Gerald P. Luttikhuizen's recent *Gnostic Revisions of Genesis Stories and Early Jesus Traditions*. But as indicated in the very title of his work, Luttikhuizen treats this insight into the *sequential* nature of the creation account as a *revision* of the early Genesis accounts rather than as an elucidation of the original meaning of those accounts. "The authors of [Gnostic texts, in this case the *Apocryphon of John* and *Letter of Peter to Philip*] read biblical and early Christian texts through the lens of their own Gnostic thought system.... Indeed, the response of Gnostics to biblical and early Christian texts was greatly determined by the relationship of these texts to their own favourite traditions. The intertextual tension between the biblical texts and their Gnostic interpretations betrays that on essential points the thought structure of the interpreters differed from what they found in the texts."[151]

---

[148] Benjamin H. Dunning, "What Sort of Thing Is This Luminous Woman? Thinking Sexual Difference in *On the Origin of the World*," *Journal of Early Christian Studies* 17 (2009): 55–84, quoting 69.

[149] Citing both Wayne Meeks and Rabbi Samuel bar Nachman, Pagels also recognizes the "two-stage process" implied in both Gen 1:27 and Genesis 2; see Elaine H. Pagels, "Exegesis of Genesis 1 in Thomas and John," *Journal of Biblical Literature* 118 (1999): 482–83.

[150] On the seven in the *Apocryphon of John*, see n. 160.

[151] Gerald P. Luttikhuizen, *Gnostic Revisions of Genesis Stories and Early Jesus Traditions* (Nag Hammadi and Manichaean Studies 58; Leiden: Brill, 2006), 4–5.

What the academy has done over the last several decades to hand down to us the NHL is of immense value in understanding the wide variety of Christian faith and practice before the ascendance of orthodoxy in the fourth century. And within its own halls some scholars are aware that the gnostic texts in the NHL interpret Genesis 1–3 as two different stages in one sequential creation account. This is contrary to the common view of scholars to date that these three chapters present two different creation accounts. It is my position that the gnostic texts more nearly reflect the intent of the creation myth, and that interpreting that myth as it appears in the canon without knowledge of the content of the ancient mysteries as set out in the RSAM misses the underlying truth that the myth passes down to us. Indeed, so many of the ancient myths take on new meaning in the light of that content from the ancient mysteries. We are still in the early stages of discovering what the NHL has to reveal.

Two Names for God

We will return shortly to Gen 2:4a as well as the question of whether there are two creation stories each telling in its own way of one singular event, or one creation story that describes two different stages in the long process of creation as suggested herein. For now it only needs to be said that in these early chapters it was fairly obvious that two different names were used for God, the plural elohim in the first portion (Gen 1:1–2:3) and the singular Yahweh, or YHWH, in the second (Gen 2:4b through Gen 3 and portions beyond).

Scholars clearly recognize that elohim is a plural term. *The Anchor Bible Dictionary* recognizes the plurality of the term, but it follows the general understanding, here deemed in error, that it refers to "the one God of Israel," stating, "The striking feature of the OT texts lies in the use of this plural form 'elohim' in order to designate the one God of Israel."[152] Dunning describes the Septuagint's use of "us" in Gen 1:26 (which in *On the Origin of the World* he says is understood as referring

---

[152] Martin Rose, "Names of God in the OT," *Anchor Bible Dictionary* 4:1006 (item 7 under "Non-Yahwistic Divine Names").

"to Ialdabaoth and his cohort of archons") as "a perennial problem for early Jewish and Christian exegetes."[153] He is eminently correct in this latter assessment, the problem still being inadequately resolved to this day absent the insights from the contents of the ancient mysteries.

That the Genesis creation story in fact pictures the elohim as a plurality is noted early in the RSAM, where they are characterized as having the sevenfold nature of creation itself that is common at all levels of the hierarchies—a reflection, so to speak, of the elliptical journey of creation and the human journey (Prov 9:1). It is on this issue of the respective and sequential roles of the elohim and Yahweh in Genesis 1–3 that the RSAM and the NHL are so relevant.

To a considerable extent the general confusion over where v. 2:4a of Genesis belongs, namely, to what went before it or to what comes after, is due to the real spiritual difference in the divinities represented by the elohim on the one hand and the singular eloha-Yahweh on the other. The Hebrew term *elohim*, the Greek term *exousiai*, the English term "Authorities," and Steiner's phrase "Spirits of Form" are all one and the same, the sevenfold sixth rung of the ancient ninefold hierarchical structure (the seraphim and cherubim as the first two down through the archangels and angels as the last two), comprising three ranks of three each.[154] The fourth Condition of Consciousness is the Earth Condition, and it was toward the end of the third major Epoch of that Condition, known as the Lemurian, when in the course of the progressive separations within our solar system the moon separated from the earth as we know it, that Yahweh sacrificially descended from the sun sphere to the moon sphere in order to work more directly with humanity than would have been possible from the greater distances in space (all as explained early in the RSAM).[155]

English Bibles virtually from the first have followed the convention of translating the plural elohim with the word "God" and the

---

[153] Dunning, "What Sort of Thing," 69.

[154] See n. 333.

[155] The order in which the bodies of our solar system separated from the original solar nebula, according to Steiner, is given in chart I–27 in Smith, *Burning Bush*, derived from Rudolf Steiner, *The Influence of Spiritual Beings upon Man* (Spring Valley, N.Y.: Anthroposophic Press, 1961), 35–46 (CW 102, lect. 3, February 15, 1908).

singular Yahweh (YHWH) as "Lord God." This is most noticeable in these early chapters of Genesis. For instance, only the term God is used in Gen 1:1–2:3. Then from 2:4 through chapter 3 only the Lord God is used, except where the serpent speaks. Interestingly, the serpent does not speak of Yahweh but of the plural elohim.

Genesis 2:4a

It is of great importance that we have a proper understanding of the meaning and function of the entirety of the fourth verse of Genesis 2, for, as shown below, its meaning is obscured by present translations. The King James Version combines vv. 4 and 5 in a single sentence as follows:

> ⁴These *are* the generations of the heavens and of the earth when they were created, in the day that the Lord God made the earth and the heavens,
> ⁵And every plant of the field before it was in the earth, and every herb of the field before it grew: for the Lord God had not caused it to rain upon the earth, and *there was* not a man to till the ground.

This is the version to which Steiner directed attention in his lecture cycle on Genesis when, as we shall shortly see, he said that it is ambiguous, having no "reasonable meaning," and that its generations should be understood as referring to those who followed rather than those formed earlier.

Without removing the ambiguity, the New King James Version ends the sentence in the middle of v. 5, reading as follows:

> ⁴This is the history of the heavens and the earth when they were created, in the day that the Lord God made the earth and the heavens, ⁵before any plant of the field was in the earth and before any herb of the field had grown.

The Revised Standard Version (RSV) probably represents the prevalent modern approach where v. 4 reads as follows:

⁴ᵃThese are the generations of the heavens and the earth when they were created.

⁴ᵇIn the day that the Lord God made the earth and the heavens,

The RSV and several other versions treat the latter sentence as continuing through v. 7 (the formation of man from dust); some place the period a bit earlier, at the end of v. 6 (the watering of the earth by a mist). A few abandon the reference to generations in v. 4a and simply state, similar to the Anchor Bible, "Such is the story of heaven and earth as they were created." The effect of these decisions about punctuation seems clearly to make v. 4a refer back to all that preceded it. It is beyond our purpose to compare structure through all these verses, our main interest being whether the first sentence quoted above from the RSV, placed as a separate paragraph between v. 2:3 and v. 4b, refers to what went before or what comes after.

In his lecture of August 26, 1910, in Munich contained in his cycle Genesis, predating most of what we today call modern translations, Steiner said relevant to this passage:

And now we must call attention to something else of importance. If everything that I have just been saying is correct, then we must regard the Yahweh-man, the man into whom Yahweh impressed his own Being, as the direct successor of the more etheric, more delicate man who was formed on the sixth "day." Thus there is a direct line from the more etheric man, who is still male-female—from the bi-sexual man—to the physical man. Physical man is the descendant, in a densified form, of the etheric man. If one wanted to describe the Yahweh-man who passes over into Atlantis, one would have to say: "And the man who was formed by the Elohim on the sixth 'day' of creation developed further into the unisexual man, the Yahweh-man." Those who followed after the seven "days" of creation are the descendants of the Elohim-men, and thus of what came into being during the first six "days."

Again the Bible is sublime when, in the second chapter, it tells us that the Yahweh-man is in fact a descendant of the heavenly man, the man who was formed by the Elohim on the sixth "day." The

Yahweh-man is the descendant of the Elohim-man in precisely the same way as the son is the descendant of the father. The Bible tells us this in the fourth verse of the second chapter, which says "Those who are to follow are the descendants, the subsequent generations, of the heavenly man." That is what it really says. But if you take a modern translation, you find the remarkable sentence: *These are the generations of the heavens and of the earth when they were created, in the day that the Lord God made the earth and the heavens.* Usually we find the whole hierarchy of the Elohim called "God," and Yahweh-Elohim called "the Lord God"—*the Lord God made the earth and the heavens.* I ask you to look at this sentence carefully and try honestly to find a reasonable meaning for it. Anyone who claims to do so had better not look on ahead in his Bible, for the word used here is *tol' doth,* which means "subsequent generations"; and the same word is used in the later chapter which tells of the subsequent generations of Noah. Thus here it is speaking of the Yahweh-men as the descendants, the subsequent generations, of the heavenly Beings, in the same way as there it speaks of the descendants of Noah. Thus this passage must be translated something like this: "In what follows we are speaking of the descendants of the heaven-and-earth beings who were created by the Elohim and further developed by Yahweh-Elohim." Thus the Bible too looks upon the Yahweh-men as the descendants of the Elohim-men. Anyone who wants to presuppose a fresh account of the creation, because it says that God created man, should also look at the fifth chapter, which begins *This is the book of the generations* (the word used there is the very same as in the other passages—*tol' doth*), and should assume a third account there—thus making his Rainbow Bible really complete! That way you will get a whole knocked up out of Bible fragments, but will no longer have the Bible.[156]

He continues by explaining that the original myth was perceived by the seer in clairvoyance, who thus presented it pictorially, and was

---

[156] Rudolf Steiner, *Genesis: Secrets of the Bible Story of Creation* (trans. Dorothy Lenn and Owen Barfield; 2d ed.; London: Rudolf Steiner Press, 1982), 133–34 (CW 122). The spelling "Yahweh-man" has been substituted for "Jahve-man."

acquired by Steiner himself in the same manner—which he elsewhere stated was before he had read the Bible. But his explanation should be tested in light of the sense it makes and the way it comports with the otherwise baffling plurality of the elohim and the order of their appearance in the text.

And not only so, but that its substance comes from the ancient mysteries as presented in the RSAM can be seen reflected in the tractates of the NHL, albeit in a decadent manner fuzzed away and splintered by the progressive loss of spiritual vision. The yearning for the ancient spiritual truths was there, but vision was no longer clear. The Mystery of Golgotha, according to Steiner, was the enactment of the substance of the ancient mysteries on the world stage for all to see, hear, and eventually come to understand.[157] Both of the two major classifications of gnostic works (Valentinian and Sethian) contained in the NHL show that the god of creation was not the highest, the ineffable God and that the savior, whose nature derived not from the god of creation but from that highest God, was higher than all the heavenly hierarchies, as Paul proclaimed (Eph 1:21; Col 1:15–16).

While the *Apocryphon of John*, coequal in length with one other Sethian work (*On the Origin of the World*), is fairly representative of that body of material in the NHL, the channels of Valentinian gnosticism divert more from its philosophical median and are thus not so easily summarized in any uniformity of structure. It is this that makes Einar Thomassen's comprehensive work *The Spiritual Seed: The Church of the "Valentinians"* such a valuable contribution to Valentinian scholarship.[158]

By far the longest work in the NHL is the Valentinian *The Tripartite Tractate*, more than twice the length of the longest Sethian works. Thomassen calls this long treatise "a comprehensive and systematic work of Valentinian theology" as well as "the only completely preserved

---

[157] This is the substance of Steiner's *Christianity as Mystical Fact*, first published in 1902, as there evident and in his later works made explicit.

[158] Einar Thomassen, *The Spiritual Seed: The Church of the "Valentinians"* (Nag Hammadi and Manichaean Studies 60; Leiden: Brill, 2006).

Valentinian systematic treatise transmitted to us directly," though by Coptic translation, from which "we get a full and accurate presentation of a system, which is not the case with the systems reported to us by the heresiologists."[159]

The Apocryphon of John

But the greater variety within Valentinian gnosticism suggests that we use the Sethian *Apocryphon of John* as an example for closer inspection of a gnostic system. An understanding of its content is important. For that reason such content is condensed in the abstract below. Those already familiar with the treatise may wish to skip to the text beyond. In the abstract that follows, page and line citations are from Wisse in the NHL volume, and bracketed words are not identified as such:

A light being identifies itself to John as the one with him always, being Father, Mother, and Son (2:14).

Who has come to teach about the race of the perfect Man (2:20), who is above everything and is pure light into which no eye can look (2:29–32).

The Monad is God and Father of everything: invisible, more than a god, eternal, total perfection, illimitable, unsearchable, ineffable, unnameable in whom all things exist, needing nothing, having no one prior to him nor able to comprehend him or give him a name (2:26–3:17).

Further the Monad is immeasurable light, immaculate, incorruptible, incorporeal, unknowable, not within time, an aeon-giving Spirit (3:17–4:3).

The Monad gazes upon his image in and essence of pure water-light that surrounds him (4:19–26). In the shine of that water-light she, Barbelo, appeared to him as the first power that came forth from him, the forethought of the All with a light that shines like his

---

[159] Thomassen, *Spiritual Seed*, 46, 166.

light as the perfect power that is the image of the invisible, virginal Spirit, the perfect glory in the aeons (4:27–5:4). She is the first thought, the womb of everything, his image (5:4–11).

Barbelo requested five divine qualities, namely, thought, foreknowledge, indestructibility, eternal life, and truth, these five composing the androgynous pentad of the aeons, which is the Father (5:11–6:10).

The Father looked at Barbelo with the pure light which surrounds the invisible Spirit and with his spark, and she conceived and bore the only begotten Son, the perfect light, of the Mother-Father (6:10–18).

And this only begotten Son requested a fellow worker, the mind, which came forth and wanted to produce a deed through the word which arose from the will, the word following the will, and by virtue of the word Christ the divine Autogenes created everything, and the virginal Spirit placed Autogenes over everything making him a name exalted above every name (6:31–7:30).

From the light of Christ, the divine Autogenes, four lights appeared to attend him. One such light was assigned to each of four powers or light-aeons, being in order named Armozel, Oriel, Daveithai, and Eleleth (7:30–8:18). To each of these four was assigned three subordinate aeons, being twelve in total, thus four lights and twelve aeons to attend Autogenes, the Christ (8:18–28).

Through the wills of the invisible Spirit and Autogenes, the perfect Man appeared as the first revelation, called Pigera-Adamas, who was placed over the first aeon with Autogenes by the first light Armozel and his three subordinate powers (8:28–9:3).

And Adamas placed his son Seth over the second aeon in the presence of the second light Oriel, and in the third aeon the seed of Seth was placed over the third light Daveithai where the saints were also placed, and in the fourth aeon the souls were placed of those who do not know the pleroma and who did not repent at once, but who persisted for a while and repented afterwards, all by the fourth light Eleleth, and all of these creatures glorified the invisible Spirit (9:11–25).

Here Sophia appears as an aeon (*epinoia* or thought), and through the power in her invested by the invisible Spirit and foreknowledge, but without the consent of her male consort, satisfied her own desire to bring forth a likeness of herself (9:25–31). And she did through that power bring forth something that was imperfect, not in her own likeness but in another form which she cast away from her calling its name Yaltabaoth (Yaldabaoth) (9:31–10:19).

Yaldabaoth was the first archon, taking a great power from his mother but removing himself from her (10:19–23). He created other aeons with a flame of luminous fire that still exists, joining with his own arrogance and begetting twelve authorities for himself and naming them (10:24–11:4). He placed seven, called kings, over the seven firmaments of heaven and five over the depth of the abyss, sharing his fire with them but not the power of the light he had taken from his mother, for he is ignorant darkness (11:4–10). At this point Yaldabaoth and the archons create seven named powers who create angels, 365 in total, the seven powers representing the days of the week (11:11–35).[160]

From the power of the glory he possessed of his mother's light he called himself God but did not obey the realm from which he came (11:35–12:10). What he created through his mother's light was a likeness of the cosmos of the first aeons, and looking upon it he declared, "I am a jealous God and there is no other God beside me," suggesting to the angels around him that there was another God, for otherwise he would not have been jealous (12:11–13:12).

Then the mother Sophia, noticing that her light was diminished, began moving to and fro (13:12–17). When John asked the Lord

---

[160] The complexity of the Sethian accounts as they refer to the archons is taken up in Andrew J. Welburn, "The Identity of the Archons in the 'Apocryphon Johannis,'" *Vigiliae christianae* 32 (1978): 241–54. He resolves the bewildering array of names assigned to these spiritual beings in the *Apocryphon of John* into an array of seven, the seven traditional planets of the solar system as Origen assigned them, and an array of twelve representing the zodiac, while dividing the latter into the seven day signs and the five night signs. One also detects a prominence of the seven in two other Sethian tractates dealing with the archons, the *Hypostasis of the Archons* and *On the Origin of the World*. Steiner's position was always that the elohim, which are really the archon level, were sevenfold.

what that meant, he said it was not as Moses said (i.e., Gen 1:2, the Spirit of God moving over the face of the waters) (13:17–21). Rather it was that she had seen the theft of her powers her son Yaldabaoth had committed, whereupon she repented in shame, moving about to and fro (13:21–26).

Sophia wept in repentance, and the whole pleroma heard her prayer, praising her to the invisible, virginal Spirit, who consented, and the Holy Spirit poured over her from the whole pleroma, and she was taken up above her own aeon and that of her son Yaldabaoth (13:32–14:13).

A voice came forth from the exalted aeon, "The Man exists and the son of Man" (14:13–15). Yaldabaoth heard it and thinking it had come from his mother taught the archons the complete foreknowledge, the image of the invisible one, the Father through whom the first Man came into being whose likeness was revealed in human form (14:15–24).

And the whole aeon Yaldabaoth trembled and the foundations of the abyss shook, and "of the waters which are above matter, the underside was illuminated by the appearance of his image" (14:25–29). And when all the authorities and the chief archon looked, through the light they saw on the underside "the form of the image in the water" (14:30–34). And Yaldabaoth said to the authorities, "Come, let us create a man according to the image of God and according to our likeness, that his image may become a light for us" (15:1–4). And through their powers creating a being according to that likeness, the first perfect Man, they said, "Let us call him Adam" (15:5–13).

The various powers and the 365 angels and even others with them worked on the natural body of Adam until it was completed, but for the detail on these "others" reference is made to "the book of Zoroaster" where it is "written" (15:13–19:12).

But Adam was lifeless (19:13). The mother, wanting to retrieve the power that went out of her to Yaldabaoth, petitioned the Son, the Mother-Father, who sent down the lights to the level of Yaldabaoth's angels so that they could bring forth the power of the mother, and the lights said to Yaldabaoth "Blow into his face something of your spirit and his body will arise," and he blew the power of his mother into the natural body of Adam that had been fashioned in the image of the highest God (19:14–32). And the body moved and became luminous (19:33).

But when the archons and their subordinates realized that Adam had become luminous and could think better than they, they "threw him into the lowest region of all matter" (19:34–20:9). But the Son (Mother-Father) had mercy on the power of the mother and sent luminous *epinoia* (thought) to assist Adam "by teaching him about the descent of his seed and … about the way of ascent, which is the way he came down," thus correcting the deficiency of the mother (20:9–28).

But because Adam's thinking was superior to all those who had made him, they brought him into the shadow of death in order to again form him from the elements and the spirit in matter, which is the ignorance of darkness and desire of their counterfeit spirit (20:28–21:9). "This is the tomb of the newly-formed body," the bond of forgetfulness of mortal man, "the first one who came down.… But the light that was in him would awaken his thinking" (21:9–16).

And the archons placed him in paradise telling him to eat at his leisure from the tree of "their life," which is the promise of death, standing themselves in front of the tree of knowledge of good and evil, which is the *epinoia* of the light, thinking to hide it from Adam (21:17–22:15). Due to the light that was in him Adam knew he was disobedient to the archon, who in turn "brought a forgetfulness over Adam" (22:15–20). It was not as Moses wrote about the deep sleep of Adam, but that this forgetfulness dulled his perception, and the *epinoia* of the light hid herself in Adam (22:20–28). Yaldabaoth wanted to bring this out of Adam's rib, but he could not grasp it, so he brought out of Adam another creature in the form of a woman fashioned according to the likeness of the *epinoia* that had appeared to him (22:28–39). So it was not as Moses said that the woman came from the rib bone of Adam (22:39–23:4).

In them their thinking was awakened and they recognized their nakedness. And when Yaldabaoth noticed that they withdrew from him, he cast them out of paradise and clothed them in gloomy darkness (23:4–24:8).

Then the chief archon saw the virgin who stood by Adam, and he seduced her, begetting two sons: unrighteous Cain (called Eloim) and righteous Abel (called Yave) (24:8–18). Abel he set over the elements fire and air, and Cain he set over water and earth (24:18–25).

At this point sexual desire and intercourse was implanted by Yaldabaoth in order to produce copies of their bodies, inspired by his counterfeit spirit (24:25–31). Two archons [sun sphere and moon sphere?] were set over principalities (archai) to "rule over the tomb" (24:32–34).

"When Adam recognized the likeness of his own foreknowledge, he begot the likeness of the son of man," calling him Seth (24:33–25:2). "The mother [presumably Sophia] also sent down her spirit,... a copy of those ... in the pleroma, to prepare a dwelling place for the aeons which will come down" (25:3–7). And they were made to drink Yaldabaoth's water of forgetfulness so they would not know whence they came (25:7–9). But the seed remained in him so that it might be raised by the Spirit when it came (25:10–16).

Then John asks the savior, "Who will be saved?" (25:16–18). The savior explains in progressive chapters that most will eventually be saved (25:18–29:5). In the process, it is again said that it is not as Moses said in regard to Noah and the flood, which was brought about by Yaldabaoth, for it was not in an ark that they hid themselves but in a luminous cloud (29:6–12). But while the light was with Noah, Yaldabaoth planned with his powers; they sent angels to the daughters of men, who, when they could not propagate with them, created a counterfeit spirit to pollute the souls they produced (29:12–30:4). "And thus the whole creation became enslaved forever and all became hardened through the counterfeit spirit" (30:5–11).

But the Christ speaks to John, "I, therefore, the perfect *pronoia* of all, changed myself into my seed.... And I went into the realm of darkness and I endured till I entered the middle of the prison (30:11–19). And the foundations of chaos shook (30:19–20). And I hid myself from them because of their wickedness, and they did not recognize me" (30:20–21). And the Christ came a second and third time (30:22–31:2). "And I entered into the midst of their prison which is the prison of the body (31:3–4). And I said, 'He who hears, let him get up from the deep sleep'" (31:5–6). And the Christ said, "Arise and remember ... and follow your root, which is I, the merciful one" (31:6–32). And the Christ raised them up and then went to the perfect aeon having completed everything for them (31:22–27).

Memories from the Ancient Mysteries

Considering the above summary of King's comparisons between Valentinian and Sethian works, it will suffice for our purpose to observe that the two systems are alike in recognizing that the creator god(s), the god (Yahweh) or gods (elohim) active in the early chapters of Genesis, are not the ineffable Father God. Thus it appears that the body of gnostic works is fairly uniform in this one respect.

This fairly uniform aspect of the gnostic writings in the NHL resembles Steiner's description of the content of the ancient mysteries decades before the discovery at Nag Hammadi. At the same time his assertion that as the Christian era approached the true gnostic content of the ancient mysteries had become decadent is borne out by the great diversity among gnostic believers, Christian and otherwise. Indeed this is one of its flaws that Irenaeus and others pointed to as showing its error inasmuch as truth could not be so divided. On the other hand, according to Steiner, though "no man is free from error in this field, no matter how high he stands," there was more agreement between the seers throughout the ages than between historians of even a single century.[161]

In regard to the relationship between the demiurge/Yaldabaoth and the supreme God, the Valentinian writings tended to, as King put it, "portray the world creator in a partially positive light, while Sethian myth paints a more sharply critical portrait."[162] In this respect the Valentinian was nearer to Steiner's exposition, which put the elohim in a completely favorable light. According to it, save for those hierarchical

---

[161] Rudolf Steiner, *Cosmic Memory* (trans. Karl E. Zimmer; Blauvelt, N.Y.: Rudolf Steiner Publications, 1959), 40 (CW 11).
[162] King, *What Is Gnosticism?* 159.

spirits that broke away from their fellow spirits at progressively lower stages in the descending portion of the long parabolic and evolutionary journey of humanity (namely, the Asuric, Ahrimanic, and Luciferic), all nine levels of the hierarchies that participated in the creative process did so in harmony with the highest divine will.[163] As the RSAM shows, by the time in the progression that the Earth Condition of Consciousness (evolution) had arrived, the elohim (*exousiai*) or Spirits of Form, led by the eloha-Yahweh, were the hierarchical rung in charge. Before the Lemurian Epoch ended, the lower three kingdoms had descended into a stage of materiality, as had the human physical body though still in a grotesque, gelatinous form. The human *I Am* that had been created through the sacrifice by the elohim had not yet descended but was still in the lap of the gods. Before the Luciferic influence had effectively grasped the human astral body it was the intent and desire of the elohim that the human merely look down upon what existed in its body on earth and see its reflection there and recognize its own *I Am*, without ever descending out of the spiritual realm into the material physical body.[164] This is in keeping with the biblical instruction the eloha-Yahweh gave Adam not to eat of the tree of life. That the human being through the Luciferic influence did thus "eat" and consequently descend into a material body thus became, in spite of the intent of these Spirits of Form (elohim), a fait accompli with which Yahweh and the threefold hierarchical rank below him (archai, archangels, and angels) had to deal.

The die was then cast, and humanity would have to overcome the world of matter before it could again return to dwell in the spiritual

---

[163] For an indication of the ruptures in the spiritual realm that produced these breakaway spirits, and the parts they played in the creative process, see charts I–22 and I–32 in Smith, *Burning Bush*, and their cited sources.

[164] In Steiner, *Outline of Esoteric Science*, 201 (ch. 4) we read: "Thus, we can say that at this level of existence, the human being consisted of a sentient soul, an astral body, a life body, and a physical body woven of fire. The spiritual beings involved in human existence surged up and down in the astral body [cf. Jacob's 'ladder' dream, Gen 28:12], while the sentient soul made the human being feel bound to the body of the Earth. Human consciousness at this stage was primarily a pictorial consciousness in which spiritual beings disclosed themselves. The human being lay in the bosom of these spiritual beings, and the sensation of a personal body appeared only as a point within this consciousness. The human being looked down from the spiritual world on an earthly possession, so to speak, and had the feeling, 'This is yours.'"

realms free of earthly attachment. Human rest in those spheres would not be complete until not only the human but also the lower kingdoms had been redeemed from materiality (cf. Rom 8:19–23). In so many ways, aspects of this account given by Steiner scintillate in the various gnostic texts though without the coherence that existed before human conscious contact with the spiritual realms became so completely veiled.

There is another aspect of Valentinian gnosticism that reflects something of a remnant of spiritual reality from of old, namely, the threefold nature of the human being. Paul alone within the canon articulates it as body, soul, and spirit (1 Thess 5:23), a fundamental principle of anthroposophy. Within gnosticism, this ancient spiritual truth seems to have found its reflection in the nature of humanity rather than of the individual human.

Scholars have given the primary Valentinian treatise, *The Tripartite Tractate*, its name because it divides humanity into "three essential types, the spiritual, the psychic, and the material, conforming to the triple disposition of the Logos" (118:14–19; see all of 118:14–122:12). It is immediately apparent that these are precisely the respective elements of the individual earthly human, a central feature of anthroposophy.

And just as the Valentinian tripartite division was given near the end of that tractate as the matter of redemption of humanity from the fallen state was addressed, one might also see this threefoldedness in the concluding portions of the Sethian version dealing with the period of redemption. In the *Apocryphon of John* (30:5–31:25), Christ tells John that he comes three times in the process of raising humanity up. Whatever was in the minds of the authors who produced them, these gnostic texts bear an intriguing conceptual similarity to the progressive purification by the Christ-imbued human Ego (I Am) of its three bodies and their related three lower kingdoms.

But in both of these texts there is something that is less satisfying than the perception Steiner tells us existed in the ancient mysteries. They are, in the language of Paul, like seeing "in a mirror dimly" (1 Cor 13:12).

The Apocalypse of Adam

In the introduction to her famous book, Pagels discusses how even before 1945 scholars were divided on the provenance of gnosticism, identifying it variously as Persian (Iranian, Zoroastrian), Judaistic (cf. kabbalistic), Greek, or simply Christian (including Jewish Christians).[165] This, especially in light of early church fathers such as Clement of Alexandria and even Augustine in his *Retractions* ("What is now called the Christian religion existed already among the ancients, and was not lacking at the very beginnings of the human race"), witnesses to another Steiner assertion, namely, that the mysteries have existed since the time of Atlantis and throughout the great diversity of races since then.

This brings us to another Sethian treatise, one that has been said to contain no trace of Christian influence in its development while at the same time showing the source of the genealogy of Matthew's Jesus child, the reincarnated prehistoric Zarathustra. This treatise is the *Apocalypse of Adam*. Andrew J. Welburn's recent, penetrating work on the Sethian *Apocalypse of Adam* makes a powerful case that its roots go back to the prehistoric, legendary Zarathustra.[166] The section "Incarnation of Christ" in the RSAM speaks of the very different genealogies for the two Jesus children, the Matthew Jesus child being the reincarnation of this legendary individuality. Welburn's 1991 *The Book with Fourteen Seals*, published largely for an anthroposophical readership, purported to trace all the incarnations of this ancient being through the ages of preparation until he finally appeared in this holy infant.[167] Welburn's recent book *From a Virgin Womb*, a more academic version of this

---

[165] Pagels, *Gnostic Gospels*, xxxi–xxxii. A far more detailed discussion of this search for sources is contained in King, *What Is Gnosticism?* chs. 3–5, which deal with the situation in the twentieth century prior to the emergence of the NHL.

[166] Andrew J. Welburn, *From a Virgin Womb: The Apocalypse of Adam and the Virgin Birth* (Leiden: Brill, 2008). Clearly a substantial background for Welburn's book is reflected in his article "Iranian Prophetology and the Birth of the Messiah: The Apocalypse of Adam," *Aufstieg und Niedergang der römischen Welt* II.25.6:4752–94, and his article "Identity of the Archons."

[167] Andrew J. Welburn, *The Book with Fourteen Seals: The Prophet Zarathustra and the Christ-Revelation* (London: Rudolf Steiner Press, 1991).

account, provides a highly scholarly basis for what Steiner had said so many decades before about the provenance of Matthew's Gospel, certainly at least its first two chapters.[168] Welburn's *The Book with Fourteen Seals* is never mentioned in *From a Virgin Womb*, which relies instead for its related background upon his 1988 article "Iranian Prophetology and the Birth of the Messiah." This article was obviously also the academic basis for *The Book with Fourteen Seals*.

Welburn makes the case that the *Apocalypse of Adam* is an Essene writing having similarities with certain Qumran scrolls and manifesting no essentially unique Christian influence. Its contacts with the infancy narrative in Matthew therefore suggest, in keeping with Steiner's indication, that the Gospel of Matthew was directed to a Jewish Essene audience.[169] Thus, though coming from a Jewish background, the highly esoteric *Apocalypse of Adam* appealed to the sensibilities of those who assembled the collection found at Nag Hammadi, though virtually every other treatise found in those codices manifested some, if not primary, Christian influence.

One of the most striking things in the *Apocalypse of Adam* is that the account of each of the thirteen kingdoms that precede "the generation without a king" ends with the cryptic phrase, "And thus he came on the water."[170] The reference to primal waters over which the elohim moved in Gen 1:2b ("and the Spirit of God was moving over the face of the waters") at a point when the earth was not only without

---

[168] Other scholars, members of the NHL team, have taken different approaches to the interpretation of the *Apocalypse of Adam*. See Charles W. Hedrick, *The Apocalypse of Adam* (Chico, Calif.: Scholars Press, 1980; repr., Eugene, Oreg.: Wipf & Stock, 2005) and Douglas M. Parrott, "The 13 Kingdoms of the Apocalypse of Adam: Origin, Meaning and Significance," *Novum Testamentum* 31 (1989): 67–87.

[169] Steiner, *According to Matthew*, lect. 6; see also the closing paragraphs of Steiner's lecture on November 13, 1910, in Nuremburg, published as "The Wisdom Contained in Ancient Documents and in the Gospels: The Event of the Christ," *Anthroposophic News Sheet* 5, no. 26 (June 27, 1937): 105–7; 5, no. 27 (July 4, 1937): 109–11; 5, no. 28 (July 11, 1937): 113–15; 5, no. 29 (July 18, 1937): 117–18, http://wn.rsarchive.org/Lectures/19101113p01.html (CW 125).

[170] The preposition "on" is Welburn's translation. Parrott ("13 Kingdoms," 75) translates "upon," and Hedrick (*Apocalypse of Adam*, 141) sees either "upon" or "to" as permissible, without mentioning "on," which is synonymous with "upon."

form but also "void" (1:2a) is most baffling without understanding the nature of those waters. Certainly they were not the tangible water consisting of matter as we know it. Anthroposophy asserts that in the descent of a reincarnating soul from the higher spiritual realms it passes through different levels, the last being the etheric realm, from which it unites with its earthly body during fetal development.[171] The etheric realm is often described esoterically in terms of water.

The entry into earthly life through a watery realm resembles the classical myth about the river of forgetfulness (Lethe); ordinary souls drink from that river before incarnating, whereas the more spiritually advanced, the initiates, might drink from a river of remembrance (Mnemosyne).[172] I suggest that Ezekiel's "river that could not be passed through" (47:5) depicts the River Lethe. The water that accompanies birth might be seen as an earthly reflection of this suggested spiritual reality.

This understanding then invites unique meaning from the concluding words of each of these thirteen kingdoms in the *Apocalypse of Adam*, "and thus he came to [or on] the water." The somewhat similar passage describing the birth of Moses (Exod 2:10, "and she named him Moses, for she said, 'Because I drew him out of the water'") can then also take on new and deeper meaning.[173]

---

[171] For a schematic of the fourfold etheric realm and its relation to the descending soul, see chart 1–22 in Smith, *Burning Bush*, showing the descent from higher spiritual worlds through the etheric world toward earthly life as a progression through the etheric fire (warmth), the etheric gas (air), the etheric fluid (water), and finally the life ether, the soul entering the solid (earth) body as its etheric or life body. See n. 82, above, discussing Christ's "water and Spirit" explanation to Nicodemus in John 3:5. Water and Spirit (air or gas) are the last two etheric realms before the descending soul incarnates in a body, and in order to leave the flesh and be born into the spiritual world one must again pass upward through those two etheric realms, which happens within about three days after each death but is a pattern that reflects what the human spirit must ultimately master to enter the higher spiritual realms, the kingdom of God.

[172] Cf. the conclusion of the Myth of Er at the end of Plato's *Republic* (10.620–621) and *Apocryphon of John* 25:7–9; see also the entry on Lethe in Wikipedia.

[173] See Steiner's lecture on Moses on March 9, 1911, in Berlin, published in Rudolf Steiner, *Turning Points in Spiritual History: Zarathustra, Hermes, Moses, Elijah, Buddha, Christ* (trans. Walter F. Knox; Great Barrington, Mass.: SteinerBooks, 2007), 106–41 (CW 60). See also Steiner, *Gospel of St. Mark*, lect. 8, regarding the initiation of Moses.

One could go on drawing instances where passages in the NHL texts call to mind things from what Steiner proclaimed to be the substantive, unwritten content of the ancient mysteries. This is so not because those mysteries are adequately reflected in the various NHL codices but because in the by then decadent state of the mysteries the NHL texts appear to reflect, though skewed as in faulty memory, aspects from that ancient content.

The presence in these later-discovered NHL tractates of so many basic aspects of what Steiner had previously given (in a more coherent form) as content of the ancient mysteries is a meaningful circumstance to take into account in evaluating what he said. This is especially true when the result of heeding what he said is to peel away the veil over and give deeper meaning to so many otherwise strange or obscure passages of scripture—passages whose past interpretations have become less and less satisfying over time. The most significant aspect of this for our purposes is the nature of the raising of Lazarus that pervades the rest of this book.

Appendix One: *The Giving of a Name*

"In Jewish thought, a name is not merely an arbitrary designation, a random combination of sounds. The name conveys the nature and essence of the thing named. It represents the history and reputation of the being named."[174]

The naming of infants in the Bible seems to reflect the ancient recognition that the essence of an infant (i.e., an incarnating soul) was to be reflected in a name having that meaning. Thus, with reference to the naming of the child Samuel (1 Sam 1:20), "We recognize in these passages wordplay upon the name of the child, a common feature of Old Testament birth narratives."[175] The name Abram ("the father is exalted") was changed to Abraham ("father of a multitude") after his spiritual experience with Melchizedek, and the deep sleep that fell upon him (see Genesis 14–17, esp. 17:5). His wife Sarah was told by God to name her child Isaac (17:19). Moses was given his name because he was drawn "out of the water," the significance of which is offered near the end of the previous section. The many instances of such naming in the Old Testament is carried forward into the New. Joseph is told to name the child Jesus "for he will save his people from their sins" (Matt 1:21), and Zechariah is told by the Lord's angel to name his child John for all of the many godly characteristics that are then described of him (Luke 1:13–17).

In *The Temple Legend* Steiner speaks of the giving of a new name after the temple sleep initiation is completed.[176]

Of greatest significance is the name that the Lord first gave to Moses on Mount Sinai when Moses asked the Lord for his *name*. The name given was *I Am*. John's Gospel has Christ using that phrase of

---

[174] Tracey R. Rich, "The Name of G-d," Judaism 101, http://www.jewfaq.org/name.htm.
[175] P. Kyle McCarter Jr., *I Samuel: A New Translation with Introduction, Notes, and Commentary* (Anchor Bible 8; Garden City, N.Y.: Doubleday, 1980), 62–63.
[176] Rudolf Steiner, *The Temple Legend* (trans. John M. Wood; London: Rudolf Steiner Press, 1985), 216–18 (CW 93, lect. 16).

himself many times, and his Apocalypse (Revelation) also indicates that it is the same name that will be given to those who through their own perfection have brought the Christ into their own being. The "new name" that is to be given to them is this *I Am*. Steiner seems to have stood alone in showing us that the name "which no one knows except him who receives it" is the *I Am* (Rev 2:17; 3:12; 19:12), for it can only be spoken of the one who speaks it, the one to whom it is given. There is no other name of which that can be said.

APPENDIX TWO: *Steiner Lecture April 13, 1908, in Berlin*[177]

Why was spiritual vision a natural condition in the far distant past? The reason is that the connection between the physical body and the etheric body was different. The connection existing today did not develop until the later phases of the Atlantean Epoch. Before that time the upper part of the etheric head extended far outside the boundaries of the physical head; toward the end of Atlantis the etheric head gradually drew completely into the physical head until it coincided with it. This gave rise to the later form of consciousness which became natural in Post-Atlantean man, enabling him to perceive physical objects in sharp outlines, as we do today. The fact that man can hear tones, be aware of scents, see colors on surfaces—although these are no longer expressions of the inmost spiritual reality of things—all this is connected with the firm and gradual interlocking of the physical body and etheric body.

In earlier times, when the etheric body was still partly outside the physical body, this projecting part of the etheric body was able to receive impressions from the astral body, and it was these impressions that were perceived by the old, dreamlike clairvoyance. Not until the etheric body had sunk right down into the physical body was man wholly bereft of his dim clairvoyance. Hence in the ancient Mysteries it became necessary for the priests to use special methods in order to induce in the candidates for Initiation the condition which, in Atlantis, had been natural and normal.

---

[177] See n. 90.

When pupils were to receive Initiation in the Mystery-temples, the procedure was that, after the appropriate impressions had been received by the astral body, the priests conducting the Initiation induced a partial loosening of the etheric body, in consequence of which the physical body lay for three and a half days in a trance-like sleep, in a kind of paralytic condition. The astral body was then able to imprint into the loosened etheric body experiences which had once come to Atlantean man in his normal state. Then the candidate for Initiation was able to see around him realities that henceforth were no longer merely preserved for him in scripts, or in tradition, but had become his own, individual experiences.

Let us try to picture what actually happened to the candidate for Initiation. When the priests in the Mysteries raised the etheric body partially out of the physical body and guided the impressions issuing from the astral body into this released etheric body, the candidate experienced in his etheric body the spiritual worlds. So strong and intense were the experiences that when he was restored from the trance and his etheric body was reunited to the physical body, he brought back the memory of these experiences into his physical consciousness. He had been a witness of the spiritual worlds, could himself bear witness to what was happening there; he had risen above and beyond all division into peoples or nations, for he had been initiated into that by which all peoples are united; the primal wisdom, primal truth.

APPENDIX THREE: *A Giant in Human Evolution*[178]

"Among those born of women there has risen no one greater than John the Baptist" (Matt 11:11). Christ here tells us of John's incomparable greatness, but also implies that he, Christ, was not born of woman. Even for those who hold that Christ was born of a virgin in the common sense of the word, Jesus of Nazareth was still born of a woman. Christ's words are compatible with Steiner's position, that the

---

[178] This appendix, referred to in n. 97, relates to the discussion about the testimony of John the Baptist in John's Gospel, discussed on p. 61.

incarnation—the "birth"—of Christ can be dated no earlier than when John baptized Jesus and the Spirit descended upon him. Only then did he become, only then was he born as, Jesus Christ.

Over the first quarter of the twentieth century as his hearers were prepared for his revelations, but especially toward the end of his life, Steiner gave clear indications of the individualities that incarnated in given earthly personalities.[179] I described five of those that were powerfully involved in the biblical story in the final essay in *The Burning Bush*, entitled "Pillars on the Journey." The one individuality that is here pertinent is the first one there listed and is as follows:[180]

Adam Kadmon
Phinehas
Elijah (Naboth)
John the Baptist
Raphael
Novalis

---

[179] Every human being with the exception of the Nathan-Jesus child, his birth mother, and avatars such as Melchizedek went through the fall (Genesis 3) and is thus burdened by the karma resulting from that "original sin." All human sin has resulted from the Ego's yielding to the impurities of the astral body resulting from the fall. Steiner says, however, that the original fall occurred before the human Ego had entered into the human being. Since it is only the Ego's failures in relation to the influence of its infected astral body that produces guilt, the innocence of humanity for guilt for the fall is balanced on the scale of divine justice by the unmerited grace bestowed by the shed blood of Christ (Steiner, *Concepts of Original Sin and Grace*). Karma and reincarnation constitute the instrument of that grace, giving every human being the opportunity, over long eras and many lives, to make restitution to every creature ever wronged by it. The term *individuality* designates the eternal aspect of every human being, the part that goes through many incarnations on its long journey to perfection. The individuality can address, in any one incarnation, only a portion of the individuality's accumulated karma from past lives. The *personality* is only that portion of an individuality necessary to address the karma that comprises the spiritually fashioned destiny of an individuality for a given lifetime (destiny is a biblical term: Job 15:22; Isa 23:13; 65:11–12; Hos 9:13; Acts 4:28; Rom 8:29–30; Eph 1:5, 11; 1 Thess 5:9; 1 Pet 1:2; 2:8). Metaphorically speaking, the *personality* is to the *individuality* as the visible portion of an iceberg is to its entirety. The entirety of the iceberg represents the accumulated karma that must be addressed and overcome in the long journey. The *individuality* is the spiritual reality that Moses perceived in the burning bush on Mount Sinai, the "bush" that is always burned but never destroyed.
[180] This individuality is the subject of Sergei O. Prokofieff's book *Eternal Individuality: Towards a Karmic Biography of Novalis* (London: Temple Lodge, 1992).

Steiner gave two lectures on Elijah, the first one exclusively on him, the second significantly so.[181] It was in the second that Steiner emphasized how the ancient spirit that dwelled in both Elijah and John the Baptist "could not wholly enter into" either of them, in contrast to the Christ Spirit that entered wholly into the three bodies of Jesus.[182] The earthly embodiment of this ancient Elijah spirit in Naboth and then in John the Baptist was of such nature that in both cases it hovered over them, and in each case its activity was not limited to the presence of the physical body either before or after the death of its earthly body.[183] This feature is brought out in the earlier lecture where Steiner describes how Elijah-Naboth was initiated into all seven steps of the Persian Mithraic mysteries and how the nature of the Elijah spirit confused Ahab but not Jezebel.[184]

There is ample biblical warrant for understanding that John the Baptist was Elijah returned.[185] Elijah himself had gone through the name-changing experience (from Naboth to Elijah) by initiation into the Mithraic mysteries, where he would have seen his own past.[186]

---

[181] Steiner, *Turning Points*, 142–78 (CW 61, December 14, 1911); idem, *Gospel of St. Mark*, 39–62 (lect. 3).

[182] Steiner, *Gospel of St. Mark*, 52–53 (lect. 3).

[183] This aspect of the Elijah spirit appearing after the death of its body (Naboth) is reflected in 1 Kings 21. Jezebel plots to have Naboth killed. Immediately after he is killed, the Elijah spirit pronounces doom upon Ahab, which pronouncement is consummated upon Ahab's line in 2 Kgs 9:21–26.

[184] See n. 122, concerning the seven-step initiation. The earlier lecture interprets the story of Elijah in the book of Kings, showing how what seems to be a description of two different persons is really a description of only one as a result of the nature of the Elijah spirit. The account is condensed in Smith, *Burning Bush*, 375–86.

[185] See Mal 4:5; Matt 17:1, 9–13; Mark 9:2, 9–13. See also Smith, *Burning Bush*, 131–33, 486–87; idem, *Soul's Long Journey*, 24–25, 210–11.

[186] Modern scholarship on Mithraism focuses upon the Roman Mithraic Mysteries, placing the origins of the latter in the first centuries B.C.E. or the earliest centuries C.E.; David Ulansey, *The Origins of the Mithraic Mysteries* (New York: Oxford University Press, 1989); Roger Beck, "The Mysteries of Mithras: A New Account of Their Genesis," *Journal of Roman Studies* 88 (1998):115–28, http://www.jstor.org/stable/300807. Such scholarship dates the origins of the Roman cult to the first appearances of the tauroctony (bull-killing), but both authors recognize an earlier worship of Mithra in which there was no tauroctony (Ulansey, *Origins*, 8; Beck, "Mysteries," 119–20, 123–27). The ancient roots of Mithra worship in Zoroastrianism are said to have gone back as far as the fifth millennium B.C.E.; Mary Boyce, *Zoroastrianism: Its Antiquity and Constant Vigour* (Costa Mesa, Calif.: Mazda, 1992), 52–61.

When Lazarus-John went through his own initiation (raising) and, as indicated in the main text, was penetrated and indwelled by the Elijah individuality, it was as though the consciousness of Lazarus-John himself went all the way back to Adam, the first individuality to be able to remain incarnated as an earthly being (Gen 4:25). In that consciousness, he would have experienced in his own soul the effect of the fall to which he and all other human beings save the Christ were burdened.[187] Hence, through that indwelling Elijah recognition, he could say (and later write) with the deepest of comprehension, "After me comes he who is mightier than I, the thong of whose sandals I am not worthy to stoop down and untie" (John 1:26–27; Mark 1:7; Matt 3:11; Luke 3:16; Acts 13:25). As we will see later, the part of Adam that had fallen (John in Elizabeth's womb) jumped with joyful recognition as the part that did not go through the fall (Jesus in Mary's womb) approached him (Luke 1:41–45). It is as though, at the baptism of Jesus by John, we have a reprise of that deep soul recognition during the gestation of the two infants.[188] Paul spoke of the first Adam, who became a living being, and of the last Adam, who became a life-giving spirit (1 Cor 15:45; see also Rom 5:14). The babe John in Elizabeth's womb was the first Adam, while the one in Mary's womb was, upon the baptism by the first Adam, to become the last Adam, the life-giving spirit.

This accords with Steiner's indication that the most ancient Zarathustra, not his far later namesake called Zoroaster by the Greeks, the one who observed the Ahura Mazda, was the leading spirit of the Ancient Persian cultural era that commenced in 5067 B.C.E.

Of this aura, the ancient Zarathustra "knew that this being was guiding the evolution of humanity but would only be able to descend to Earth from cosmic space at a certain point in the future" (*Outline of Esoteric Science*, 258–62, quoting 261). As the Christian era approached, Steiner said, "The worship of Mithras was a last powerful remembrance of the Christ Who had not yet reached the earth but was descending"; Rudolf Steiner, *Festivals of the Seasons* (CW 156; London: Anthroposophical Publishing Co., 1928), 87 (December 26, 1914).

[187] The avatar Melchizedek as well as the Nathan-Jesus child and mother in Luke's Gospel would also have been free from the karmic burden of the fall.

[188] At the baptism the recognition is between individualities, while in the nativity account the recognition is between etheric (life) bodies, the one that went through the fall recognizing the pure one that was not sullied by that experience in the higher realms.

CHAPTER TWO—JOHN

The Tetrad (Four)

There is something basic about the number four, a sacred geometry. Irenaeus noted this with respect to the four gospels (*Against Heresies* 3.11.8). Mystery inheres in each, Matthew, Mark, Luke, and John. As we turn our attention to the last of these, let us start with some reflections on their authorship. We note that, at present, while the tradition of quasi-apostolic authorship on the middle two, Mark and Luke, retains a respectable following, the apostolic origin of the first and last faces tougher sledding.

Rudolf Steiner gave lecture cycles on all four of the gospels. He presented insights into the authorship of the Gospels of John and Matthew, while leaving the traditional views on the other two undisturbed, referring to them simply as Luke or Mark. He specifically recognized Mark as a pupil of Peter, saying that Mark remained with Peter for some time before coming to Alexandria; he arrived at a time when its environment made it "possible for [him] to be stimulated to give his description of the cosmic greatness of Christ. This was a period when ... Jewish-philosophical-theosophical learning in Alexandria had reached a certain culmination. He could take up in Alexandria what at that time were the best aspects of pagan gnosis.... From the pagan gnosis he could accept everything that was told him about the origin of man out of the cosmos when our planet came into being."[189]

The early view that Matthew was written by the tax collector is now widely rejected, and few other likely candidates are yet on the general scene. Steiner also offered his insights into the authorship of the Matthew Gospel, though without suggesting a known personality. Contrary to sixth-century rabbinic authority, as we shall see, he

---

[189] Steiner, *Gospel of St. Mark*, 188 (lect. 10).

said that the great teacher of the Essenes, "the righteous one," was Jeshu ben Pandira, who suffered martyrdom on account of alleged blasphemy and heresy, a hundred years B.C.E. This Jeshu had five pupils, Mathai, Nakai, Nezer, Boni, and Thona, each of whom took over a special branch of his general teaching. It was Mathai's teaching, Steiner said, that the Zarathustrian genealogy in Matt 1:1–17 reflected, and he said it is from his name that the gospel derives its title.[190] Most likely, in such event, it was a disciple in Mathai's line who, whether or not himself named Matthew, or perhaps Matthias, pseudonymously wrote the gospel in the time frame normally suggested. That the gospel came from such a spiritual descendant of this Jeshu is also suggested by Matt 2:23, "And he went and dwelt in a city called Nazareth, that what was spoken by the prophets might be fulfilled, 'He shall be called a Nazarene.'" More than any other gospel, Matthew calls upon the authority of the prophets, but in this one instance alone, no canonical prophet can be identified. But if Matthew was directed primarily to the Essenes, the reference, which is plural, would most likely have included, above all, the righteous teacher of the Essenes. Welburn's *From a Virgin Womb*, discussed earlier in the *Apocalypse of Adam* section, supports Matthew's Essene connection. Steiner also said that another of those five pupils of Jeshu was named Netzer (or Nezer), for whom the little settlement called Nazareth (Netzereth, or Nezereth), composed of Nazirites, got its name.

The time frame in which the Righteous Teacher lived and died generally covers the approximate period Steiner gave, 100 B.C.E.[191] Among scholars there is no consensus on his identity or whether he was martyred.

In identifying Jeshu as the Essenes' Teacher of Righteousness, Steiner was rejecting the polemical portrait of this individual in the

---

[190] Steiner, *According to Matthew*, 94–108 (lect. 6). See also Smith, *Burning Bush*, 39–40; and the latter part of Steiner, "Wisdom Contained in Ancient Documents."

[191] See, for instance, Sarah Klitenic, "The Teacher of Righteousness and the End of Days," *Sources* 3 (Spring 1997), http://humanities.uchicago.edu/journals/jsjournal/klitenic.html; and F. F. Bruce, *The Teacher of Righteousness in the Qumran Texts* (London: Tyndale, 1957), http://www.biblicalstudies.org.uk/pdf/qumran_bruce.pdf.

sixth-century C.E. rabbinic text *Sanhedrin* 43a, which identified this Jeshu (Yeshua, or Yeshua ben Pantera) as the Jesus of the Christians, claiming that he was hanged on the eve of the Passover along with all five of his pupils.[192] Contrary to this rabbinic tradition, Steiner said that Jeshu was sent to serve as a guide to the Essenes about a century before Christ, during the reign of King Alexander Jannaeus (ca. 125–70 B.C.E.):

> In esoteric circles, this personality is well known as an Essene precursor of Christianity. Exoteric Talmudic literature calls him Jeshu ben Pandira (Jesus the son of Pandira) and reports all sorts of slanderous falsehoods about him, which have recently been revived. The fact is, however, that Jeshu ben Pandira was great and noble, though he is not to be confused (as some Talmudic scholars do) with Jesus of Nazareth. We know that Jeshu ben Pandira, after discovering blasphemy in Essene doctrines, was accused of blasphemy and heresy himself. He was stoned and then, to add insult to injury, hanged from a tree. His fate is known to esotericism, but it is also reported in the Talmud.[193]

In his lecture the following day he added, "Beginning in the second century A.D., he was repeatedly confused with the Jesus of the Gospels; nevertheless, Jeshu ben Pandira is not the same as the Christian Jesus. We must, however, acknowledge that a historical connection does exist, though we can confirm it today only through spiritual-scientific research."[194]

But it is to the identity of evangelist John that we now, again, turn our attention.

---

[192] For the text of *Sanhedrin* 43a, see http://www.come-and-hear.com/sanhedrin/sanhedrin_43.html. For discussion, see James D. Tabor, *The Jesus Dynasty: The Hidden History of Jesus, His Royal Family, and the Birth of Christianity* (New York: Simon & Schuster, 2006), 63–73.

[193] Steiner, *Gospel of St. Mark*, 78–79 (lect. 4).

[194] Steiner, *Gospel of St. Mark*, 80 (lect. 5). The exalted stature of the one who was Jeshu ben Pandira is more fully expressed by Steiner in *From Jesus to Christ*, 178–80 (lect. 10).

Who Was Evangelist John?

THE CANDIDATES

The word, as we approached our first final exams in law school, was that if we could identify all the issues posed in the exam question we would score at the summa cum laude level whether we knew any of the answers or not, the assumption being that in practice the answers could be found if the issues were recognized.

In John's Gospel scholars have encountered a bountiful harvest of issues. Anyone with the thought of descriptively identifying all of them must surely recognize the ponderous nature of the under-taking. Even the thought of listing all the formidable scholars who have written meaningfully on the gospel or identity of its author over the modern era is intimidating. Prominent names that spring immediately to mind, Rudolf Bultmann, Raymond E. Brown, Oscar Cullmann, C. H. Dodd, Martin Hengel, Ernst Käsemann, D. Moody Smith, John Ashton, D. A. Carson, R. Alan Culpepper, Marinus de Jonge, Robert T. Fortna, Robert Kysar, and J. Louis Martyn don't begin to express the endless array. One surveying the terrain today might even be excused for irreverently wondering if the search for new issues has surpassed further deliberation on the old. Anyone attending all fifty-eight papers of the John sessions at the SBL convention in San Diego in November 2007 must surely have come away lightheaded from the dizzying blizzard presented. Though the specific identity of the author was apparently not the theme of any of the papers, it nevertheless seems to be a critical thread woven through virtually all of them.

But on the issue of authorship, and at the risk of being overly selec-tive, I have found no work more helpful in focusing jointly on the issues of authorship in general and the naming of those scholars who have staked out clear positions on author identity in particular than *The Beloved Disciple* by James H. Charlesworth. On the matter of authorship in general, the threshold question is whether the beloved disciple is a real person or only idealized, fictional, or symbolic. And if real, is the beloved disciple the one who actually wrote the gospel or at least was the writer's immediate source? To do much more than recognize the existence of these issues and postulate some general answers before going on to our specific concerns is beyond the scope of this work. Readers desiring to do so are encouraged to probe more deeply into the areas of their concerns that are not fully pursued here, and Charlesworth's book would be a decent place for general readers to start.

While I find Charlesworth's book helpful, our respective candidates for evangelist John are not the same. Fascinating is it that his candidate, Thomas the Apostle, is also supported by the respected Hans-Martin Schenke. But Charlesworth differs from Schenke on the vital question of whether the beloved disciple is a real or fictitious person. Schenke considers him fictitious, whereas Charlesworth and I both accept his personal reality but differ on who he is and whether or not he wrote the gospel (or was the writer's immediate source of information). Obviously, in Schenke's view, the beloved disciple could not have written the gospel, nor does Charlesworth suggest that Thomas wrote the gospel. On that matter, I find it difficult to go with the idea that the one who wrote "This is the disciple who is bearing witness to these things and who has written these things; and we know that his testimony is true" (21:24) was writing a falsehood.

Literary-critical analysis of the text has been a helpful tool in many instances, and many scholars have concluded that the verse just cited cannot be taken seriously, but when knowledge of the full content of the ancient mysteries is taken into account, it can be seen that powerful reasons support the truth of the statement. I leave for later the discussion of whether chapter 21 was written by the evangelist or one close to him (commonly impersonalized by the term "redactor," an agency scholars often use to break texts into a profuse series of altered or amended texts, though there has been a tendency since the early 1980s to look at the final product of texts as a whole, such as with the books of Isaiah and John). And it should be noted that the use of the third-person "his" is consistent with the third-person references to the beloved disciple throughout the book. Particularly noticeable, though, is its use along with the "we" in the final clause of v. 24, "and *we* know that *his* testimony is true." Some reason that the writer's first-person use of "we" rather than the second-person "you" distinguishes himself from the disciple described in the third-person. One wonders, however, how much weight can be accorded the argument based on these pronouns. For instance, in the not improbable event that the beloved disciple was aged and was providing the story to a younger person to write down for him, thus being the immediate source of the story, then as discussed later I would consider him the author.[195] In that case, both pronouns would be consistent with the elder's authorship, for the "we" is written from the perspective of the secretary and the intended readers (cf. the greeting by Paul's secretary Tertius in Rom 16:22). The widely held view among scholars that v. 23 means the beloved disciple has died and thus cannot have written the concluding chapter is an astute observation. There is a viable, and in my view likely, alternative, as we shall see.

The writings of one of Schenke's scholarly stature cannot be dismissed cavalierly, nor in disagreeing with his conclusions do I intend such. I refer to his paper "The Function and Background of the Beloved Disciple in the Gospel of John."[196]

To begin with, the paper is placed in the context of the 1983 Springfield, Missouri, conference on the NHL, which focused on its relationship to early Christianity. The connections Schenke cites between a few verses of the *Book of Thomas* (not the *Gospel of Thomas*) and a few verses of John's prologue, while indeed noteworthy, do not, standing alone, seem of great probative force nor does the simple fact that in both it and John's Gospel the savior's "dialogue partner(s) frequently misunderstand him."[197] A more plausible surmise as to why Schenke chose Thomas, at least as against Lazarus, as the gospel's source is his explanation later in the paper of why he thinks the beloved disciple is "only a simple fiction of the redactor."[198]

---

[195] For instance, there is a tradition that Prochorus was with John in the cave on Patmos and wrote the book Revelation as John dictated.

[196] Hans-Martin Schenke, "The Function and Background of the Beloved Disciple in the Gospel of John," in *Nag Hammadi, Gnosticism, and Early Christianity* (ed. C. W. Hedrick and R. Hodgson Jr.; Peabody, Mass: Hendrickson, 1986), 111–25.

[197] Schenke, "Function and Background," 112.

[198] Schenke, "Function and Background," 119; also 116.

Perhaps what I admire most in Schenke's paper is his following observation:

> Finally, I cannot avoid asking a very subtle but irresistibly suggestive question, although I feel unable to judge whether it warrants pursuit: is the relationship between *Trimorphic Protennoia* and the prologue of John only a specific example of a much more general relationship between Sethianism and the whole Gospel of John?[199]

Surely anyone with an anthroposophical background must love the question and the direction in which it leads. The *Trimorphic Protennoia* is shot through with content so similar to what Steiner gave us as the content of the ancient mysteries. But to pursue it more fully here would lead us too far afield.

Recognizing that not all the issues regarding the beloved disciple can be addressed in any one paper, Schenke states candidly the two premises upon which his conclusions are based about the identity of the beloved disciple and the authorship of chapter 21. They are "(1) that neither the Gospel of John as a whole nor certain parts of it can be thought of as guaranteed by a historically trustworthy person or regarded as written by an eyewitness; and (2) that the whole of chapter 21 is redactional."[200]

Before moving to our principal proposal, that Lazarus is both the disciple whom Jesus loved and the author of the gospel, two counter postulates must be either established or assumed: first, leaving aside for the moment the issue of chapter 21, the gospel was written by the disciple whom Jesus loved; and second, the matter of authorship need not distinguish between the act of writing, on the one hand, and providing the content for another to do the writing, on the other hand.

The prevailing consensus of scholarship on these two points seems to be that the beloved disciple did not "write" the gospel but was only the source behind it, considering that one is deemed to have written a document if he or she directs another to write it, as in the

---

[199] Schenke, "Function and Background," 113.
[200] Schenke, "Function and Background," 116.

case of a secretary (*amanuensis*).[201] My position is contrary to that consensus on the first point; the beloved disciple *wrote* the gospel within the broader, generally accepted meaning of that term, though on that second point I would opt for the possibility of stretching the strict amanuensis theory a bit. If the beloved disciple was the "source," he would have been very directly so as, for instance, in the case of an author having narrated the events to one with the understanding that the latter would very soon reduce the account to writing for the author's review and approval. In view of the fact that Lazarus-John would have been quite elderly when the gospel was written, the prospect of having another actually do the writing is fairly likely.

Also contrary to the prevailing judgment on the matter, the position adopted here is that Lazarus-John also "wrote" chapter 21, but discussion of that will be deferred till later.

We come then to the case for Lazarus as the disciple whom Jesus loved and the one who became John and wrote the gospel.

THE CASE FOR LAZARUS AS PRESENTED BY STEINER

We return to the situation at the beginning of the twentieth century, the fall of 1900 C.E. At thirty-nine years of age, his foundational years behind him, Steiner transitionally begins to lecture on matters of a more spiritual nature. Only the year before, 1899, as he tells us in the *Autobiography*,[202] written and dictated during his last illness, "I stood spiritually before the Mystery of Golgotha in a deep and solemn celebration of knowledge." A year later, in the fall of 1901 he begins a series of twenty-five lectures that were then revised and published in 1902 as *Christianity as Mystical Fact*. In the pages of his *Autobiography* leading up to his description of these lectures, he tells of his decision to depart from the ancient and then still widely held

---

[201] Richard Bauckham, *Jesus and the Eyewitnesses: The Gospels as Eyewitness Testimony* (Grand Rapids: Eerdmans, 2006), 358 – 62; Charlesworth, *Beloved Disciple*, 24 – 26. The latter part of the portion cited from Bauckham deals specifically with John 21:24 though its rationale applies to the larger content.

[202] Steiner, *Autobiography*, 239.

view that knowledge of the ancient mystery content should not be revealed exoterically but only applied as the foundation for personal service in the outer world. Of these lectures he says: "My intention was not merely to present the mystical meaning of Christianity. My purpose was to describe evolution, from the ancient Mysteries to the Mystery of Golgotha, in a way that would reveal forces active in evolution that were not merely earthly, historical forces, but spiritual and extra earthly. I wanted to show that the meaning presented in the ancient Mysteries assumed the form of ritualized images of cosmic processes that were then transferred from the cosmos to Earth in the Mystery of Golgotha as a sensory-perceptible artifact brought about on the level of history."[203]

Steiner died on March 30, 1925. His last lecture was on September 28, 1924, when he became too ill to complete it. His *Autobiography* was published monthly throughout 1924. His last illness prevented its completion beyond that point in his life story somewhere in the year 1907. Correspondence between him and his wife, Marie, who continued to travel giving performances related to his anthroposophical teachings, continued throughout his illness. During the course of his final months of correspondence it was evident that he had become aware as early as January 1923 that his life body was beginning to separate from his physical body. Obviously, by the time he completed the passage quoted above he was nearing the end. What he said must surely have been with the deepest solemnity in reflection upon what he had been about to launch into human understanding with those lectures and their subsequent publication.[204]

It was in *CMF*, after six chapters of background regarding the mysteries, that he revealed in chapter seven ("The 'Miracle' of Lazarus") the nature of the raising of Lazarus followed in chapter eight by the keys to understanding the cosmic significance and meaning of the Apocalypse of John. In the remaining four chapters,

---

[203] Steiner, *Christianity as Mystical Fact*, 259.

[204] For such correspondence, see Rudolf Steiner, *Correspondence and Documents, 1901–1925* (ed. Joan M. Thompson; trans. Christian von Arnim and Ingrid von Arnim; London: Rudolf Steiner Press, 1988) (CW 262).

from the Essenes and Therapeutae through "the gnostic crisis" to Augustine he laid the groundwork for understanding the submergence of the mystery knowledge until he undertook to reveal it early in the twentieth century.

From that point for the next twelve years (until the beginning of the war in 1914) he laid the groundwork for, and provided, I suggest, the most astoundingly profound insights into the biblical message that have been offered since the beginning of the Christian era.

His radical revelation about the nature of the raising of Lazarus and the Gospel of John constituted the opening salvo of this spiritual cornucopia.

Only in understanding this background is it possible to evaluate whether the publication of Kreyenbühl's thoughts on Lazarus had any influence on the essentially contemporaneous account that Steiner was beginning to bring forth in such a complete way. We shall now briefly compare their disclosures in further reflection on this question, but the position taken herein is that Steiner was the one who first laid the complete foundation to establish Lazarus as the evangelist John and that Kreyenbühl's publication one year earlier of his account, which was somewhat at variance with Steiner's, though astute for the time, is unlikely to have had any meaningful effect, if he was even aware of it, upon the course of revelation Steiner was undertaking.[205] Whenever hereafter I refer to Steiner as the first to identify Lazarus as the evangelist, it is with this understanding.

What, then, was it that Kreyenbühl said in his 1900 publication?[206]

Essentially, as it relates to our inquiry, it is what Charlesworth described in one paragraph in *The Beloved Disciple*: that the evan-

---

[205] Robert Eisler writes, "The late Dr. Rudolf Steiner of Vienna, the founder of the Anthroposophic movement, taught the same interpretation of Jn xi. 3—independently of Kreyenbühl, whose work he does not seem to have known—in 1903 in his book [*Christianity as Mystical Fact*]" (*The Enigma of the Fourth Gospel: Its Author and Its Writer* [London: Methuen, 1938], 190). From what has previously been said, clearly Steiner knew Kreyenbühl's other, earlier works, though the contemporaneity of their writings on the beloved disciple lends credibility to Eisler's statement.

[206] The following discussion of Kreyenbühl's *Evangelium der Wahrheit*, 1:151–52, 156–62 derives from the translation kindly provided to me by my friend Paul V. O'Leary, of St. Lucie, Florida.

gelist was a Palestinian Jew and that the designation "the disciple whom Jesus loved" was the evangelist's self-designation that was sufficiently clearly pointed to by the passages describing the savior's love for him in chapter 11.[207] To Charlesworth's summary should be added another Kreyenbühl observation. Contrary to Steiner's position, Kreyenbühl categorically rejects chapter 21 as being by the evangelist. The matter seems to have been raised to controvert any effort to show that the evangelist was the apostle John (son of Zebedee), based upon some "Ephesian parochialism," though the traditional Ephesian locus for the writing of John's Gospel was not questioned. It all seems to stem from v. 23, the saying about the disciple who was not to die, that continues to be the prime grounds for the same prevailing view on chapter 21 today. Kreyenbühl seems to make the point that if other scholars choose that rationale to attribute John's Gospel to the apostle John they do so with great ineptitude.

Kreyenbühl offers one other glimmer when he says that all the effort "to make, directly or indirectly, [John's] gospel into a work of the historical *or idealized* John rests only and alone upon … Chapter 21, which does not have the least to do with the gospel" (emphasis mine). He seems to be rejecting any theory that John the evangelist was merely an "idealized" disciple.

It is to the credit of Kreyenbühl that he was willing to part with tradition and tie the authorship to Lazarus as both a Palestinian Jew and the one Jesus is said to have "loved." But these discussions were a relatively minor part of his book. In view of the likelihood that Steiner and Kreyenbühl were at least somewhat acquainted, as previously suggested, and of what had occurred in Steiner's life shortly before the publication of Kreyenbühl's book, and the far greater elaboration by Steiner of Lazarus as John, it seems as likely that Steiner's early views may have triggered those of Kreyenbühl as that it was the other way around, if indeed either influenced the other rather than them being spontaneous, independent, and contemporary proponents in which perhaps higher worlds were involved.

---

[207] Charlesworth, *Beloved Disciple*, 186.

The radical difference between Steiner's presentation of Lazarus and of John's Gospel from that of Kreyenbühl, and indeed from the vast majority of other John scholars, is due in part to his privileging of what he calls Spiritual Science over historical criticism. Consider what he said in the second paragraph of his first lecture in the primary John cycle in May 1908:

> In order to make this absolutely clear, we shall have to express ourselves in quite radical terms. Let us suppose that through some circumstance all religious records have been lost, and that men possessed only those capacities which they have today; they should, nevertheless, be able to penetrate into life's mysteries, if they only retain those capacities. They should be able to reach the divine-spiritual creating forces and beings which lie concealed behind the physical world. And Spiritual Science must depend entirely upon these independent sources of knowledge, irrespective of all records. However, after having investigated the divine-spiritual mysteries of the world independently, we can then take up the actual religious documents themselves. Only then can we recognize their true worth, for we are, in a certain sense, free and independent of them. What has previously been independently discovered is now recognized within the documents themselves. And you may be sure that for anyone who has pursued this path, these writings will suffer no diminution in value, no lessening of the respect and veneration due.[208]

In this approach Steiner is complying in the fullest way with the second commandment given to Moses (Exod 20:4, "graven image"; 2 Cor 3:6b, "not in a written code but in the Spirit; for the written code kills, but the Spirit gives life"). When one reads the Bible in light of what Steiner has to say, one may not only confirm his statements, by seeing them conveyed there, but also acquire new and deeper insight into the greatness of its message.

---

[208] Steiner, *Gospel of St. John*, 16 (lect. 1).

Steiner's preference for Spiritual Science led him to identify Lazarus as the beloved disciple and author of John's Gospel in a unique way by focusing on the ancient mysteries and the knowledge of higher spiritual truths that is available only to an initiate yet is reflected in the Gospel of John.

Of significance also is his identification of the three parts of the gospel, namely, the prologue (1:1–18), the testimony of John the Baptist (1:19–10:42), which is made possible by the penetration of the being of John down through the consciousness soul of Lazarus, and the testimony of Lazarus himself (11:1–21:25). This trichotomy has been noted by other prominent scholars. Bultmann, speaking about John 10:40–42, said, "The public activity of Jesus has reached its end.... The situation, however, gives occasion for making the testimony of the Baptist, with which 1:19ff. began, to be confirmed out of the mouth of the people."[209] Raymond Brown also felt that John 10:40–42 brought the ministry of Jesus to an end. But whereas Brown says that Bultmann "treats these verses as the introduction to ch. xi," Brown himself considers John 11–12 as "an editorial addition to the original gospel outline" in which John 10:40–42 "was followed by the opening of the Book of Glory in ch. xiii."[210] Gail R. O'Day notes that John 10:40–42 "return[s] Jesus to the place where John the Baptist first bore witness to him (1:28) ... [and] moves the witness of John the Baptist into view for the last time."[211]

Steiner also attributes a distinctive meaning to the word "loved" as used in connection with the beloved disciple: "What does 'to love' mean in the language of the Mysteries? It expresses the relationship of the pupil to the teacher. 'He whom the Lord loved' is the most intimate, the most deeply initiated pupil."[212] In recent years a few scholars have come to realize basically the same thing, that Jesus' special love for

---

[209] Rudolf Bultmann, *The Gospel of John* (trans. G. R. Beasley-Murray; Philadelphia: Westminster, 1971), 393–94.

[210] Brown, *Gospel according to John*, 1:414. Brown notes how jumping over John 11–12 results in greater similarity to the synoptic account.

[211] Gail R. O'Day, "The Gospel of John: Introduction, Commentary, and Reflections," *The New Interpreter's Bible* 9:678.

[212] Steiner, *Gospel of St. John*, 64 (lect. 4).

the beloved disciple signals the depth of the latter's initiation into his master's teaching. Charlesworth, for instance, commenting on J. Edgar Bruns' thesis that Ananda is the beloved disciple, proposed that Arjuna's relationship to Krishna in the Bhagavad Gita presents "a far more stunning parallel to the Beloved Disciple," for like the beloved disciple in John, Arjuna is said to have been "loved" by his master, who "imparts salvific knowledge to his favorite disciple."[213] Similarly, Sjef van Tilborg showed that this particular form of relationship, characterized by love, between a teacher and the disciple he chose to have "a special role in the future succession of teacher and pupil" was so prevalent in antiquity as to be "an institutional reality."[214]

THOSE WHO CHOSE LAZARUS

Charlesworth identifies twenty-two candidates for the beloved disciple that scholars have suggested. While not exhaustive, his coverage, indicated below, is impressive:

Suggested Identity	Number of Scholars
1. Impossible to Decide	5
2. Ananda[215]	2
3. An Ideal, Fictitious, or Symbolical Figure	1
4. A Symbol of the Apostolic Prophet	3
5. A Symbol of the Church	1
6. A Real Human Whose Identity Is Lost	26

---

[213] Charlesworth, *Beloved Disciple*, 132–33. For Bruns, see n. 215, below.

[214] Sjef van Tilborg, *Imaginative Love in John* (Leiden: Brill, 1993), 77–81, quoting 59.

[215] Ananda was a disciple of Gautama, the Buddha. For the connection of Ananda to the identity of the beloved disciple, Charlesworth (*Beloved Disciple*, 132) cites, among others, J. Edgar Bruns, "Ananda: The Fourth Evangelist's Model for 'the Disciple Whom Jesus Loved'?" *Studies in Religion* 3 (1973): 236–43, as seeing in Ananda the pattern of a beloved disciple.

7.	Matthias	1
8.	Apollos	3
9.	Paul or a Paulinist	3
10.	A Second Benjamin (cf. Deut 33:12)	1
11.	The Rich Young Ruler	5
12.	Judas Iscariot	2
13.	Andrew, Simon Peter's Brother	1
14.	Philip	1
15.	Nathanael	3
16.	Lazarus	13
17.	John Mark	7
18.	Judas, Jesus' Brother	1
19.	John the Apostle	29
20.	John the Elder	4
21.	John the Elder Blended with John the Apostle	3
22.	One of the Two Anonymous Disciples Noted in 21:2	2

It is immediately apparent that there is at least one other candidate, namely, Thomas the Apostle, for Charlesworth devotes a chapter in support of Thomas as the beloved disciple, noting the same identification by P. de Suarez and H.-M. Schenke. Charlesworth differs with Schenke on one point. Schenke sees the beloved disciple as "a redactional fiction who functions to give the Fourth Gospel the appearance of being authenticated and written by an eyewitness."[216] But Schenke is not listed in category no. 3 above. Charlesworth points out that

---

[216] Charlesworth, *Beloved Disciple*, 419.

neither de Suarez nor Schenke developed their conclusion on the basis of an interpretation of the Gospel of John.[217]

While Charlesworth, de Suarez, and Schenke, with variant rationales, identify Thomas as the beloved disciple, Pagels in stark contrast sees the Gospel of John as having been written "in the heat of controversy, in order to oppose, among other things, "what the Gospel of Thomas teaches."[218]

A few scholars have also suggested Mary Magdalene as the beloved disciple, so the absence in the listing of that popular figure might surprise some. For whatever other reasons, Charlesworth points out early that the beloved disciple could not be a woman "because from the cross Jesus told his mother, 'Behold your son.'"[219] Proponents of Mary as the beloved disciple have found a way around that constriction.[220]

Still another scholar points to James, the brother of Jesus as the beloved disciple.[221]

Charlesworth's 1995 listing illustrates the spread and general drift of thinking. Aside from those who think the identity is forever lost (26 in no. 6) and those who contend for John son of Zebedee, generally known as John the Apostle (29 in no. 19), those opting for Lazarus are more numerous than any other. Charlesworth generalizes that the traditional John son of Zebedee identification is "usually [made] without any independent research" and that the position appeared "in the precritical period and is coin in 'Sunday-school-type' literature."[222]

---

[217] Charlesworth, *Beloved Disciple*, 224–25 n. 495.

[218] Pagels, *Beyond Belief*, 34.

[219] Charlesworth, *Beloved Disciple*, 5–6.

[220] Some authors suggest that a redactor added the male reference. See Ramon K. Jusino, "Mary Magdalene: Author of the Fourth Gospel?" http://ramon_k_jusino. tripod.com/Magdalene.pdf; Esther A. de Boer, *The Gospel of Mary: Beyond a Gnostic and a Biblical Mary Magdalene* (New York: T&T Clark, 2004), 178–90; idem, "Mary Magdalene and the Disciple Jesus Loved," *Lectio difficilior* 1 (2000), http://www.lectio. unibe.ch/00_1/m-forum.htm; and Robin Griffith-Jones, *Beloved Disciple: The Misunderstood Legacy of Mary Magdalene, the Woman Closest to Jesus* (New York: HarperCollins, 2008).

[221] Tabor, *Jesus Dynasty*, 81, 91, 165, 206–7, 238, 258; idem, "The Identity of the Beloved Disciple," Tabor's Blog, http://jamestabor.com/2009/08/30/the-identity-of-the-beloved-disciple/.

[222] Charlesworth, *Beloved Disciple*, 197–98.

The strength of Lazarus as the candidate of choice is enhanced if, as I contend, he is also the rich young ruler (no. 11—with 5 proponents) and John the Elder (no. 20—with 4 proponents). Only F. W. Lewis is listed by Charlesworth in both nos. 11 & 16 (Lazarus and The Rich Young Ruler), and none of those in no. 20 (John the Elder) were included by him under either of such other two listings.

The trend in recent times seems clearly to be away from the idea that John son of Zebedee is the beloved disciple. Among the reasons behind the trend are the strongly Judean setting of the gospel; the lack of interest in the twelve (referred to only in two passages; 6:67–71 and 20:24); the familiarity of the beloved disciple with the high priest of the temple (18:15); the unlikelihood that a Zebedee from Galilee owned a home in or near Jerusalem; and the unlearned nature of the Galilean fisherman.

Aside from Steiner and other anthroposophical authors, as well as Kreyenbühl, scholars who have named Lazarus as the beloved disciple include, in chronological order, William Kaye Fleming (1906), K. Kirkendraht (1914), H. B. Swete (1916), B. Grey Griffith (1920), H. M. Draper (1920), F. W. Lewis (1921), Robert Eisler (1938), Floyd V. Filson (1949), J. N. Sanders (1953), K. A. Eckhardt (1961), W. H. Brownlee (1972), N. Walker (1973), Desmond Stewart (1981), J.-M. Léonard (1983), Vernard Eller (1987), Poul Nepper-Christensen (1990), Mark W. G. Stibbe (1992), Frederick W. Baltz (1996), J. Phillips (2004), Herman C. Waetjen (2005), and Ben Witherington III (2006).[223] Along with these, a tip of the hat should also be made to Richard Bauckham, who fleshes out many supporting aspects, including the argument that the beloved disciple is both the primary

---

[223] For the documentation, see Charlesworth, *Beloved Disciple*, 188–92. Those in this list not included by Charlesworth are: William Kaye Fleming, in an article (according to Eisler, *Enigma*, 191) contributed first to *The Guardian* in 1906 and, again, to *The Spectator* of August 7, 1926; N. Walker, "Fourth Gospel Authorship," in *Studia evangelica VI: Papers Presented to the Fourth International Congress on New Testament Studies Held at Oxford, 1969* (ed. E. A. Livingstone; Berlin: Akademie-Verlag, 1973), 599–603; Desmond Stewart, *The Foreigner*; Frederick W. Baltz, *Lazarus and the Fourth Gospel Community* (Lewiston, N.Y.: Mellen, 1996); J. Phillips, *The Disciple Whom Jesus Loved* (3d rev. ed.; Kearney, Nebr.: Morris, 2004); Herman C. Waetjen, *Gospel of the Beloved Disciple*; and Ben Witherington III, whose work I discuss later.

witness and the author of the gospel.[224] Only he concludes that John
the Elder is both, but is not Lazarus. We consider this further below.

Of the scholars named above who chose Lazarus as the beloved
disciple, only Eisler and N. Walker cite Steiner as one who had previously named Lazarus as the beloved disciple.

Before considering Bauckham's book, let us direct attention to the
views of Witherington and Cullmann, taking the latter first.

Charlesworth did not include Cullmann in his list of Lazarus
proponents, putting him instead in the well-populated no. 6 category,
"A Real Human Whose Identity Is Lost," citing Cullmann's 1975
book *The Johannine Circle*.[225] But Cullmann dismisses Apostle John
and notes that two names "in particular," John Mark and Lazarus,
have been proposed as the beloved disciple.[226] He gives more attention to Lazarus, cites a number of the factors cogently supporting
his candidacy, and clearly feels that there is nothing to preclude the
conclusion that one person is both the beloved disciple and author.
Yet almost wistfully he concludes, "We must ... be content with
remaining in ignorance about the name of this beloved disciple."[227] He
tiptoed right up to the threshold of Lazarus believer but did not step
into the household—at least not at that time. But we have to ponder
whether this eminent theologian did not himself step into that household at a later time.

Charlesworth cites J.-M. Léonard as indicating that Cullmann did
come to accept Lazarus as the "most likely" candidate for the beloved
disciple, although Charlesworth's comment does not tell us whether
Cullmann arrived at this conclusion before or after he wrote *The
Johannine Circle*.[228] In any event, I cannot help but think that Cullmann's difficulty in affirming the Lazarus candidacy was the result

---

[224] Bauckham, *Jesus and the Eyewitnesses*.

[225] Oscar Cullmann, *The Johannine Circle* (trans. J. Bowden; Philadelphia: Westminster, 1975), 63–85.

[226] Cullmann, *Johannine Circle*, 76–85, quoting 76.

[227] Cullmann, *Johannine Circle*, 77–78.

[228] J.-M. Léonard, "Notule sur l'Évangile de Jean: Le disciple que Jésus aimait et Marie," *Études Théologiques et Religieuses* 58 (1983): 355–57, cited in Charlesworth, *Beloved Disciple*, 190–91.

of the obfuscation inherent in the Johannine community thesis so prevalent among modern scholars.

Relevant to this and to my own view expressed herein that the Gospel of John was the earliest of the gospels, though in final written form it was the last, is Cullmann's statement, "If we are right in seeing the author as eyewitness of at least some events, I am now inclined to change my earlier opinion and put the original composition of the Gospel [of John] at least as early as the synoptic gospels, and probably even earlier than the earliest of them. None of them is written by an eyewitness."[229]

Witherington's brief but trenchant article "The Last Man Standing" can be divided into three parts, the first devoted to negating John son of Zebedee as the beloved disciple and the third to what follows as a logical conclusion to the second. The second opens with the inquisitive supposition that the beloved disciple was Lazarus, based upon the love expressed in John 11:3, 5. The unique, so far as I know, observation Witherington offers is how "it clears up another conundrum: Where was the Last Supper held?" In a synoptic-gospel passage immediately foreshadowing the Last Supper, Jesus instructs his disciples on where they shall find the house where it is to be held (Mark 14:13–15): "Go into the city, and a man carrying a jar of water will meet you; follow him, and wherever he enters, say to the householder, 'The Teacher says, Where is my guest room, where I am to eat the passover with my disciples?' And he will show you a large upper room furnished and ready; there prepare for us." Witherington then quickly cuts to the bone:

> The owner of the house clearly knows Jesus and even seems to be expecting the Teacher and his disciples. But the owner is not one of the twelve who come with Jesus ("When it was evening, he came with the twelve" [Mark 14:17])…. John 13:23 indicates that the Beloved Disciple was present at the Last Supper, reclining next to Jesus on a couch. Now it was customary for the owner of the house to recline with the chief guest, in this case Jesus. But who

---

[229] Cullmann, *Johannine Circle*, 97.

do we find on Jesus' couch? The Beloved Disciple! In other words, the Last Supper was probably held in a house owned by Lazarus (a.k.a. the Beloved Disciple) in Bethany, a suburb of Jerusalem. That the Beloved Disciple had a home near Jerusalem is reflected in the notice that, after the crucifixion, the Beloved Disciple took his mother "into his own home."[230]

This gospel's setting is mainly in Jerusalem and its environs, including Bethany, while the Synoptic Gospels' *twelve* are Galilean. And while they may have often spent their evenings in Bethany (Mark 11:11–12; 14:3), the twelve, whether or not they had previously met Lazarus, apparently did not know the location of the particular house to which they were being led, or perhaps they had not been told that the Last Supper would be at Lazarus's house. Hence the need for such instruction. Possibly the prearrangement with the host was thus "coded" so that Judas could not thwart this last important meal together by intercepting the instructions that Jesus would subsequently give to the messengers. Witherington also speaks of "*a house* owned by Lazarus," not *the house* so owned, in obvious recognition of his wealth and the probability that he indeed owned more than one, a scenario which could help preserve the secrecy to the last. Witherington's proposal could also apply if the house in question was one owned by Lazarus in Jerusalem.

Witherington fleshed out this argument in a much fuller treatment titled "The Historical Figure of the Beloved Disciple in the Fourth Gospel," which he presented at the SBL convention in November 2006.[231] It was one of only four papers in the panel session, the last two being by Bauckham and Witherington. In his paper Witherington refers to Bauckham as his "friend and colleague," as seems appropriate since Witherington, a professor at Asbury Theological Seminary in Kentucky, is also doctoral supervisor at Bauckham's institution. What

---

[230] Ben Witherington III, "The Last Man Standing," *Biblical Archaeology Review* 32, no. 2 (March/April 2006): 24–25, 76.

[231] Ben Witherington III, "The Historical Figure of the Beloved Disciple in the Fourth Gospel" (paper presented at the annual meeting of the SBL, Washington, D.C., November 20, 2006), http://benwitherington.blogspot.com/2007/01/was-lazarus-beloved-disciple.html.

is interesting is that they have different candidates for the beloved disciple as expressed in basically contemporary works of which it is inconceivable that each was not aware of the position of the other. Bauckham's book *Jesus and the Eyewitnesses* cites Witherington many times on other matters but never on this one.

Witherington, whose undergraduate degree was in literature, skillfully presented his Lazarus thesis in the form of a novel.[232] While perhaps a bit unusual in academia, this avenue, when sufficiently notorious, has proved to be a fruitful entry into public awareness—witness Dan Brown's *The Da Vinci Code*. In Witherington's narrative, a labyrinthian web of intrigue is woven around the contemporary archaeological discovery of a burial crypt behind the "Church of Mary and Martha, home of the oldest known graveyard in Bethany."[233] Inside the crypt was an ossuary (box of bones) with an encrusted inscription *Eliezer, son of Simon*. Later, evidence of Mary and Martha having also been entombed there at one time was discovered.

Witherington also has our archaeologist find in the tomb a scroll that constituted "an Aramaic telling of the Gospel story that we now call John's Gospel" except that it is called "Eliezer's memoirs," and quite conveniently the portions are absent that some scholars now feel were not part of the original gospel, namely, the prologue, the account of the woman caught in adultery, and the last chapter. The circumstances indicate that these memoirs were early, written by Lazarus before 38 C.E., thus indicating that this was the earliest of any of the gospels.[234]

In order to employ the archaeological intrigue of the Holy Land and his own obvious expertise on that locus, the novel has Lazarus, Mary, and Martha all entombed in Bethany. This flies in the face of the tradition that evangelist John wrote his gospel in Ephesus and died there.

We will return to the Witherington-Bauckham relationship and look at some of their respective positions relative to each other and to Steiner, but first let us look at Bauckham's book.

---

[232] Ben Witherington III and Ann Witherington, *The Lazarus Effect: A Novel* (Eugene, Oreg.: Pickwick, 2008).

[233] Witherington and Witherington, *Lazarus Effect*, 3.

[234] Witherington and Witherington, *Lazarus Effect*, 126, 159.

While only four of its sixteen chapters deal specifically with John, its thesis is that all the gospels derive from eyewitness testimony as distinguished from oral tradition, secondhand reports, and/or other written sources, and it argues that the only gospel that comes directly from an eyewitness is John.

The substantial impact the book has made is reflected in the number of critiques, published or otherwise, it has spawned.[235] The fact that it draws a *somewhat* different final conclusion as to the identity of the beloved disciple does not keep me from embracing it as a book that supports conclusions either declared by Steiner or warranted by the anthroposophical principles he initially established clairvoyantly.

Bauckham's candidate for both the beloved disciple and the author is Elder John, for whom he presents a plausible case.[236] But the significant considerations that lead him to this conclusion could also apply to Lazarus, as we will see later. Bauckham rejects Lazarus solely because he is one of those named in the Gospel, thus losing the benefit of anonymity. "Attempts to identify the Beloved Disciple with one of this circle who is named in the Gospel (Lazarus, Thomas, or Nathanael) fail because they require us to think that the Gospel sometimes refers to the Beloved Disciple as an anonymous figure and sometimes names him." It is not clear to me why this should be a problem, and Bauckham does not explain. He then immediately adds, "Whatever the function of anonymity in the Gospel's portrayal of the Beloved Disciple, it would be defeated if it were not consistently employed."[237] The key word is "whatever." He is indicating that *any* function of anonymity the author might have intended would be defeated if the beloved disciple's name appeared

---

[235] It was promptly scheduled for a panel review at the 2007 SBL convention and has been followed by other panel reviews. See, e.g., the book symposia in *Nova et Vetera* 6 (2008): 483–542, which includes responses by Samuel Byrskog, Frank J. Matera, Rodrigo J. Morales, Christopher Seitz, and Gregory Tatum, followed by Bauckham's "Response to the Respondents"; and in *Journal for the Study of the Historical Jesus* 6 (2008): 157–253, which includes responses by Samuel Byrskog, David Catchpole, Howard I. Marshall, Stephen J. Patterson, and Theodore J. Weeden Sr., followed by Bauckham's "In Response to My Respondents: *Jesus and the Eyewitnesses* in Review."

[236] Bauckham, *Jesus and the Eyewitnesses*, 412–37, esp. 416.

[237] Bauckham, *Jesus and the Eyewitnesses*, 414–15.

somewhere in the gospel. On this point I think Bauckham has over-generalized. The appearance of the beloved disciple's name in the gospel would not impinge on this character's anonymity, for the fact remains that every time the character described as "the disciple whom Jesus loved" appears in the story, his name is withheld. And so for all intents and purposes, the beloved disciple always remains anonymous.

Bauckham's position above seems inconsistent with the one he adopted elsewhere. Recognizing that the chief priests planned to put Lazarus to death, he states, "Lazarus could not have been protected in the early period of the Jerusalem church's life by telling his story but not naming him. His story was too well known locally not to be easily identifiable as his, however it was told."[238] And there could hardly have been an anonymity element involved in leaving out Lazarus's name when the gospel was finally put in full written form in Ephesus because by then he was known as John.

It is possible that the beloved disciple's identity is concealed as a deliberate mystery which the reader has to figure out by considering which named disciple is the same person. Bauckham himself presumes that the beloved disciple is also the anonymous disciple in John 1:35–40 and 21:2 and the anonymous disciple in 18:15–16, two figures who are not described as loved by Jesus.[239] If these are legitimate identifications, as I think they are, then it is clear that the reader is supposed to wonder whether the beloved disciple is a character who is identified in a different way elsewhere in the narrative. His identity could be an intentional puzzle, and if it is, the author has to give enough clues for a reader to figure it out. That would *require* a named appearance and hints that link the named character with the beloved disciple (e.g. "he whom you love," in John 11:3).

The anonymity rationale seems very weak, and in any event is not preemptive, clearly overpowered by the increasingly obvious identification of Lazarus as the one who is loved, especially when

---

[238] Richard Bauckham, *The Testimony of the Beloved Disciple: Narrative, History, and Theology in the Gospel of John* (Grand Rapids: Baker Academic, 2007), 189.
[239] Bauckham, *Jesus and the Eyewitnesses*, 391, 397.

the meaning of "loved" as so used and the nature of the raising as an initiation in the mode of the ancient temple sleep are taken into account.

Otherwise Bauckham's conclusion is itself not necessarily incompatible with the anthroposophical standpoint, for there is considerable likelihood that Elder John was indeed Lazarus himself. While I cannot presently say that Steiner ever specifically so identified him, it is clear that he spoke of Lazarus as being a very elderly disciple in Ephesus who wrote not only the gospel but also the three letters of John.[240] The fact that Steiner spoke of Lazarus as the author of all three letters when the second and third clearly identify the Elder as the writer suggests that he considered the Elder to be Lazarus. While I've been unable as I write this to find the source of the information, I have it in my mind from my years of intense reading of Steiner's work that he indicated that Lazarus lived to a very ripe old age, even, I believe, into the early second century. That it was not so unusual for some persons to live long lives is suggested by Josephus. Of the Essenes, he wrote, "They are long-lived also; insomuch that many of them live above a hundred years, by means of the simplicity of their diet; nay, as I think, by means of the regular course of life they observe also."[241]

While we do not know that Lazarus was an Essene, he seems to have been a disciple of John the Baptist (John 1:35–40), whose lifestyle appears similar to that of the Essenes and who may have been affiliated with them. The writings of other anthroposophical writers accord with

---

[240] According to Raymond E. Brown (*The Epistles of John* [Anchor Bible 30; Garden City, N.Y.: Doubleday, 1982], 20), a significant minority of scholars deny common authorship to the Gospel and First Epistle. Not all who accept that commonality of authorship are willing to extend it to the Second and Third Epistles. The Second Epistle speaks of "doctrine" (vv. 9–10), suggesting to some a stage of early church development beyond the lives of the evangelists themselves. See C. Clifton Black, "The First, Second, and Third Letters of John," *The New Interpreter's Bible* 12:376. Bauckham is one of the academic scholars who subscribe to the view that the evangelist also wrote all three of the letters.

[241] Josephus, *Jewish War* 2.8.10 (151), as translated in William Whiston, trans., *The Works of Josephus* (Peabody, Mass.: Hendrickson, 1987), 607.

this indication about the longevity of Lazarus.[242] Bauckham himself makes the point in support of his own candidate for beloved disciple and author. Having earlier accepted the common view that John's Gospel was written in Ephesus, he noted the view "that appears first in Irenaeus and was then common among the fathers: that John's Gospel was the last of the four Gospels to be written and that its author lived longer than most of his fellow disciples (Irenaeus says he lived into the reign of Trajan, which began in 98 C.E., *Adv. Haer.* 3.1.1; 3.3.4)."[243] Since his John the Elder, as the beloved disciple, would have "lain on the breast of Jesus" at the Last Supper, he must surely have been a contemporary of Lazarus in terms of age.

Bauckham's book superbly treats the issues addressed. The present proposal that the name of Lazarus was changed upon his initiatory experience is the most significant difference between Bauckham's conclusions and those herein. Bauckham reasons that we need a candidate named John, and that criterion is satisfied if Lazarus became a John, as suggested.

It is well to again consider the significance of a *name*.[244] Today names do not have the significance accorded them in ancient times. As can be seen in the RSAM, clairvoyance, the ability to perceive in the spiritual realm, was universal among humanity in the earlier stages

---

[242] René M. Querido, introduction to *The Book of Revelation and the Work of the Priest,* by Rudolf Steiner (London: Rudolf Steiner Press, 1998), 7; Emil Bock, *The Apocalypse of St. John* (Edinburgh: Floris, 1957), 20, having earlier, in his *The Three Years: The Life of Christ between Baptism and Ascension* (Edinburgh: Floris, 1955), 156–59, named Lazarus as the John who wrote both the Gospel of John and Apocalypse of John; James H. Hindes, introduction to *Reading the Pictures of the Apocalypse,* by Rudolf Steiner (Great Barrington, Mass.: Anthroposophic Press, 1993), 9. Whether the introductions by Querido and Hindes will appear in the CW volumes in which the Steiner lectures will appear (CW 346 and 104a, respectively) is uncertain.

[243] Bauckham, *Jesus and the Eyewitnesses*, 420.

[244] See Appendix One: The Giving of a Name, in chapter one of Book Two. Steiner often emphasized the importance of names in ancient times: *Gospel of St. John*, 180 (lect. 12); *Gospel of St. John and Its Relation to the Other Gospels*, 134 (lect. 7); *Temple Legend*, 28 (lect. 16); *Genesis*, 81 (lect. 6); *Bhagavad Gita and the West*, 39–41; *Background to the Gospel of St. Mark*, 196 (lect. 11); *According to Luke: The Gospel of Compassion and Love Revealed* (trans. Catherine E. Creeger; Great Barrington, Mass.: SteinerBooks, 2001), 69 (CW 114, lect. 3); *An Occult Physiology* (London: Rudolf Steiner Press, 1951), 70 (CW 128, lect. 3).

of its descent into matter, fading only gradually as the ages progressed. Before clairvoyance as a general human trait faded, the nature of the soul descending toward incarnation was known, and the infant was given the name that described that nature. Similarly, when an event (e.g., an initiation) so affected a person as to bring about a perceptible change in character, that person sometimes received a new name. For instance, Abram was given the new name Abraham after the spiritual encounter with Melchizedek (Genesis 14–17), and Jacob was named Israel after his encounter with the angel of God at the river Jabbok (Genesis 32). These phenomena can be seen in the names of the patriarchs and even down to Moses.[245] In the same way, when Lazarus was raised from the tomb, according to Steiner, he was "so completely transformed that [he] became the individuality of John in the Christian sense."[246]

To understand what Steiner meant, it is necessary to consider what the name "John" means and why it was necessary that Lazarus become a "John being" upon his high initiation by Christ. Literally, the name John meant "Yahweh is gracious." To appreciate how this applies to Lazarus, we go to what would seem to be its most fundamental meaning as given by Steiner in his lecture in Munich on May 3, 1911, on the concepts of original sin and grace.[247] Simply stated, at the stage of human development in the supersensible realm, before its descent into materiality, the human being comprised only the three bodies. At that point, the astral body, desirous of what it saw in the material realm below, influenced by Luciferic forces, yielded to the temptation, precipitating what is known as the fall (Genesis 3). But the inchoate human being had not yet, at that point, been invested with an Ego. While it was, like an animal, without an Ego and thus not guilty of

---

[245] Cf. Andrew F. Key, "The Giving of Proper Names in the Old Testament," *Journal of Biblical Literature* 83 (1964): 55–59, http://www.jstor.org/pss/3264907.

[246] Steiner, *Gospel of St. John and Its Relation to the Other Gospels*, 134 (lect. 7). It is clear that Steiner meant that the individuality of Lazarus came to be known as John, not that he became the individuality of John the Baptist, although as we've seen, Steiner said on his deathbed that when Lazarus was raised, the being of John the Baptist penetrated him down to his consciousness soul.

[247] Steiner, *Concepts of Original Sin and Grace*.

any moral lapse, it was nevertheless plunged into an earthly existence infected by what we call "original sin." The consequence, if left to its own devices, was a continual materialization which would eventually reach a point of no return; the human Ego would not be capable of its salvation and return into the spiritual realm. It was at the "right time" that the higher Christ I Am incarnated. Through the shedding of the Ego-carrying blood of the Christ, the eventual salvation of the human being was assured. As Steiner put it, "We fell without being ourselves guilty and we must therefore be able to ascend without merit of our own." It is the "inflowing power [that] repairs the astral body to the same extent to which it has deteriorated ... that is the Atonement,... what in the true sense is called *'Grace'*. Grace is the concept that is complementary to that of Original Sin."[248] The concept was pronounced in the prologue of John's Gospel, "And from his fullness have we all received, grace upon grace. For the law was given through Moses; grace and truth came through Jesus Christ" (1:16–17). The name John therefore epitomizes the message of redemption through grace that his gospel announces.

In his lecture in Hamburg on May 22, 1908, Steiner said, "John the Baptist called himself—literally interpreted—the forerunner, the precursor, the one who goes before as herald of the ego."[249] Luke's Gospel strongly emphasized the imperative that Zechariah and Elizabeth name their child John, indicating of him, "He will go before him in the spirit and power of Elijah ... to make ready for the Lord a people prepared" (1:13, 17). The imperative is again emphasized by the fact that Zechariah's ability to speak was restored only when he complied with the angel's instruction to name the child John (1:18–23; 57–64). According to John's Gospel, Christ referred to himself in so many deeply significant ways as "I Am"; for example, "I Am the way, and the truth, and the life; no one comes to the Father but by me" (14:6). And it was Steiner who showed us that the "I Am" is the new name to be given to those who are redeemed (Rev 2:17; 3:12; 19:12). Speaking about evangelist John's proclamations about

---

[248] Steiner, *Concepts of Original Sin and Grace*, 18, 25.
[249] Steiner, *Gospel of St. John*, 74 (lect. 4).

Jesus, Witherington said it well: "He is the incarnation of the great I Am."[250]

We saw previously that Steiner said on his deathbed that upon Lazarus's raising, the spirit of John the Baptist entered the being of Lazarus down through his consciousness soul. Luke's Gospel shows us how important it was that the messenger of Christ be named John. And just as John was the one to both prepare the way and recognize the Christ who descended into Jesus of Nazareth at his baptism, so Lazarus was to become the first to recognize the significance of the empty tomb (John 20:8) and to provide the spiritual guidance of humanity through the writing of his gospel, with its high Christology and emphasis upon the I Am.

Thus, through his initiation, and because of the role he was thence to fulfill, Lazarus became John.

For some, it might seem sufficient to understand Lazarus's name-change to John to reflect merely the fact that the spirit of John the Baptist had penetrated Lazarus's being down through the level of his consciousness soul. We've seen that Steiner said the first ten chapters of John's Gospel, following its prologue (1:1–18), were at least largely what came to Lazarus through John the Baptist. But that cannot account for the rest of the gospel, nor can it reflect what really happened when the astral body of Christ passed to Lazarus at the foot of the cross, as described presently. What happened then, and what is expressed from John 11 forward, is really the passing of the baton, so to speak, of the Elijah forces, those of ancient Israel, from John the Baptist as announcing messenger, to John the evangelist, the messenger of the Christ forces of the new Israel, an aspect of John's own "He must increase, but I must decrease" (3:30). And the one who was to be the messenger of those forces till Christ's return was the new John, the former Lazarus.

Whereas on his deathbed Steiner spoke of the penetration of Lazarus by the soul and spirit of John the Baptist, previously Steiner had indicated that upon the death of John the Baptist he became the group soul of the twelve, hovering over them much as the spirit of Elijah had

---

[250] Witherington, "Historical Figure."

hovered over Israel in the days of Ahab and Jezebel (cf. 1 Kgs 18:17; 21:15–19).[251] Because of their special character as messengers of the Christ, the penetration of the later John (Lazarus) by the earlier (the Baptist) was doubtless far more profound. But it was at the time of the initiation of Lazarus himself by Christ that the Baptist's spirit could also penetrate his being, and his John-mission was confirmed when the mantle of the astral body of Jesus of Nazareth was bestowed upon him from the cross. He was then fully John in his own nature, subsuming also the Baptist's spirit.

Aside from this narrow, though significant, difference with Bauckham regarding the name change from Lazarus to John, his *Jesus and the Eyewitnesses* is a very close academic parallel to so much of what Steiner revealed.

One final thing before returning to the relative positions of Witherington and Bauckham. Bauckham, properly as Witherington notes, places emphasis on things Papias says about the Elder John.[252] He then devotes a section to Polycrates' less reliable statement that John was he who "leaned back on the Lord's breast, who was a priest, wearing the high priestly frontlet (*to petalon*)...."[253] There was only one petalon, said to have been the one formed by Moses for the head of Aaron, on which the holy name itself was inscribed. The petalon could be worn only by the high priest and apparently only on certain occasions. There are recognized errors in what Polycrates said in this context. Nevertheless, the statement tends to indicate some tradition about John's high priestly status, which would be consistent with his having been "known to the high priest" (I assume that the "other disciple" who gains Peter's access to the high priest's court in John 18:15–16 is the beloved disciple). Some writers, mentioned though not followed by

---

[251] Steiner, *Gospel of St. Mark*, 102–22, esp. 113–14 (lect. 6). John's was not the only power hovering over the twelve. In *Fifth Gospel*, 80–81 (lect. 5), Steiner spoke of how during the ministry of Christ his disciples were specially empowered by the extension of his own etheric body over them so that it was as if the Christ himself were speaking or acting through them.

[252] Bauckham, *Jesus and the Eyewitnesses*, 12–38, 417–25. For Witherington's approval, see n. 260, below.

[253] Bauckham, *Jesus and the Eyewitnesses*, 438–52, esp. 442.

Bauckham, have suggested that the evangelist is the John mentioned in Acts 4:5–6, where the high priest's family is said to include someone named John: "On the morrow their rulers and elders and scribes were gathered together in Jerusalem, with Annas the high priest and Caiaphas and John and Alexander, and all who were of the high-priestly family." If Lazarus was both the beloved disciple and evangelist known as John, as I propose, it seems nigh unto impossible that he was also the John of Acts 4:6 at the time Peter and John son of Zebedee were appearing before that Jewish tribunal. Bauckham carefully reviews the matter, finally deciding that Polycrates identified the beloved disciple with the John of Acts 4:6, not because he had any historical information, but simply as scriptural exegesis.[254] Be that as it may, there is some possibility that the beloved disciple had in fact been the high priest as early as in his late teen years.

Frederick Baltz helps us here. The high priest Annas, who served through 15 C.E., had five sons, each of whom subsequently served as high priest, the eldest one succeeding him and serving for the very short period 16–17 C.E.[255] The name of this son was Eleazar (Lazarus). He could have been quite young. Relying on Joachim Jeremias, Baltz notes that "the High Priests were generally appointed by the Romans *at about the age of twenty.*"[256] If Eleazar was appointed at that young age, considering that Jesus was likely born somewhere up to four years prior to the turn of the calendar, Lazarus would have been almost identical in age to Jesus and, as previously noted with reference to the Essenes, could have become the Elder John in Ephesus, assuming his name was changed after his substantially later encounter with and initiation by the Christ. And if such were the case, Lazarus (and Elder John) would certainly have been a person familiar to the temple authorities.

Now let us look at the relative positions of Witherington and Bauckham. An interesting variant has to do with how the gospel came to be named *According to John.* Bauckham concludes that Jesus had a

---

[254] Bauckham, *Jesus and the Eyewitnesses,* 451.

[255] Bauckham recognized that "in the late Second Temple period the Jewish high priest mostly held office for short periods only" (*Jesus and the Eyewitnesses,* 451).

[256] Baltz, *Lazarus and the Fourth Gospel Community,* 73–74, quoting 74 (emphasis mine).

very close disciple from Jerusalem who was not one of the twelve but was present at the Last Supper and lay on Jesus' breast; this disciple, when elderly, lived in Ephesus, became known as the Elder John, and was both the beloved disciple and author of the gospel.[257] As support, Bauckham notes that Papias thought that Elder John was the evangelist. By contrast, Witherington concludes that "Lazarus was the Beloved Disciple and the author of most of the traditions in this Gospel," and conjectures that the gospel was named for John "because John of Patmos was the final editor of this Gospel after the death of Lazarus," having gone from Patmos to Ephesus, where he was known as the Elder.[258] Witherington identifies John of Patmos as "a prophet from the Johannine community operating at a time when there is apparently no apostolic presence left in that community."[259] Evidently Witherington supposes that John of Patmos came into possession of the writings of Lazarus within that community, though it should be noted that Witherington approved Bauckham's reliance upon Papias's information that the Elder was a disciple of the Lord.[260] Bauckham and Witherington both conclude that the Elder John is the evangelist, though Bauckham sees the Elder as the beloved disciple while Witherington sees him only as the final editor of the gospel, "most of the traditions" of which were written by Lazarus, the beloved disciple. Each considered it necessary to find a person named John, other than the son of Zebedee. Neither appears to have considered the possibility that the name of Lazarus was changed as a result of the changes he had undergone through his

---

[257] Bauckham, *Jesus and the Eyewitnesses*, 412–37, esp. 433.

[258] Witherington, "Historical Figure."

[259] Ben Witherington III, *Revelation* (Cambridge: Cambridge University Press, 2003), 3.

[260] Witherington, "Historical Figure": "But I defer to my friend and colleague Richard Bauckham whose new book is a wealth of information about Papias and his conclusion is right—we should take very seriously what Papias says. He knew what he was talking about in regard to both the earliest and latest of the Gospels." Bauckham refers to Papias, as recorded by Eusebius (*Ecclesiastical History* 3.39.3–4), where Papias states, "I inquired about the words of the elders ... and whatever Aristion and the elder John, the Lord's disciples, were saying (*legousin*)" (*Jesus and the Eyewitnesses*, 417). Recognizing the reluctance of some scholars on the point, Bauckham concludes that Papias was saying that Aristion and the Elder John were Jesus' disciples and were alive when he inquired of them (419–20).

death and rebirth experience, though Witherington recognized that "This was bound to change his world view, and did so."[261]

Witherington rejects "the attempts of Lincoln and others to suggest that the author drew on earlier Gospels, particularly Mark."[262] Bauckham's emphasis upon John's Gospel being the only one written by an eyewitness suggests that he agrees with this position. Schenke and various others have taken a contrary position when they argue that the resurrection story in the Secret Gospel of Mark, if authentic, represents an "earlier stage, in terms of the history of tradition, of the narrative we know as the resurrection of Lazarus in the Fourth Gospel."[263] My position (and that which Cullmann expressed above) that John's Gospel, in its essence, was the earliest of the gospels accords with both Witherington and Bauckham.

These illustrations are perhaps sufficient to demonstrate how interwoven the conclusions of Bauckham and Witherington are, and, except for the matter of Lazarus's name change, how similar they are to Steiner's as presented elsewhere herein, even though Steiner's pathway to understanding is dramatically different.

Additional Insights of Steiner on Lazarus and John's Gospel

Considering what has already been given as content of the ancient mysteries and the nature of the raising of Lazarus, perhaps the most basic and vital portion of what is relevant to our inquiry from Steiner's work is already in. There is much more unique disclosure in his lecture cycles on John's Gospel [264] that has scarcely been scratched and yet is not so directly pertinent to our present undertaking to

---

[261] Witherington, "Historical Figure."

[262] Witherington, "Historical Figure."

[263] Schenke, "Function and Background," 120. But Schenke considered the beloved disciple to be a fictitious disciple.

[264] The texts of his lectures most directly focused upon John's Gospel are found in Steiner, *Gospel of St. John*; idem, *Gospel of St. John and Its Relation to the Other Gospels*; idem, "Gospel of St. John"; idem, "John's Gospel" and "John's Gospel as a Record of Initiation: The First Twelve Chapters," in *Christian Mystery*, 249–65 (February 3, 1907; February 12, 1906). These are all that have come to my attention specifically on John's Gospel in English; I know of no others in the German archives in Dornach, Switzerland.

warrant its extended discussion here. We can only hint at some of this by concluding this John chapter with a discussion of that mysterious final chapter.

John 21

So far as I know, Steiner never specifically addressed the question of whether John 21:23 implied that the beloved disciple had died before chapter 21 was written. The position had been taken at least as far back as Kreyenbühl that it did and that therefore the beloved disciple could not have authored that chapter. Clearly this is the position of the majority of scholars who have considered the matter. However, it is clear that Steiner considered Lazarus-John to have written the entire gospel, including chapter 21. He begins the fourth chapter of his main lecture cycle on John's Gospel (published in *The Gospel of St. John*) by stressing the architectural integrity of the twenty-one chapters: "Authors of the past ... introduced into their works much more of an architectural structure, much more of an inner arrangement than is usually imagined"—citing an example from Dante's *Divine Comedy*.[265] He shows how the first post-prologue section of the Gospel is the testimony of John the Baptist (the section between "And this is the testimony of John ..." [1:19] and "And many came to him; and they said, 'John did no sign, but *everything that John said about this man was true*" [10:41]), comprising ten chapters. (We saw earlier that upon the raising of Lazarus the being of John the Baptist penetrated him down through his consciousness soul so that he could give the Baptist's testimony.) Steiner then points out that at the end of the last ten chapters of the Gospel we find its corresponding verse, "This is the disciple who is bearing witness to these things, and who has written these things; *and we know that his testimony is true*" (21:24). And then he says, "In the middle of the Gospel of St. John a fact is presented [the raising of Lazarus] which, if not understood, would render this Gospel incomprehensible.... With this chapter

---

[265] Steiner, *Gospel of St. John*, 60 (lect. 4).

the whole Gospel falls into two parts. At the end of the first part it is pointed out that the testimony of John the Baptist should be accepted ... and at the very end of the Gospel it is pointed out that all that follows the chapter on the raising of Lazarus should be accepted on the testimony of ... 'the Disciple whom the Lord loved.'"[266]

In the last lecture of that John cycle, Steiner speaks of the mother of Jesus at the foot of the cross. He points out that nowhere in the gospel is the mother of Jesus named. We then come to another one of those places where the evangelist embodies a double meaning in what he writes. "When Jesus saw his mother, and the disciple whom he loved standing near, he said to his mother, 'Woman, behold, your son!' Then he said to the disciple, 'Behold, your mother!' And from that hour the disciple took her to his own home." Steiner's explanation of the deeper meaning of this passage brings to mind the passing of Elijah's mantle to Elisha (2 Kgs 2:9–14), for Steiner says that with these words Christ passed to the beloved disciple the force in his own astral body that enabled it to be the bearer of the Holy Spirit, imposing upon him the mission of writing down what this astral body had been able to acquire—and the disciple took that force unto himself and wrote the gospel. The disciple became the genuine interpreter of the Messiah.

Clearly in this deeper meaning of the passage, this "son" of the "mother of Jesus" would remain until the Parousia ("until I come," 21:22), for he would live through the gospel itself. Without giving such an esoteric interpretation, Bauckham endorses this also as the meaning of the beloved disciple not dying.[267]

"The saying spread abroad . . ."

The saying spread abroad among the brethren that this disciple was not to die; yet Jesus did not say to him that he was not to die, but, "If it is my will that he remain until I come, what is that to you?"

---

[266] Steiner, *Gospel of St. John*, 60–61 (lect. 4).
[267] Bauckham, *Jesus and the Eyewitnesses*, 129, 367–68, 388, 392–93.

A majority of scholars feel that John 21 was a later addition to the gospel and that it was written by a different author. This verse, John 21:23, has furnished a principal rationale, namely, the implication that the beloved disciple had in fact died. Also important is the observation that 20:30–31 functions as an adequate conclusion to the whole narrative. This fact suggests that chapter 21 is an epilogue added later.[268] Such arguments are not without merit, in the normal sense of things. But it is possible to read the evidence differently, in a way that illustrates this gospel's ability to convey deeper meanings.

Let us first consider the significance of the double ending, which most scholars view as evidence that the authorship of chapter 21 differed from that of the main work. We can agree that a later date for this chapter is possible, perhaps probable, given the likelihood that this gospel took shape over several decades. But the possibility that chapter 21 is an epilogue does not demonstrate that its author was a different person. The same person could have resumed his narrative in order to add some information that had become more pertinent as he grew older—indeed, the very information given in 21:23.[269]

So let us ask ourselves why the beloved disciple might have recorded such a saying. Given the late date when this gospel, including this chapter, was written, the beloved disciple would have been advanced in years, and the Christ would not yet have returned. That his own death was near he certainly knew, and the last thing he would want to do is suggest to future readers, after he was gone, that "the saying" was mistaken, since he too had died. So he explained that it did not refer to his remaining alive until the Parousia. So what then could the verse mean? Only that in some way he was in fact to survive till the Parousia.

We have just seen that the disciple's taking the mother of Jesus into his home should also be understood as his receiving the astral body of the Christ, enabling him to write the gospel that proclaimed the Christ in a way that was to remain in the hearts of humanity until the

---

[268] Significant proponents of this view are Brown, *Gospel according to John*, 2:1055–61, and Bultmann, *Gospel of John*, 700.

[269] The architecture of the gospel noted by Steiner, above, takes no position on whether this chapter was added at a later time to the main work.

Parousia. But there is also a further way of understanding how he was to remain.

Previously I have shown that some of the most deeply esoteric books or passages of the Bible can be understood only if we grasp the meaning of those three cases in the Bible where it is said that some thing is not consumed by fire or some person could not die.[270] They are the burning bush (Exod 3:2), Cain (Gen 4:13–16), and Job (1:12). Such resistance to termination in each case should be a clue to something more important than the literal meaning of the words. Each of these should be understood only in a figurative sense, as metaphor, illustrating an aspect of every human being. Each one testifies to the existence of an element in every human being that goes on and on and on and cannot pass out of existence from one incarnation to another.

In the case of the burning bush we are talking about the human Ego, the "I Am."[271] It is "burned" both in earthly life and in the purification period between lives but cannot be consumed. There is an unperfected element of the creative Christ "I Am" in every human being, the Christ representing the higher "I Am" so evident in John's Gospel, and the human Ego representing the lower "I Am" working, in its long journey, toward the required perfection (Matt 5:48).

In the case of Cain we must conceive, not of a man by that name, whether or not one existed, but of that element that is the astral body, the blemished body of sense and desire cast into every human being tainted by the events described in Genesis 3 that are now known as the fall. It becomes a wanderer through the ages (i.e., "east of Eden") until it is purified by the Christ element in the Ego into the higher manas element to accompany that Ego eternally.[272]

Job is among the least understood books of the Bible. Libraries exist on it dealing with the quandary in which Job finds himself and the travails that bedevil him. But I have yet to read a book or analysis of this poor man that expresses what this book is about or has to be saying. Indeed it deals with the question of why the innocent

---

[270] See Smith, *Soul's Long Journey*, 73–121.

[271] See also Smith, *Burning Bush*, 283–94.

[272] See Smith, *Soul's Long Journey*, 195–204.

suffer, as so many have written so eloquently. Yet that is not what the book is about. Rather, it is a metaphor that portrays the human being, the fourfold human being, comprising three bodies (the three "friends": Eliphaz, the physical body; Bildad, the etheric or life body; and Zophar, the astral or sense body) as well as the Ego, which arrived last on the scene of human evolution (Elihu, the youngest, who spoke last because the others were all older than he). It is only in the context of this understanding of the spiritual structure of the fourfold human being that we can approach with a deeper comprehension the meaning of this cryptic twenty-third verse of John's concluding chapter.

So while Steiner did not elaborate specifically on John 21:23, the creative principles that anthroposophy contains demonstrate a more profound meaning of remaining until the Parousia. One of those is that the higher bodies (etheric and astral), which have been perfected by high initiates (such as Lazarus-John was), remain alive and working on behalf of humanity after the death of the earthly physical body.[273] The etheric body in particular is known as the life body. There is a relationship of this principle to Christ's statement that "whoever lives and believes in me shall never die" (11:26). Indeed, we learn from anthroposophy that the Parousia itself will occur only in the etheric, and not the mineral-physical, realm.[274] But that topic is outside our present quest.

Taking into account the likelihoods that Lazarus-John lived in Ephesus until a very old age and was one and the same as John the Elder, and the depth of meaning of passages such as this, the position adopted here is that Lazarus-John wrote the entire gospel, including its final chapter. Some passages, however, such as the woman caught in adultery, might be subsequent additions, as the variants in the manuscript tradition demonstrate.[275]

---

[273] See Steiner, *Principle of Spiritual Economy*, 12–55 (lects. 2 and 3).

[274] See Smith, *Burning Bush*, 213–43.

[275] On the question of whether the account of the woman caught in adultery (John 7:53–8:11) was a later addition, see Bart D. Ehrman, *Misquoting Jesus: The Story behind Who Changed the Bible and Why* (New York: HarperCollins, 2005), 3–5.

Penetrating the Mysterious

That Jesus performs seven signs in John's Gospel is well known.[276] Steiner shows how they present a profound picture of increasing spiritual power of the Christ force, reflective of the seven stages of initiation of humanity.[277] We may infer that they were also reflective of stages that Lazarus had moved through as he became ill and approached death itself, which Christ, through his power over the hovering etheric body, could convert into an initiation akin to the ancient temple sleep. This inference is supported especially by Steiner's implication that Lazarus's descent into a death experience was the final step initiating him into a profound spiritual consciousness and insight. Only Lazarus among the disciples could write in a knowledgeable way of these seven "signs" because through his association with the Christ during the three years and the penetration of his being by John the Baptist he had personally experienced them, and then in his "three days' journey" he perceived their significance and relationship to the pathway of humanity itself.

Some of these signs (called miracles by some) have been difficult for many to accept in the light of their seeming impossibility, as in the case of the feeding of the five thousand or the walking on water. We've already seen how the raising of Lazarus has a profound meaning that is different from the common understanding of one being raised from the dead. The other "miracles," without regard to whether they occurred in the manner the language otherwise suggests to modern thought, do have meaning on a more esoteric level as Steiner's explanations show. Immediately after the entry of the Christ Spirit at Jesus' baptism we are

---

[276] The seven signs comprise the following: 1. turning of the water to wine (2:1–11); 2. healing of the nobleman's son (4:46–54); 3. healing of the man by the pool of Bethesda (5:2–9); 4. feeding of the five thousand (6:1–14); 5. walking on the Sea of Galilee (6:16–21); 6. healing of the man born blind (9:1–41); and 7. raising of Lazarus (11:1–46). While the gospel makes many references to the signs that Jesus performed, the four that are specifically referred to as signs are nos. 1 (2:11), 2 (4:54), 4 (6:14), and 7 (12:18).

[277] The initiatory character that the seven signs reflect is portrayed in Steiner, *Gospel of St. John*, 78–94 (lect. 5). A discussion of the progressive increase of the Christ force in each one is given in Steiner, *Gospel of St. John and Its Relation to the Other Gospels*, 157–78 (lect. 9).

told how it had to penetrate his three bodies. Again, metaphor is used as each is referred to as a temptation. In one of them he specifically rejected the miraculous as a means of ministry. Everything he did, his "mighty works," can be better understood in the light of the nature, and inherent power, of the individual human being, of which he represented the perfected state toward which each must move.

Most of these seven signs have some parallel in the Synoptic Gospels. Raymond Brown says that "Only the Cana miracle has no parallel in the Synoptic tradition."[278] We would digress unduly to look at all of these. There are many aspects to the Cana wedding, the first of the signs. One of those is the uncharacteristic statement Jesus makes to his mother, "O woman, what have you to do with me?"— though it has been variously translated due to the quizzical nature of its intent. Brown says that this statement is a Semitism that literally says "What to me and to you?" Steiner's translation of this retort is probably closer than any standard translation to this literal meaning: "Oh Woman, that passes here from me to you!"[279] Steiner explains how the entire Cana wedding episode is a sign pointing to the movement of the human Ego from the time of blood love to the time of the development of agape love, the love that extends to every creature, hence the setting of this marriage in Cana, a Galilean community of mixed blood.[280] A full explanation of this Cana marriage is available elsewhere and not directly pertinent to our immediate mission.[281]

What is most significant for our purpose, however, is that the culmination of these seven signs was the raising of Lazarus. Having already looked at it in both of these first two chapters, it suffices in

---

[278] Brown, *Gospel according to John*, 1:101. Even here, in the light of anthroposophy, one can see some connection; see Smith, *Burning Bush*, 137.

[279] Steiner, *Gospel of St. John and Its Relation to the Other Gospels*, 167 (lect. 9).

[280] According to Steiner, *Gospel of St. John*, 83 (lect. 5), "The term Galilean means "mixed-breed," "mongrel"; see also Rafael Frankel, "Galilee," *Anchor Bible Dictionary* 2:879, which indicates that "throughout history" the area's valleys "were more densely populated than the central mountain area, often with peoples of diverse character and origin." The literal meaning of the Hebrew root *gll* means "circularity," as noted in Frankel's article. See also Smith, *Soul's Long Journey*, 121–33.

[281] See Steiner, *Gospel of St. John and Its Relation to the Other Gospels*, 165–70 (lect. 9); *Gospel of St. John*, 82–90 (lect. 5).

closing this second chapter only to point out the place it occupies not only in John's Gospel but, by extension, in the essential journey of every human soul.

What is said in this gospel brings out in great clarity the status of Lazarus, now become John, among all the disciples. As Bauckham makes so clear, this is the only gospel that claims to be written by an eyewitness. As is clear from the works of Steiner, and should be clear from what has been said herein, Lazarus was the most highly initiated of Christ's disciples during Christ's earthly sojourn. One other was initiated directly by Christ after Christ was risen—Paul. It is my position that almost all of the New Testament comes directly or indirectly from these two high initiates. Although many scholars might not follow this reasoning (and it is beyond our present scope to discuss it here), only the Gospel of Matthew and the letters of James and Jude can be thought outside this pervasive influence. Mark's Gospel and the letters of Peter must surely carry at least some influence from Lazarus because of the relationship of the beloved disciple to Peter in John's account. It is that relationship that must have carried from Peter into the raising and instruction narrative in the Secret Gospel of Mark, which Mark, Peter's disciple, placed in the tenth chapter of Mark following the reference to the wealthy ruler whom Jesus *loved*. Such placement was between vv. 34 and 35. A further insertion then expanded v. 46 and referred to "the young man whom Jesus loved."

We can begin to see the preeminent status of John's Gospel in relation to the Synoptic Gospels when these things are deeply contemplated.

It is now time to turn our attention to the concluding chapter of Book Two.

CHAPTER THREE—MARK'S FLEEING YOUTH

In our transition from John to Mark, it is appropriate to consider the egregious incident of the fleeing young man (*neaniskos*) in Mark's Gospel. Its relationship to the account of the young man (*neaniskos*) in the Secret Gospel of Mark is noted by Helmut Koester, who argues that the passage was added to canonical Mark by the same person (whom he calls a "redactor") who added Secret Mark.[282] It is one of the more mystifying passages in Mark and can be seen as a link between Mark and John's Gospel. "And a (certain) young man followed him, with nothing but a linen cloth about his body; and they seized him, but he left the linen cloth and ran away naked" (Mark 14:51–52). Is this the same "young man" (*neaniskos*) who appears to the women inside Jesus' tomb in 16:5? "And entering the tomb, they saw a young man sitting on the right side, dressed in a white robe; and they were amazed." In each of these two, and only two, appearances of *neaniskoi* in canonical Mark, we must also ask, Is it historical, or symbolical, or both? It is hardly surprising that a large variety of answers have been imagined.

In his Anchor Bible commentary, Joel Marcus suggests the fleeing youth passage "may enshrine a historical memory but ... also have

---

[282] Helmut Koester, "Was Morton Smith a Great Thespian and I a Complete Fool?" *Biblical Archaeology Review* 35, no. 6 (November/December 2009): 58; also idem, "History and Development of Mark's Gospel (From Mark to *Secret Mark* and 'Canonical' Mark)," in *Colloquy on New Testament Studies: A Time for Reappraisal and Fresh Approaches* (ed. Bruce Corley; Macon, Ga.: Mercer University Press, 1983), 35–57. Koester considered Secret Mark to be part of a late first-century expansion of Mark's Gospel from which the canonical version was derived early in the second century. That Secret Mark was written after canonical Mark is the position of Scott G. Brown, "On the Composition History of the Longer ('Secret') Gospel of Mark," *Journal of Biblical Literature* 122 (2003): 89–110; idem, *Mark's Other Gospel*, 111–20. Brown believes that Mark wrote both the canonical and secret forms of his gospel in the 70s c.e. and that the stories that Mark added to the canonical form in order to produce Secret Mark were already available to Mark (as part of his notes) when he wrote the canonical gospel.

a symbolical" aspect. And though he surmises, as do others, that the "young man" in 16:5 is an angel, he theorizes that the two young men are identical.[283] In her commentary, Adela Yarbro Collins also takes the "young man" in 16:5 to be an angel, but she thinks he is contrasted with, rather than identical to, the youth in 14:51–52, as does Raymond Brown.[284] Pheme Perkins considers the young man in 16:5 to be an angel, whereas, seeming to follow Brown, she sees the one in 14:51–52 as historical, not symbolical, fleeing in abandonment in stark contrast to the one at the tomb.[285]

The obvious relevance of the Secret Gospel to this passage in Mark is suggested by the fact that all of these scholars, Koester, Marcus, Collins, Brown, and Perkins, refer to the Secret Gospel in their commentaries. Brown specifically disagrees with Morton Smith about the latter's "hypothetical common Aramaic source" for the Secret Mark story, seeing it rather as "material picked up from hearing or reading at times past other canonical Gospels, especially John (the Lazarus story)." Brown thinks that the Secret Gospel "was composed considerably before Clement came to Alexandria in 175, most likely ca. 125 when Carpocrates was active."[286] This view conflicts with Clement, who attributed the Secret Gospel to evangelist Mark, who would doubtless have died much earlier than 125. Raymond Brown is thus suggesting, like Koester, that it originated with a redactor other than Mark himself, a position contrary to that of Scott Brown, to which I subscribe.[287]

Michael J. Haren, without rejecting a symbolical meaning, takes Mark 14:51–52 to depict a historical person, Lazarus, the only "figure besides Jesus who was the object of a projected arrest by the authorities" and one "on whom an arrest is known to have been actually

---

[283] Marcus, *Mark 8–16*, 1124–25, 1080.

[284] Collins, *Mark*, 795. Raymond E. Brown, *The Death of the Messiah: From Gethsemane to the Grave: A Commentary on the Passion Narratives in the Four Gospels* (2 vols.; New York: Doubleday, 1994), 1:302–4, citing Gnilka, Gourgues, Monloubou, Neirynck, Pesch, and Fleddermann of like persuasion.

[285] Pheme Perkins, "The Gospel of Mark," *The New Interpreter's Bible* 8:710.

[286] Brown, *Death of the Messiah*, 1:297.

[287] Brown, *Mark's Other Gospel*, 200–30; also Dart, *Decoding Mark*.

attempted."[288] Haren does not consider what relationship, if any, exists between this passage and the appearance of the "young man" at the tomb (Mark 16:5). This is only a representative sample of scholarly opinions about the young man in Gethsemane.

Scholars have long wondered how an event so momentous in nature as the raising of Lazarus could have gone unmentioned in the Synoptic Gospels. The answer to that, I propose, is that it didn't. Canonical Mark, the earliest of the Synoptic Gospels, embodies it in its two *neaniskos* passages, the fleeing young man in the linen garment and the young man in the white robe in the tomb. The puzzlement these passages in canonical Mark have occasioned is due to their deeply esoteric nature, a nature consistent with the passages unique to Mark's longer gospel. Koester, based upon the astute observation that Matthew and Luke used a version of Mark that lacked the young man in Gethsemane, sees the fleeing youth passage as being from the same hand that wrote the Secret Gospel. All three of these *neaniskos* passages were of such esoteric character as to defy comprehension except for the more advanced, a point stressed by Clement with respect to the Secret Gospel, which he characterized as "a more spiritual gospel," the interpretation of the unique content of which "would, as a mystagogue, lead the hearers into the innermost sanctuary of that truth hidden by seven veils." This form of Mark's Gospel was read "only to those who are being initiated into the great mysteries" (*Letter to Theodore* I.21–22, 25–26; II.1–2).

How, then, can these *neaniskos* passages in canonical Mark be understood esoterically? Here I propose dual meaning, corresponding to the higher "I Am" of the Christ, the lower "I Am" of the human being (Lazarus), and their union implied by the *neaniskos* in the white robe in the tomb.

At the outset, let me draw attention to the way the Secret Gospel sheds light on the identities of the young man in Gethsemane and the young man inside Jesus' tomb. It is Secret Mark's parallel to the raising of Lazarus that depicts this man, who is here unnamed, as

---

[288] Michael J. Haren, "The Naked Young Man: A Historian's Hypothesis on Mark 14,51–52," *Biblica* 79 (1998): 525–31, http://www.bsw.org/project/biblica/bibl79/Ani10.htm.

wearing nothing but a linen cloth around his naked body, just like
the unnamed young man in Gethsemane. The connection is all but
explicit: the young man in Gethsemane is Lazarus. That Lazarus is also
the young man inside the tomb in Mark 16 is also made clear by the
parallels between Secret Mark's account of Jesus raising this unnamed
young man from the dead inside a rock-hewn tomb and the account
of an unnamed young man announcing Jesus' own raising from the
dead inside Jesus' rock-hewn tomb. A linen cloth is mentioned in both
places, as the material Joseph of Arimathea wrapped around Jesus'
body and the material wrapped around the young man as Jesus taught
him the mystery of the kingdom of God. This is of course the young
man's own burial sheet, in which he was wrapped inside his tomb.[289]
We must therefore see Lazarus in all three of these Markan narratives.

Rudolf Steiner says, "Who is this youth? Who was it who escaped
here? Who is it who appears here, next to Christ Jesus, nearly
unclothed, and then slips away unclothed? This is the youthful
cosmic impulse, it is the Christ who slips away, who now has only a
loose connection with the Son of Man.... The new impulse retains
nothing of what former times were able to wrap around man. It is the
entirely naked, new cosmic impulse of Earth evolution. It remains
with Jesus of Nazareth, and we find it again at the beginning of the
sixteenth chapter," after which, he notes, "the Gospel quickly comes
to an end."[290] It is important to distinguish between the question of
whether the Christ Spirit had become flesh, on the one hand, and
whether it had died on the cross, on the other (see the appendix to
this chapter). Anthroposophy affirms the first but not the second.
The Christ Spirit withdrew from the bodies of Jesus of Nazareth as
the end approached. However, as Steiner noted, only Mark's Gospel
describes this.[291] While the traditional view of Mark 15:34 ("And at
the ninth hour Jesus cried with a loud voice ... 'My God, my God,
why has thou forsaken me?'") is that in his last breaths Jesus was recit-
ing Psalm 22, Steiner says of it that Jesus, who had been "abandoned

---

[289] Brown, *Mark's Other Gospel*, 158, 168, 180–81, which notes several more parallels.
[290] Steiner, *Gospel of St. Mark*, 175–76 (lect. 9).
[291] Steiner, *Gospel of St. Mark*, 174 (lect. 9).

by those He had chosen," was "then abandoned ... by the cosmic principle"—hence the final cry.[292] While only Matthew copies Mark in telling of this cry (Matt 27:46), only Mark situates it between the two "young men" passages.[293] As noted by Raymond Brown, this withdrawing-Christ interpretation is similar to that of the gnostic Cerinthus, according to Irenaeus.[294]

Steiner gave this lecture on September 23, 1912, forty-six years before Morton Smith's discovery of the Secret Gospel of Mark in 1958. Yet he anticipated the imagery of the Secret Gospel in a way that shows he surely would have endorsed Lazarus-John as being the one who was also described as the youth in the linen cloth. Read in an anthroposophical way, this youth, in the nakedness of the soul, was united with the Christ and thus, in that union, was there in the tomb on Sunday morning disclosing that the Christ which had dwelled within the body of Jesus was no longer bound by the dead body of Jesus but was now a cosmic being.

My first awareness of the Secret Gospel of Mark, at least in a way that left its impression, was in the early 1990s when I read Andrew J. Welburn's *The Beginnings of Christianity*. In the book's epilogue, "Return of the Youth in the Linen Cloth," Welburn not only identifies the fleeing youth in Mark's Gospel with Lazarus-John, but also identifies that youth as the one who is to "remain until I come" (John 21:22).[295] I have likewise argued that recognizing Lazarus-John as the young man in Mark 14:51–52 and 16:5 is complementary, and not contrary, to Steiner's assertion that the young man represents the fleeing cosmic Christ Spirit.[296]

---

[292] Steiner, *Gospel of St. Mark*, 177 (lect. 9). In his earlier lecture cycle on Matthew, in comparing how each of the gospels tells in its own way about "the dying Jesus on the Cross," Steiner, apparently for the first time, also gives this meaning of the final cry of Jesus in Mark's Gospel; see Rudolf Steiner, *The Gospel of St. Matthew* (trans. Catherine E. Creeger; Great Barrington, Mass: Anthroposophic Press, 2003), 219–21 (CW 123, lect. 12).

[293] Matthew changes Mark's "young man" (*neaniskos*) at the tomb to an angel (Matt 28:2).

[294] Brown, *Death of the Messiah*, 1:301; Irenaeus, *Against Heresies* 1.26.1–2.

[295] Welburn, *Beginnings of Christianity*, 294–303.

[296] Edward Reaugh Smith, *The Disciple Whom Jesus Loved: Unveiling the Author of John's Gospel* (Great Barrington, Mass.: Anthroposophic Press, 2000), 24–25, 45–54; *Burning Bush*, 404–5.

The meaning of the young man's nakedness is, I propose, diametrically opposite of that ascribed to it by Raymond Brown in his interpretation of this passage. Brown says of the young man: "That he is described as being 'clothed with a linen cloth over his nakedness' is to prepare the reader for the denouement, for when his garment is abandoned, he will be naked.... This young man's attempt to follow Jesus ... is a miserable failure; for when seized as Jesus had been, he is so anxious to get away that he leaves in the hands of his captors the only clothes he wears and chooses the utter disgrace of fleeing naked—an even more desperate flight than that of the other disciples. Nakedness is not something good, *as it is in the symbolic interpretation*; it is something to be avoided, as in Matt 25:36; John 21:7; James 2:15; Rev 3:17; 16:15."[297] The italicized words show that Brown rejects any symbolism and interprets this passage in the most mundane way. His indication that nakedness "is something to be avoided" is used in the same way that you and I would say we do not want to walk out on the street without our clothing on, or would want sufficient wraps in cold weather to stay warm. The scriptures he cites, with the exception of the Revelation passages, which have an esoteric meaning quite different from the others, support that conception of nakedness. Generally speaking, however, nakedness in scripture, save in such mundane usage as he cites above, should be understood in the more spiritual way that realizes the essential being, the Ego or "I Am" (or soul and spirit), as distinct from the body (or three bodies) with which it is clothed.[298] Paul's description in 2 Cor 5:1–10 of death in terms of losing "the earthly tent we live in" and putting on "our heavenly dwelling, so that by putting it on we may not be found naked" is an obvious example.

As Scott Brown suggested, another very relevant example appears in Philo's *Allegorical Interpretations* 2.15–16. Philo, whose work often influenced Clement of Alexandria, likewise equates "nakedness" with "absence of corporality." For Philo, the mind/soul is "naked" when it

---

[297] Brown, *Death of the Messiah*, 1:303 (emphasis added).

[298] Smith, *Burning Bush*, 401–10; April D. DeConick and Jarl Fossum, "Stripped before God: A New Interpretation of Logion 37 in the Gospel of Thomas," *Vigiliae christianae* 45 (1991): 123–50; Kovacs, "Concealment and Gnostic Exegesis," 434–35.

has "put off the body and the affections which are dear to it," a concept which refers to the way the body, with its physiological needs and cravings, and the body's senses, which are designed to perceive material realities, inhibit the soul from perceiving supernatural realities that are akin to its own nature. One who is naked in this metaphorical sense has mastered the body, "is entirely free from all vices, and has discarded and laid aside the covering of all the passions." Such a person has also "put off the robe of (human) opinion and vain fancy of the soul" and is able to see supersensible realities, "to behold the secret mysteries of God." Philo credits Abraham, Jacob, and Moses with this "most excellent nakedness" (trans. C. D. Yonge). Significantly, Philo describes the high priest's removal of his linen robe inside the holy of holies on the Day of Atonement as a symbol for the "naked" soul's ability to apprehend the mysteries of the immaterial realm. As Brown points out to me, the *Letter to Theodore*, just like Clement's *Stromateis*, elaborates this metaphor of entering the innermost sanctuary, applying it to readers of the Secret Gospel. In this way Clement indicates that initiation into the great mysteries involves the soul's ability to "put off" the body and see the invisible realities of the spiritual world (*Letter to Theodore* I.24–26; II.2; *Stromateis* V.6.39.2–40.1; cf. *Excerpta ex Theodoto* 27.3). I suggest that this understanding of nakedness, as an element in the soul's unimpeded vision of spiritual realities, is reflected in the account of the youths in both Mark 14:51–52 and the *Letter to Theodore* III.8–10.

As an aside, I have long suspected that Clement's *Who Is the Rich Man That Shall Be Saved?* (*Quis dives salvetur?*) had some connection with the Lazarus account.[299] It was therefore of interest to me when I read in Scott Brown's prepublication draft of an article on the "sevenfold veiled truth" in Clement's letter that Alain Le Boulluec found evidence in *Quis dives salvetur?* for Clement's knowledge of the story of the young man in Secret Mark and Clement's association of this young man with the rich young man in Mark 10:17–22. As Brown notes in this paper, the impression is strengthened by Clement's opinion that Jesus' demand to the rich young man that he surrender his wealth

---

[299] Smith, *Burning Bush*, 538.

would "render his soul pure, that is, poor and naked" (*Quis dives salvetur?* 16.1: trans. Butterworth, Loeb Classical Library), a state which would be aptly symbolized by him coming to Jesus wearing a linen sheet over the naked body.[300]

As can be seen in the RSAM, over the course of one's perfection, involving many incarnations, the Ego must work to perfect the three bodies (astral, etheric, and physical) into their three higher counterparts. These higher counterparts are "the treasures stored up in heaven" (Matt 6:21; Luke 13:33–34), the wedding garments (Matt 22:2–14), the fully leavened loaves (Matt 13:33; Luke 13:20–21), and perhaps also the Pauline "whole armor of God" (Eph 6:11, 13) and "armor of light" (Rom 13:12), to name but a few illustrative passages. When one passes through the gates of death, the three bodies are left behind, and the soul (the Ego or "I Am") stands in judgment, naked, except to the extent that it has purified the lower bodies into their higher counterparts (wedding garments).

What we have been discussing to this point is a *symbolical* understanding—though I prefer to think of it as spiritual reality rather than symbol, on the assumption that the spiritual realm is a reality. Let us now consider how the flight of the young man can also be seen to contain a historical element on the physical plane, for it is here that Lazarus, representing the lower "I Am," fills the bill more closely than any other.

It is Karl König, whose work we noted in the introduction, who now gives us the link that helps to solve the mystery of the streaker in Mark 14:51–52.[301] König postulates that Lazarus-John, having been present at the Last Supper, and "having linked himself with the destiny of Judas, follows him to the palace of the High Priest. He could not, must not, delay the imminent destiny that was about to unfold, for he knew that his Master had to go through the Mystery of Golgotha. His office was to be consciously present at every event. Thus it was also his duty to go with Judas and the band of the High Priest's men to Gethsemane so as to be present when Christ was taken prisoner. What came about

---

[300] Alain Le Boulluec, "La Lettre sur l' 'Évangile secret' de Marc et le *Quis dives salvetur?* de Clément d'Alexandrie," *Apocrypha* 7 (1996): 27–41.
[301] König, *Mystery of John*, 151.

through Judas had to be consciously experienced by Lazarus-John." König goes on to relate how, after all the disciples fled, Lazarus-John followed Peter to the premises of the high priest (John 18:15–16).

This scenario accords with all we have said herein, and it puts Lazarus-John at the Gethsemane scene (Mark 14:43–50), where he was uniquely qualified to understand what was taking place and to experience it in the depth of his soul: Judas arriving with the arresting band and kissing Jesus, the bystander cutting off the ear of the slave of the high priest, the disciples fleeing—all but the young man described in vv. 51–52. I propose that Lazarus-John was this young man. König wrote his essay in 1962, and it is highly unlikely that by the time of his death in 1966 he had ever heard of Morton Smith's 1958 discovery, which was not published until 1973. His book focuses only upon John's Gospel and contains no reference to these passages in Mark. But the scenario he sketches fits with Lazarus observing the scene in Gethsemane and then following Jesus, Peter, and the capturing band to the court of Caiaphas (John 18:12–16). Given that scenario, it is highly likely that Lazarus would have been wearing more than the "linen cloth" described by Mark. Indeed, only a little later a fire was necessary to warm those in regular clothing (Mark 14:54). This contextual incongruity suggests that this imagery of linen clothing and naked flight carries esoteric meaning. Mark is combining physical facts with spiritual ("symbolic") facts in his account.

We cannot leave König's account without noting another of its aspects. Steiner had said that the "inner being" of each of the twelve represented a different one of the twelve zodiacal influences, as a "collective Body of Christ," and that "the part representing the 'I' dominated by egotism, which causes the death of the Christ, is Judas Iscariot."[302] Because of the importance of the zodiacal twelve, König says that from the time of Judas's betrayal until the time when Matthias was elected to take his place (Acts 1:12–26), Lazarus-John, who had been the thirteenth, laying on the bosom of Christ, became the

---

[302] Rudolf Steiner, *Isis Mary Sophia: Her Mission and Ours* (Great Barrington, Mass.: SteinerBooks, 2003), 52–53 (CW 94, lect. November 5, 1906).

twelfth. "The Eagle, Lazarus, has now taken the place of the Scorpion, Judas." "He has become the Eagle of the new knowledge, the bearer of the Holy Spirit."[303]

As we ponder this, we cannot avoid considering the relevance of the zodiacal creatures mentioned by Ezekiel (1:10) and by John in his Apocalypse (4:7). Both refer to four creatures that are at ninety degrees from each other on the ecliptic circle, and John puts them in precisely the order in which they there appear, namely, lion, ox, human face (Aquarius, or "water-bearer"), and eagle.[304]

What immediately strikes us as we compare these four canonical figures with the four zodiacal counterparts, Leo, Taurus, Aquarius, and Scorpio, is that the last one in each series, the eagle and Scorpio, does not, on the face of it, equate to its counterpart. It is widely recognized that from ancient times attempts have been made to align the four canonical figures with the four gospels. While they were variously aligned by different early Christian writers, the alignment most commonly accepted by scholars today is that of Jerome, as follows:[305]

Aquarius	Leo	Taurus	Scorpio
Human/Angel	Lion	Ox/Bull	Eagle
Matthew	Mark	Luke	John

This is the alignment Steiner also recognized.[306] He noted in his lectures on Mark's Gospel how Mark, writing in Alexandria, had been exposed to the pagan gnosis and the lofty revelations manifest in Egyp-

---

[303] König, *Mystery of John*, 149, 156.

[304] In their order among the twelve constellations on the ecliptic, the four (in bold) are: **Leo (lion)**, Cancer, Gemini, **Taurus (ox, or bull)**, Aries (lamb), Pisces (two fish), **Aquarius (face of a man)**, Capricorn, Sagittarius, **Scorpio (scorpion)**, Libra, and Virgo (virgin).

[305] Felix Just, "Symbols of the Four Evangelists," Electronic New Testament Educational Resources, http://catholic-resources.org/Art/Evangelists_Symbols.htm. See also WGBH Educational Foundation, "Emergence of the Four Gospel Canon," From Jesus to Christ: The First Christians, http://www.pbs.org/wgbh/pages/frontline/shows/religion/story/emer gence.html.

[306] Steiner, *Deeper Secrets*, 14–23 (lect. 1).

tian architecture, including the Sphinx.[307] Elsewhere he spoke often
about how the deep wisdom of human evolution had been incorpo-
rated into the Egyptian Sphinx, noting the lion body, eagle wings, bull
form, and human face.[308] The wings of an eagle and the human face
are immediately obvious, but the wings of the eagle also comprise the
mane of the lion. According to Steiner's *Wonders of the World*, the earliest of the zodiacal forces to work upon the human embodiment was
Taurus, the bull. Perhaps one can imagine the bull as the base upon
which the neck rises from the lower body. The next influence was that
of Leo, the lion, adding to that base the lion's mane, followed by Scorpio, the scorpion/eagle represented by the eagle's wings, and finally
Aquarius, represented by the human face. All of these influences are
still contained within each human body. Each influence should be
imagined separately in its own right, since each succeeding one also
contains all that went before, just as the adult contains the child.

But we return to the relationship between the scorpion and the
eagle, for it is in that cosmic relationship that we here approach the
mystery of the young man who ran away naked, only to appear later
inside the empty tomb.

If asked which one of the twelve is best described by the qualities
of the Scorpion, most people would likely choose Judas Iscariot. He is
the one here proposed.[309] Given that Judas Iscariot is the one among
the twelve with the character of the zodiacal Scorpio, yet from the
earliest centuries Christians have substituted the eagle for the scorpion
and almost universally associated the eagle with John's Gospel, we have

---

[307] Steiner, *Gospel of St. Mark*, 188–89 (lect. 10).

[308] Rudolf Steiner, *Egyptian Myths and Mysteries* (trans. Norman Macbeth; Hudson,
N.Y.: Anthroposophic Press, 1971), 85 (CW 106, lect. 8); idem, *Wonders of the World:
Ordeals of the Soul, Revelations of the Spirit* (trans. Dorothy Lenn and Owen Barfield;
London: Rudolf Steiner Press, 1963), 154–59 (CW 129, lect. 9); and idem, *Universe,
Earth and Man* (London: Rudolf Steiner Press, 1987), 155, 162 (CW 105, lect. 11).

[309] The etymology of the name Iscariot is far from clear and should probably not
be overly relied upon in its current state. At least ten different meanings have been
proposed by G. Schwarz, and are cited by William Klassen in his article "Judas Iscariot," *Anchor Bible Dictionary* 3:1091, which divides them into four main groups,
namely, "dagger-wielding assassins," "false one," "deliverer," and "hometown" (i.e.,
Kerioth, in Judea).

an indication of the strong connection—karmic if you will—between Judas Iscariot and Lazarus-John, the disciple whom Jesus loved.

Earlier Jesus had asked James and John, sons of Zebedee, "Are you able to drink the cup that I drink …?" (Mark 10:38). In order to comprehend what Mark is saying in his *neaniskos* passages, let us hear Steiner's description of this *cup*:

> Let us place ourselves with all humility—as we must—within the soul of Christ Jesus, who to the end tries to maintain the woven bond linking him with the souls of the disciples. Let us place ourselves as far as we may within the soul of Christ Jesus during the events that followed. This soul might well put to itself the world-historical question, "Is it possible for me to cause the souls of at least the most select of the disciples to rise to the height of experiencing with me everything that is to happen until the Mystery of Golgotha?" The soul of Christ itself is faced with this question at the crucial moment when Peter, James and John are led out to the Mount of Olives, and Christ Jesus wants to find out from within himself whether he will be able to keep those whom he had chosen. On the way he becomes anguished. Yes, my friends, does anyone believe, can anyone believe that Christ became anguished in face of death, of the Mystery of Golgotha, and that he sweated blood because of the approaching event of Golgotha? Anyone who could believe that would show he had little understanding for the Mystery of Golgotha; it may be in accord with theology, but it shows no insight. Why does the Christ become distressed? He does not tremble before the cross. That goes without saying. He is distressed above all in face of this question, "Will those whom I have with me here stand the test of this moment when it will be decided whether they want to accompany me in their souls, whether they want to experience everything with me until the cross?" It had to be decided if their consciousness could remain sufficiently awake so that they could experience everything with him until the cross. This was the "cup" that was coming near to him. So he leaves them alone to see if they can stay "awake," that is in a state of consciousness in which they can experience with him what he is to experience. Then he

goes aside and prays, "Father, let this cup pass from me, but let it be done according to your will, not mine" [Mark 14:36]. In other words, "Let it not be my experience to stand quite alone as the Son of Man, but may the others be permitted to go with me."

He comes back, and they are asleep; they could not maintain their state of wakeful consciousness. Again he makes the attempt, and again they could not maintain it. So it becomes clear to him that he is to stand alone, and that they will not participate in the path to the cross. The cup had not passed away from him. He was destined to accomplish the deed in loneliness, a loneliness that was also of the soul. Certainly the world had the Mystery of Golgotha, but at the time it happened it had as yet no understanding of this event; and the most select and chosen disciples could not stay awake to that point.[310]

And yet Lazarus, his closest and most highly initiated disciple, was there, awake, staying with him through the trial even to the cross.

Does the fact that the beloved disciple went all the way with Jesus in wakeful consciousness (John 19:26) mean that Jesus' prayer was answered and that he did not have to "accomplish the deed in loneliness"? The answer is a matter of perspective. Because of the uniqueness of the twelve, representing the fullness of the zodiacal influences as a "collective Body of Christ," Jesus' prayer about the "cup" seemed to relate only to these chosen ones, especially since it was only Peter, James, and John, as representatives of the chosen *twelve*, whom he had taken furthest with him into the Garden.[311] Literally, this is what Steiner seems to be saying. Moreover, as Jesus' cursing of the fig tree suggests, the method by which Lazarus was enlightened was no longer to be available, so the question remained whether the others he had been with could follow him in the full consciousness of the spiritual

---

[310] Steiner, *Gospel of St. Mark*, 167–69 (lect. 10).

[311] It appears that, aside from Judas, at least all of the *twelve* went with Jesus to the Garden, Jesus telling them to "sit here" while he took Peter, James, and John, apparently a bit farther, and then Jesus, being "distressed and troubled," went still a bit farther to pray (Mark 14:32–35; Matt 26:36–39). Luke says only that the disciples followed Jesus to Gethsemane where Jesus "withdrew from them about a stone's throw" (Luke 22:39–41).

realities of the event. On that question, Christ's prayer about the cup was not answered. If Lazarus alone was able to go with Christ in full consciousness, and if Lazarus was one to whom Christ's prayer applied, then his prayer seems to have been answered to that limited extent.

With this, a second question emerges. If Lazarus was able to go with Christ in full consciousness all the way, what then is going on at John 20:8–9? There, after Peter and the beloved disciple race to the tomb, we read, "Then the other disciple, who reached the tomb first, also went in, and he saw and believed; for as yet they did not know the scripture, that he must rise from the dead." The question of what Lazarus believed at this moment is particularly important, for if he believed *in the resurrection* only after he heard Mary's report "They have taken the Lord out of the tomb, and we do not know where they have laid him" and then witnessed the tomb himself, how could he also have been the "young man" in the tomb in Mark 16:5–6, who had earlier told the women that Jesus had risen?

The question of what it is that the beloved disciple "believed" has puzzled scholars at least from the time of Augustine, who said that this statement meant merely that the beloved disciple believed Mary's report that the tomb was empty.[312] Without citing him, Charlesworth seems at first blush to agree with Augustine's conclusion, while recognizing that "there is an amazing consensus that 20:8 denotes resurrection faith."[313] Charlesworth thinks v. 9 precludes the beloved disciple's belief in the resurrection at that point in time. It is hard not to see, however, that Charlesworth's position on the exegesis of vv. 8–9 is influenced by his postulate that Thomas, who professes belief in the resurrection only in vv. 24–29, is the beloved disciple. Augustine's view has been put down by Raymond Brown as "a trite conclusion" in comparison to the inference that the beloved disciple was "the first to believe in the risen Jesus."[314] However, it is perhaps not so trite,

---

[312] Augustine, *Tractates on the Gospel of John* 120.9. In the same place Augustine wrote, "He could not then have believed that He had risen again, when he did not know that it behoved [*sic*] Him to rise again" (trans. John Gibb and James Innes).

[313] Charlesworth, *Beloved Disciple*, 77–116, quoting 77.

[314] Brown, *Gospel according to John*, 2:987.

for the resurrection was not of the mineral body, and it is not necessary for the mineral body to dissipate in order for the spiritual body to rise.[315] Thus, the beloved disciple might well have realized that the Christ would rise, yet still have expected his material body to remain in the tomb. It is the disappearance of that body that Mary alarmingly reported to Peter and Lazarus-John (John 20:2) and that supports Augustine's conclusion. Only when they entered the tomb could they confirm the disappearance with their own eyes.

To restate this important point, Lazarus knew that the Phantom, Paul's "spiritual body," the perfected human physical body, did not mean the mineral-physical body, but he did not know why the mineral-physical body would not still have been in the grave. In other words, Mary alarmed them that the tangible body was gone. He did not anticipate that. As for v. 9, "for as yet they did not know the scripture, that he must rise from the dead," its awkwardness sticks out like a sore thumb. Certainly no New Testament scripture existed at that point in time. The nearest Old Testament scripture is probably Hos 6:2: "After two days he will revive us; on the third day he will raise us up." Joseph A. Fitzmyer, in discussing similar language in 1 Cor 15:4 ("in accordance with the scriptures"), says, "one should not press any specific OT text too much to explain the kerygmatic 'according to the Scriptures.'"[316] Bultmann is probably right on this verse, saying that it "is a gloss of the ecclesiastical redaction," though he did so while also saying that both Peter and the beloved disciple were brought to faith in the resurrection "through the sight of the empty grave."[317]

---

[315] For my own earlier treatment of this, based upon Steiner's lectures, see Smith, *Disciple Whom Jesus Loved*, 45–54, in the discussion "Mark's Mysterious Youth in the Linen Cloth." It brings together Steiner's discrete lectures that, collectively, offer an explanation of the disappearance of the mineral body such that it, as distinct from the mineral-free physical body, was in no sense an element of what rose from the dead. The perfected physical body, the "spiritual body" in Pauline terms, Steiner called the Phantom.

[316] Joseph A. Fitzmyer, *First Corinthians* (Anchor Bible 32; New Haven: Yale University Press, 2008), 548–49. See also Raymond Brown's discussion of the difficulty posed by "as they did not yet understand the scripture"; *Gospel according to John*, 2:987–88.

[317] Bultmann, *Gospel of John*, 684–85.

Richard Distasi is an anthroposophist with extensive knowledge of Steiner's works, having, in my observation and judgment, a profound depth of insight into their meaning as well as a generous and helpful disposition in sharing that insight with others. In his recent *The Fleeing Youth*, noting the above-mentioned implications of John 20:8–9, Distasi concluded that the "young man" in Mark 14:51–52 and 16:5 was not Lazarus but rather John the Baptist.[318] His analysis and reasoning as it related to the spiritual qualifications of the Baptist should not be taken lightly. Like my own, his proposal for the identity of the "young man" complements Steiner's assertion that the youth was a metaphor for the youthful cosmic Christ Spirit as it separated from Jesus. There is not, I propose, so great a difference in my identification of the young man from that of Distasi as might at first be supposed. Two statements by Steiner near the end of his life make this clear. After missing two days of lecturing, Steiner rose from his sick bed to deliver his necessarily short Last Address, which contained the following paragraph:

> When we look back into olden times, we see rise up before us within the traditions of Judaism the prophetic figure of Elijah. We know what significance the prophet Elijah had for the people of the Old Testament, and therewith for all mankind; we know how he set before them the goal and destiny of their existence. And we have shown how in the course of time the being who was present in Elijah appeared again at the very most important moment of human evolution, appeared again so that Christ Jesus Himself could give him the Initiation he was to receive for the evolution of mankind. For the being of Elijah appeared again in Lazarus-John—who are in truth one and the same figure, as you will have understood from my book "Christianity as Mystical Fact."[319]

---

[318] Richard Distasi, *The Fleeing Youth: The Cosmic Principle of Christ* (2009), 19–33, 106–15, esp. 114, http://www.lulu.com/items/volume_67/6997000/6997588/6/print/6997588.pdf (ISBN 978-0-557-08609-2).

[319] Rudolf Steiner, *The Last Address* (trans. George Adams; London: Rudolf Steiner Press, 1967), http://wn.rsarchive.org/Lectures/Dates/19240928p01.html. (CW 238). The last

The second statement, given by Steiner in response to a question by Dr. Ludwig Noll during his last illness, was quoted in full in the Ancient Mysteries chapter.[320] Distasi recognizes that the youth in the linen cloth depicts, in the first instance, Lazarus.[321] However, Distasi then notes both that Lazarus did not flee as described in Mark 14:51–52 and that John the Baptist was "interpenetrated within the consciousness soul of Lazarus" at the latter's initiation and thus his own initiation by Christ was consummated. Since it seems to be the same *neaniskos* in both Mark 14:51–52 and 16:1–8, and since Distasi takes John 20:8–9 as suggesting Lazarus could not have been the youth in the tomb because he did not yet then realize the Christ had risen, Distasi concludes that both *neaniskos* passages refer to the spirit being of John the Baptist.[322]

Distasi's thoughtful suggestion that the *neaniskos* in the tomb was John the Baptist has, on the face of it, one virtue over my proposal that it was Lazarus-John. It would seem to explain how Lazarus, as the beloved disciple, could be with Peter when Mary returns from the tomb. The clearest problem with this solution, however, is that the spirit of the Baptist was already joined with Lazarus through the latter's initiation. The Baptist's spirit could not have appeared to Mary at that point, separated from the spiritual aspect of Lazarus-John. Their common mission, even designated by the meaning of the name John, joined them. Neither could have been present *bodily*, nor could one of them have been there spiritually without the presence of the other. So the argument that the young man was the Baptist does not refute my position that he was also Lazarus-John, which, however, requires still further discussion shortly.

In nuanced contrast to Distasi, my reasons for concluding that both *neaniskos* passages refer to Lazarus-John are: the scenario outlined

---

sentence in the quotation above might appear ambiguous, but it is clear from Steiner's works that he was not saying that Elijah and Lazarus were "one and the same figure," beyond the fact that the spirit of John the Baptist, who was Elijah reincarnated, penetrated into Lazarus-John's being down through the consciousness soul at the time of the raising of Lazarus, so that they shared a common consciousness. Clearly his *Christianity as Mystical Fact* contains no such other indication.

[320] See p. 60.
[321] Distasi, *Fleeing Youth*, 32.
[322] Distasi, *Fleeing Youth*, 114.

above puts Lazarus at the scene in Mark 14:51–52; what he "believed" in John 20:8 is that, as Augustine noted, the tomb was empty, as Mary had asserted (v. 2); the implication of his ignorance of the resurrection in v. 9 was added by a later hand, as Bultmann asserted; the astral body of Jesus (the "mother of Jesus," the Virgin Sophia) that was bestowed upon Lazarus at the cross gave him the enlightenment, if any was then still needed, to anticipate Christ's resurrection; he already had the full consciousness of the spirit of John the Baptist at the time of the Mark 16:5 appearance; and the author of the Secret Gospel of Mark used the same "linen cloth" metaphor in 14:51–52 that he had applied to the youth in its version of the raising of Lazarus.

Let us be very clear about the nature of the young man (*neaniskos*) in the tomb. He was not an embodied personality perceivable through the normal human sense of sight. No historical individual can fill the bill, nor has any been meaningfully advanced. Lazarus-John could not have been there in his material body telling the three women "He has risen, he is not here; see the place where they laid him. But go, tell his disciples and Peter" (Mark 16:5–7). Had he been the one telling this to the women, even if he had been able to outrun Mary Magdalene back to where Peter was staying, he would not have responded as he did to her excited declaration in John 21:2. The young man was, rather, a spiritual entity perceptible only through enhanced spiritual, or clairvoyant, vision. No angel has ever been endowed with material body, always having been susceptible only to a higher vision. Marcus observes that the young man is "probably meant to be an angel," noting that "angels are called *neaniai* ('young men') in 2 Maccabees and Josephus."[323] As noted, the primary meaning of the two *neaniskos* passages in Mark relates to the withdrawing Christ Spirit, imprinting a highly spiritual character to the passages. It is in this context that we must contemplate Mark's message. Yet to the extent that we venture beyond the primary meaning given by Steiner, of the escaping Christ Spirit, the *neaniskos* in Secret Mark's raising narrative, widely recognized as a version of the Lazarus account, gives us the clearest indication that the young man

---

[323] Marcus, *Mark 8–16*, 1080, citing 2 Macc 3:26, 33 and Josephus, *Jewish Antiquities* 5.277.

at the tomb is nevertheless in some sense Lazarus-John, who, by then, was adorned with a "white robe," a symbol for the astral body of Christ handed down to him from the cross.

We return to the question of what it was that rose from the grave. That the tomb was empty has suggested to many that the material body of Jesus rose. This is contrary to anthroposophy, which says that the perfected physical body, which it calls the Phantom, rose. The pure physical body is not visible to the normal human sense of sight. This body only became visible as a result of the fall described in Genesis 3, when in the long course of human evolution it was gradually filled and shaped with mineral content. The Phantom is the state of the physical body when it has been sufficiently perfected to rise above its "fallen" material state. As previously indicated, there is an explanation for the disappearance of the material body of Jesus other than to say that it also rose from the dead.[324] The incarnated cosmic Christ Spirit was able to complete the purification of the astral and physical bodies of Jesus of Nazareth, the etheric body having been pure from the birth of the Nathan-Jesus child described in Luke's Gospel (see RSAM).[325] Lazarus-John's anticipation of the resurrection of the Christ Spirit did not necessarily carry with it the realization that the mineral body would have decomposed so quickly and passed into the earth at the earthquake as heretofore suggested. Hence, he needed to see that the tomb did not still contain the mineral body, as in the case of normal human beings. Many of the post-resurrection appearances of Christ are described in ways that are inconsistent with a body composed of matter, suggesting that those otherwise described are speaking of the supersensible (clairvoyant) experiences of his followers.

Mark's Gospel tells of the appearance of only one being in the tomb, the *neaniskos*. Only Matthew follows Mark in reporting but one creature, an angel whose "appearance was like lightning, and his raiment white as snow" (28:3). Luke reports "two men ... in dazzling

---

[324] See n. 315, regarding the earthquake and its aftershocks in Matt 27:51; 28:2.

[325] Actually the astral body was also pure at such birth, having been purified through the life and spiritual activity of the Buddha; for Steiner's views on this subject, see Smith, *Burning Bush*, 45–53 and the documentation provided there.

apparel" (24:4). John reports "two angels in white" who appear only to Mary after she had fetched Peter and the other disciple (20:12). She turned around from seeing the angels and saw Jesus standing (v. 14). Similarly, in Acts 1:1–11, Luke again tells of "two men" appearing to the disciples, after the forty days, when Jesus had appeared and then disappeared into a cloud. Steiner identifies the two men in the John passage as the pure etheric and astral bodies of Jesus:

> We are told that Mary Magdalene was led to the grave, that the body had disappeared and that she saw there two spiritual forms. These two spiritual forms are always to be seen when a corpse is present for a certain time after death. On the one side is to be seen the astral body, and on the other, what gradually separates from it as ether body, then passing over into the cosmic ether. Wholly apart from the physical body, these are two spiritual forms present which belong to the spiritual world.[326]

We saw earlier that the *neaniskos* that the three women saw in the tomb was the risen cosmic Christ. Steiner said that, but he also, as above, said that the two spiritual forms who appeared to Mary Magdalene as she peered into the tomb were the astral and etheric bodies of Jesus (John 20:11–12). But the astral body of Jesus, the Virgin Sophia, the truest mother of Jesus, had been passed down to Lazarus-John at the cross. Therefore, the young man (*neaniskos*) in the white robe that Mary Magdalene and the other women saw in the tomb in Mark 16:5 must surely have represented some aspect of Lazarus-John, then spiritually united with the Christ, adorned with his astral body.

One further problem with my proposal remains. If Lazarus-John was the young man who appeared to the women, announced to them that Jesus was risen, and pointed to the place where they had laid him (Mark 16:5–7), how could Lazarus-John have been surprised by the empty tomb when Mary declared to Peter and him that the tomb was empty (John 20:1–10)? The problem is not solved, at least not at first blush, by the premise that the young man was a disembodied spirit. Presumably

---

[326] Steiner, *Gospel of St. John*, 187 (lect. 12).

if the young man was a spiritual aspect of Lazarus-John, that spiritual consciousness immanent within Lazarus-John would have precluded his surprise at the empty tomb.

Scholars have long dealt with discrepancies between the different gospel accounts, which often occur in substantive content or chronological arrangement of events, or both. It seems possible that we have such a discrepancy between Mark and John that gives rise to this problem. While John's account of the raising of Lazarus and Secret Mark's account of the raising of the youth are widely thought to relate to the same incident, there are significant differences in their respective details. Similarly, we have noted that Mark and Matthew both speak of the appearance of a single entity (youth or angel) while Luke and John both speak of two entities (men or angels). We've seen how they can be understood as merely different ways of describing the observations of enhanced spiritual vision among the followers of Jesus. Is it possible that Mark is speaking of the spirit of that one, Lazarus, who gave rise to the legend behind Secret Mark, whose being was enhanced by the spirit of the Baptist, while John, that is Lazarus himself, says that two different individualities, himself and the Baptist, appeared to Mary? Lazarus and Peter had gone back to their homes (John 20:10), and only then did the dual spirits of Lazarus and the Baptist appear to Mary, which Lazarus describes as "two angels in white" (v. 12). Mark puts his version of the appearance to Mary at an earlier point than John, namely, at the time she enters the tomb before she notifies the disciples and Peter. John puts the appearance to Mary after Peter and the beloved disciple returned home and she is left alone at the tomb. Both appearances are to Mary (or to Mary and the other women) and both are at the tomb. Their chronology is different. If John's chronology, being that of an eyewitness, is accepted, it would seem to carry the greater weight.

The above suggestion that John was showing that the "two angels in white" (John 20:12) who appeared to Mary were himself (Lazarus) and the Baptist should not be understood as saying anything in conflict with Steiner's assertion that the two angels were the etheric and astral bodies of Jesus. We've seen that Lazarus received the astral body of Jesus at the foot of the cross and was conjoined at the consciousness soul and spirit level by the spirit of the Baptist. The spirits of Moses and the Baptist (Elijah) had appeared to Peter, James, and John at the transfiguration of Jesus, probably there also representing the purified astral and etheric bodies of Jesus (Mark 9:4; Matt 17:3; Luke 9:30). At least in the case of Elijah and the Christ, according to Steiner's disclosures, the higher elements of their being, such as, for instance, their etheric body, could appear to, or act through, others when their earthly bodies were actually at a different location.[327] And the higher bodies of these great individualities are multiplied and available to others who attain to the level worthy of them.[328]

With that, we summarize.

König's account puts Lazarus in a position to have observed what was occurring at Gethsemane as the young man in Mark 14:51–52. Mark was thus giving us a historical account, but one laced with spiritual meaning unique to his Gospel.

In so doing, Mark was carrying over into the synoptic tradition both the historical reality of the Lazarus account and the deeply spiritual nature of John's Gospel. It is Secret Mark that confirms that Lazarus was both the young man in Gethsemane and the young man inside Jesus' open tomb. Secret Mark also more clearly associates the linen cloth worn by this young man with Jesus' burial wrapping. Through the symbolism of this shared material, Mark indicates that Christ and Lazarus are united through the ability of the young man Lazarus to go all the way through Christ's passion, death, and resurrection in full consciousness, or, as Steiner put it above, drink the cup by remaining "sufficiently awake so that [he] could experience everything with him until the cross."

---

[327] With regard to Elijah, see Steiner, *Gospel of St. Mark*, 39–41 (CW 139, lect. 3) and *Turning Points*, 142–78 (CW 61, December 14, 1911). With regard to Christ, see Steiner, *Fifth Gospel*, 40–41 (lect. 3), 80–81 (lect. 5). Similar accounts of out-of-body appearances by certain Eastern masters have been reported in Paramahansa Yogananda, *Autobiography of a Yogi* (Los Angeles: Self-Realization Fellowship, 1972).

[328] Steiner, *Principle of Spiritual Economy*, 12–31 (lect. 2); Smith, *Burning Bush*, 96–97.

APPENDIX: *Did the Christ Spirit Die on the Cross?*

Steiner's view that the young man in Gethsemane represents the withdrawing Christ Spirit raises an important theological question: did the Christ Spirit die on the cross? A distinction must be made between the question of whether Christ had become flesh, on the one hand, and of whether the Christ Spirit had died, on the other. The Christ Spirit had actually dwelled in the human flesh of Jesus of Nazareth from his baptism until the process of his crucifixion. And it can be said that the Christ Spirit experienced the death of Jesus; that is, it passed through the experience of death with him. But we deal here with an important question of Christology, namely, did the Christ Spirit itself ever die? John has Christ saying that one who believes in him shall never die (11:26). If this is so, surely that great Spirit itself never died. On the other hand, Paul says, "Christ being raised from the dead will never die again" (Rom 6:9), suggesting that he died once. On this difficult question it is important to bear in mind what it is that, if it believes in Christ, will never die, for it cannot be said that the bodies of one who believes will never die. That part of the human being that believes in Jesus (the Ego) and those parts of the three bodies that have been perfected into their higher spiritual counterparts (in the sevenfold or ninefold human being)—it is these that will never die. Since the Christ Spirit was able to perfect the three bodies of Jesus of Nazareth into their higher spiritual counterparts (of which the transfiguration had to be some evidence), these aspects never died on the cross, though the lower bodies of Jesus of Nazareth certainly did. This distinction probably figured into those gnostic texts that mistakenly held that the Christ never became flesh. While it was lost by the time of the Nicene Creed, the earlier Apostles' Creed ("He descended to the dead" [or "into hell"]) is consistent with the descent of the Christ Spirit into hell to preach to the captives there, which suggests that the Christ Spirit proceeded, without itself dying, from the body of Jesus into the realm of those who were not then in the incarnated state in order to bring to their souls and spirits the truth of the Mystery of Golgotha.

This is in accord with scripture (Eph 4:9–10; 1 Pet 3:19; 4:6; cf. John 5:28), and is often confirmed by Steiner: "The moment when the blood flowed from the wounds of the Redeemer, when the corpse was hanging on the cross, the Christ appeared in the underworld and kindled the light that once again gave sight to the souls below."[329]

---

[329] Steiner, *Principle of Spiritual Economy*, 131 (lect. 10, May 25, 1909). See also *Outline of Esoteric Science*, 273–74 (ch. 4); *Reappearance of Christ in the Etheric*, 84 (lect. 5), 99 (lect. 6); *Christ and the Human Soul*, 50 (lect. 3); and Rudolf Steiner, *Rosicrucian Esotericism* (trans. D. S. Osmond; Spring Valley, N.Y.: Anthroposophic Press, 1978), 102–3 (CW 109/111, lect. 8), 107–8 (lect. 9).

BOOK THREE

Relevant Substance of the Ancient Mysteries (RSAM)[330]

Conditions of Consciousness

From Mesopotamia and coursing through the Latin and Germanic tongues came the ancient recognition that the names of the days of our week represent the long ages or "days" of creation. This ancient knowledge antedated Moses but was perceived by him and related to some extent in the biblical account.[331] The following three earlier, creative Conditions of Consciousness have preceded our present Earth Condition or evolution:

Old Saturn	Saturn's Day	Saturday
Old Sun	Sun's Day	Sunday
Old Moon	Moon's Day	Monday

---

[330] The information imparted in this section comes mainly from two of Steiner's early and most basic works: *Theosophy: An Introduction to the Spiritual Processes in Human Life and in the Cosmos* (trans. Catherine E. Creeger; Hudson, N.Y.: Anthroposophic Press, 1994) (CW 9); and *Outline of Esoteric Science*. A considerable portion of this RSAM adapts the overview in Smith, *Burning Bush*, 13–28.

[331] In order to distinguish between the seven major Conditions of Consciousness and the lesser conditions during Earth evolution, capital letters are used for the sun, the moon, and the five classical planets of our solar system only when describing one of these "days" of creation, or what we call "Conditions of Consciousness." Most frequently these capitals will be used in conjunction with the term "Old" or "Ancient," as in

These Conditions of Consciousness were prior to any materialization such as could have been detected by a present-day human being. Each Condition passed into a state of rest, or cosmic sleep, in effect dying to be reborn in a Condition of enhanced newness. The fourth such stage, or Condition of Consciousness, is that of Earth. The part of Earth evolution prior to the incarnation of Christ is represented by mars; the part since, by mercury, appropriately called "the morning star" in Rev 2:28.[332] Simple research confirms that Tuesday is Mars' day and Wednesday is Mercury's day. Earth (i.e., our solar system) will die or pass away and be reborn (i.e., "a new heaven and a new earth"; Rev 21:1) in the ennobled Jupiter Condition of Consciousness—this is Jupiter's (Thor's) Day, or Thursday. Today's senses will be of no use there, just as they were of no use in those Conditions prior to Earth, but consciousness will greatly increase. The Jupiter Condition will then expire phoenixlike into the Venus Condition, represented by Venus's Day, Friday. The seventh and final Condition, within the scope of spiritual investigation, is that called Vulcan that resolves into the octave, the mirror image of the first stage in humanity's creation and descent, when its perfection will be attained and all the lower kingdoms redeemed. These Conditions of Consciousness are what the largest available spiritual lens shows to constitute the seven pillars (Prov 9:1). But each Condition is again and again divided into seven, so that enormous eons of time interspersed by timelessness are involved in the marvel that humanity, with all its entanglements, represents.

Old Saturn or Ancient Saturn, Conditions that would not have been perceptible with our normal earthly senses but were preliminary stages of creative, spiritual activity. Lowercase is used when referring to the physical bodies as we observe them in our solar system as we know it even though the names of the five planets, as distinguished from the sun and moon, are otherwise capitalized in normal usage.

[332] "Both Mercury and Venus are … evening and morning stars. That is because they are nearer to the sun than the earth is, so they can never appear very far from the sun in the sky" (John P. Pratt, "The Evening and Morning Star," http://www.johnpratt.com/items/astronomy/eve_morn.html). The terms morning star and evening star nearly always refer to venus because it is by far the brighter of the two. But the terms properly apply to mercury as well.

Heavenly Hierarchies

According to evangelist John, with whom we are here primarily concerned, all of this emanated from the "Word" of God, which is the Christ. We are told that it was "with God in the beginning" (John 1:1), and if we visualize Christ as "the Son" of God, the eternal masculine, then there was also from the beginning (Prov 8:22) the fruitful eternal feminine, the highest and holiest "virgin" aspect of the Spirit. Between this Trinity (here, at this stage, the eternal masculine and feminine are still divinely one) and humanity were the hierarchies, a major part of the heavenly host. According to ancient tradition the hierarchies are ninefold, being in three ranks of three. Steiner gave each of these a name in keeping with its character in the creative process.[333] The Greek terminology corresponded with the English terms, but it is noteworthy that the Hebrew term for "authorities," or for the *exousiai* in Greek, was *elohim*, the plural term used for God in Genesis 1. Yahweh was one of the seven elohim, the one who sacrificially took up abode on the moon (that is, in the moon sphere) while the others served from the sun (the sun sphere).[334] Careful attention to the Genesis account reveals this. Notably the elohim were, by Steiner, given the name "Spirits of Form," the hierarchical rank in direct charge of Earth evolution (the Earth Condition of Consciousness), and thus in the final materialization of the Earth Condition they were the gods who served most directly as the divine agents, and in the case of Yahweh, of the particular "form" of the Hebrew folk.

---

[333] See Smith, *Burning Bush*, 556–57 (chart I–6) and sources there cited; online: http://www.bibleandanthroposophy.com/Smith/main/burning_bush/charts_tabs/i06.html.

[334] When we speak here of the "moon" or the "sun" we refer to the "moon sphere" or "sun sphere," in each case meaning the sphere that would be described whose circumference is traced by such body (moon or sun) as it travels around the earth. As our solar system travels around the ecliptic (zodiac) on its way through the heavens, all the planets circle the sun, which is the center of the solar system. But that means that sometimes the earth is racing ahead of the sun and at other times the sun is racing ahead of the earth. The sun moves on a more linear (so to speak) path, but from the perspective of each planet it circles that planet. The sun sphere is based upon the circumference that would be established when considered geocentrically (as in the Ptolemaic system). That is what I mean by the sun sphere.

Paul can be considered the source of the high knowledge of these hierarchies. It is he who used their Christian names, and he was the high teacher of Dionysius the Areopagite (Acts 17:34), who formed the School of Athens. In keeping with the ancient occult tradition, its teachings were oral, but they were finally reduced to writing by "Pseudo-Dionysius" around the early sixth century. In the account of his vision, Dante also recognized the hierarchies, and they were well known among eminent Christians, including Aquinas, until the sixteenth century when materialistic Christianity lost this spiritual view of the universe.

Evolution and Essential Nature of the Human Being

The earliest creation of humanity, during Old Saturn, began with the sacrifice by the thrones (the third level of the hierarchy); thereafter through all the stages, humanity and its lower kingdoms came into being through progressive sacrifice by the descending orders in the hierarchies, it being a sacred law that not only human beings but also beings at even such high levels advance only by sacrificing themselves, that is, dying (figuratively speaking only) to be reborn at higher spiritual levels.

All of the four earthly kingdoms—mineral, plant, animal, and human—started out during Ancient Saturn as beings of the same nature. However, not all beings reach their goals in the course of an evolutionary period. Those beings who reached their goal in each of the ancient Conditions of Consciousness (Saturn, Sun, and Moon) became human during Earth evolution. Those who failed during one or more of the three prior Conditions appear, during Earth evolution, as one of the lower kingdoms. Thus, the animal kingdom failed once, the plant twice, and the mineral all three times. In the larger sense, however, they should be looked at not so much as having failed as having been sacrificed in service to those who would become humans during Earth evolution. By reason of that, it becomes the spiritual task of the human kingdom to redeem the lower kingdoms through the progress of the last three Conditions of Consciousness (cf. Rom 8:19–23; Eph 1:9–10).

The beings which, at the end of Ancient Moon, were destined to become the animal kingdom on earth, were themselves at different levels of development. Each level, or species, became a group soul. The less developed animal species descended into materiality first, while the more advanced descended later in reverse order of their nearness to the human, the most advanced thus descending later. The naming of each animal species as it descended can be seen in Gen 2:19.

The makeup of the human being can be seen as threefold, fourfold, sevenfold, or ninefold, depending upon how it is viewed. These are demonstrated as follows:

THREEFOLD	FOURFOLD	SEVENFOLD	NINEFOLD
	Physical	Physical	Physical
Body	Etheric	Etheric	Etheric
	Astral	Astral	Astral
			Sentient Soul
Soul		Ego	Intellectual (Mind) Soul
			Consciousness (Spiritual) Soul
	Ego		
		Spirit Self	Spirit Self (Manas)
Spirit		Life Spirit	Life Spirit (Budhi)
		Spirit Man	Spirit Man (Atma)

The essential nature of the body and soul components is as follows:

COMPONENT OF HUMAN BEING	ESSENTIAL NATURE OF COMPONENT
Ego	Lasting or Eternal Individuality
Astral Body	Seat of Consciousness, Passions, and Desires
Etheric (Life) Body	Seat of Life
Physical Body	Seat of (Pattern for) Mineral Accumulation

The ninefold division corresponds with the nine hierarchies and the nine characteristics of the "one like a son of man" (Rev 1:13–16).[335] The sevenfold corresponds with the seven Conditions of Consciousness represented by the days of the week. The fourfold corresponds with the four elements and with the four Conditions that have existed thus far, namely, Old Saturn, Old Sun, Old Moon, and Earth. Finally, the threefold represents the threefold division expressed by Paul in 1 Thess 5:23: body, soul, and spirit. In fact, all such multifold divisions are merely different ways of referring to the same entity.

The highest three components in the sevenfold and ninefold characterizations are only in germinal form during Earth evolution. They will mature into spiritual reality as the three bodies (astral, etheric, and physical in that order) are purified by the Ego during the last three Conditions of Consciousness. Only then will the four kingdoms be perfected as they must be (Matt 5:48). Only in such perfection will the human have become a ninefold son of man (Rev 1:13–16).

The fourfold human of Earth evolution is composed of three bodies (physical, etheric or life, and astral or sense) plus an Ego. The physical body is not synonymous with the mineral body, for the latter is an attribute of the physical only during Earth evolution. A comprehension of this distinction is essential if one is to understand the physical body as the resurrection body. The physical body had its origin during Old Saturn, the etheric or life body during Old Sun, and the astral or sense body during Old Moon. Not until Earth evolution were these joined by the Ego—the "I Am." The existence of these bodies is represented profusely in hidden language in scripture.[336] The physical is the oldest and most perfected, the Ego the youngest and most immature; the ethe-

---

[335] The nine characteristics are in the following three groups of three: three bodies (long robe, golden girdle, and head and hair white as snow); threefold soul (eyes like flaming fire, feet like burnished bronze, and voice like the sound of many waters); threefold spirit (seven stars held in right hand, two-edged sword issuing from mouth, and face like the sun shining in full strength).

[336] Numerous references to the three bodies are found in both the Old and New Testaments. An extensive presentation of these is given in Smith, *Burning Bush*, 411–73 (three additional examples are given in the preface to the revised edition, x). An example is the otherwise obscure one-verse parable, "The kingdom of heaven is like leaven which a woman took and hid in three measures of flour, till it was all leavened" (Matt 13:33).

ric and the astral fall progressively in between. The animal kingdom has the three bodies on earth, the plant kingdom the older two, and the mineral kingdom only the oldest, the physical. Each lower kingdom has the other bodies, as well as the Ego, but only in the higher worlds.

Human beings did not evolve from the lower kingdoms; the latter evolved as by-products, so to speak, of human evolution. Although science that deals only with the material realm understands the fossil record in terms of humans evolving from earlier hominids and their simian predecessors, anthroposophy understands evolution as occurring on earth from a different direction under the auspices of the spiritual realm. Thus, the skeletons, fossils, and remains of the lower three kingdoms, in succession, demonstrate themselves to archaeology, whereas the skeletal remains of humanity are of but recent origin and do not reflect the earlier stages of the human mineral-physical body because those earlier stages were too soft or gelatinous to have left skeletal remains.

Though some apparently tried, the descending human could not survive as a human in a skeletal structure that did not stand completely upright with a skull that resembled the dome of heaven. Only in that structure could it develop the forces of the spirit. It was a yawning gulf that separated the animal kingdom from the human kingdom so that identifying a connecting link is anthroposophically impossible. The structure that was being prepared through the animal kingdom could not be called human. The completely upright structure with its domed skull oriented toward the heavens could not evolve from an ascending animal structure that could not escape the downward pull of gravity. The requisite uprightness came from the other direction, from the softer material as it rose upright on a descending time scale that mirrored the upward development of the animal kingdom. It was during the Atlantean Epoch of Earth evolution that the first human entered into and survived in such an upright form.[337] That first human is the one called Adam starting in Gen 4:25.

It is amazing how what has just been described is portrayed by the ancient book of Job. We shall hardly ever come to understand the book

---

[337] See Smith, *David's Question*, 10–14.

of Job without seeing that Job himself represents humanity and his three friends represent these progressive bodies, while Elihu, the youngest character, who refrained from speaking until the end (32:4), represents the Ego, and the two monsters that God mentions in his reply to Job (40:15; 41:1) represent the Lesser and Greater Guardians of the Threshold (terms extensively discussed by Steiner in other contexts). When Job has successfully passed these thresholds, he is restored to all that he had before he (humanity) was tempted—a clear allegorical reference to the fall and eventual ascension of the human being.[338]

Earth Condition of Consciousness

The modern age brought a tectonic shift in thinking about the age of the earth, opening what is now a great gulf between the scientific view of the earth's great antiquity and the religious view of its relative youth. Anthroposophy bridges the gulf between these views of the world by taking perspective into account. When read in a literal way, the Bible appears to describe a young earth, but the language of scripture does not always bear a one-to-one relationship to the reality it describes. This is especially true when it describes distant things, due to the inherent difficulty humans have "seeing" them. For just as distance in space makes perception more difficult, so too distance in time. The further one's vision reaches either backward into the past or forward into the future, the greater the necessity of describing it in the language of myth, allegory, or other non-literal modes of expression. Consistent with the sevenfold nature of creation expressed in the early passages of both Genesis (looking backward into the past) and Revelation (looking primarily forward into the future), Steiner has given us schematics that outline the long journey of humanity out of the spiritual world and back into it in a way that can be seen to comport with the broad sweep of the biblical account. As previously mentioned, his account reveals seven Conditions of Consciousness. The entirety of Earth evolution constitutes only the fourth, or middle, Condition.

---

[338] For an anthroposophical analysis of Job, see Smith, *Soul's Long Journey*, 99–121.

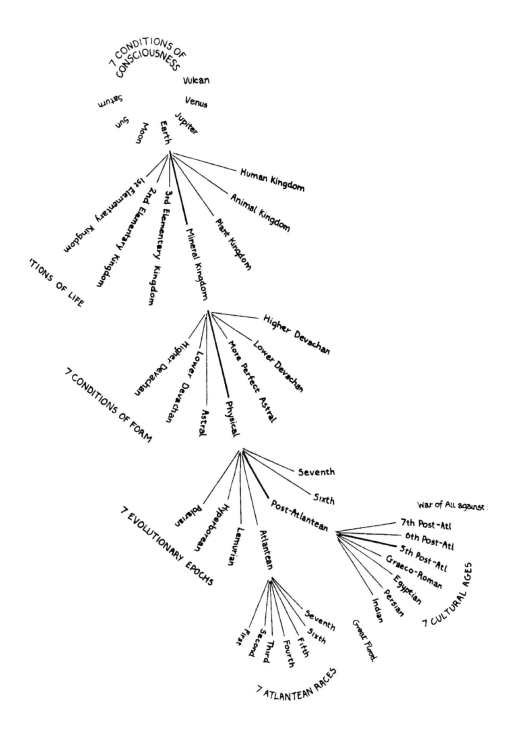

7 CONDITIONS OF CONSCIOUSNESS

Vulcan
Venus
Saturn
Sun
Moon
Jupiter
Earth

Human Kingdom
Animal Kingdom
Plant Kingdom
Mineral Kingdom
3rd Elementary Kingdom
2nd Elementary Kingdom
1st Elementary Kingdom

'TIONS OF LIFE

7 CONDITIONS OF FORM

Higher Devachan
Lower Devachan
More Perfect Astral
Astral
Physical
Lower Devachan
Higher Devachan

7 EVOLUTIONARY EPOCHS

Seventh
Sixth
Post-Atlantean
Atlantean
Lemurian
Hyperborean
Polarian

War of All against .
7th Post-Atl
6th Post-Atl
5th Post-Atl
Graeco-Roman
Egyptian
Persian
Indian
Great Flood

7 CULTURAL AGES

First
Second
Third
Fourth
Fifth
Sixth
Seventh

7 ATLANTEAN RACES

The Earth Condition of Consciousness is itself progressively divided and subdivided again and again into seven stages. The above schematic is given for perspective. The dizzying immensity of the human journey is portrayed in this chart that Steiner prepared for his thirteen-lecture cycle entitled The Apocalypse of St. John, which he delivered one month after his twelve-lecture cycle The Gospel of St. John (CW 103). Steiner's exegesis of Revelation is the only one in this writer's experience that resolves that book's otherwise profoundly obscure message in a highly meaningful and coherent way, and it stands pretty much alone in its treatment. That critical interpretation is available elsewhere and is largely beyond the scope of our present purpose.[339]

Suffice it for now to say that each level of Earth evolution, at its outset, recapitulates what has gone before but on a higher plane. It is important for us to see, for instance, particularly as we approach the conditions revealed in Gen 1:2, that this phenomenon applies to the first three Evolutionary Epochs (the Polarian, Hyperborean, and Lemurian Epochs) of the physical condition of form of the mineral condition of life of the earthly Condition of Consciousness (see the above schematic). The Polarian, Hyperborean, and Lemurian Epochs respectively recapitulate the Old Saturn, Sun, and Moon Conditions of Consciousness. These three Conditions represent the following stages of "descent" of the human being into materiality:

BODY FORMED	RELATED ELEMENT
Physical	Earth (i.e., solids)
Etheric	Water (i.e., tangible fluids)
Astral	Air (i.e., gas)

---

[339] CW 104 is not yet published, but an earlier English translation of it exists as *Apocalypse of St. John*. See also Smith, *David's Question*, 22– 69.

However, what is solid during Earth evolution was, during Old Saturn, merely warmth (fire), which became gas (air) during Old Sun, fluid (water) during Old Moon, and finally solid (earth) during Earth evolution. None of these "elements" prior to Earth evolution had any materiality to them, but were there in a spiritual, seminal state awaiting their material nature during Earth evolution. Each element moved one stage further (i.e., spiritually densified) toward its eventual earthly material counterpart with each progressive Condition. Thus, not until the fourth stage, the Earth Condition of Consciousness, was there any matter. The "In the beginning..." in Gen 1:1 denotes the beginning of the Earth Condition of Consciousness. During these six days of creation, water, air (spirit), and fire (warmth or heat, as in "moving," "brooding," or "stirring") existed but only in the supersensible realm, for all was still "void" (1:2). These three supersensible realms existed in the imagination of the creative elohim.

We must now ask ourselves what then took place during the six days of creation as expressed in Gen 1:3–31. An unwitting reader would normally take this to be describing the creation of a world that our present earthly senses could have observed at the time, but such is not the way it is understood in anthroposophy. What was being created by the elohim is the pre-material, etheric state of all four kingdoms that would emerge in matter beginning after the seventh day, the day the elohim rested (2:1–4a) before the descent into materiality began. Steiner makes this clear in his lecture of August 19, 1910, in Munich on the seven days of creation, as follows:

> In fact all that is narrated in the Bible of the six or seven "days" of creation is a reawakening of previous conditions, not in the same but in a new form.
>
> The next question which we have to ask ourselves is this—what kind of reality are we to attribute to the account of what happened in the course of these six or seven "days"? It will be clearer if we put the question in this way. Could an ordinary eye, in fact could any organs of sense such as we have today have followed what we are told took place during the six days of creation? No, they could

not. For the events there described really took place in the sphere of elementary existence, so that a certain degree of clairvoyant knowledge, clairvoyant perception, would have been needed for their observation.[340]

It may be helpful to note, in the schematic above of the seven Conditions of Consciousness, that in the Earth Condition of Consciousness there are three elementary kingdoms as conditions of life prior to the mineral kingdom (the kingdom of matter).

During the first three Epochs of Earth evolution, the Polarian, Hyperborean, and Lemurian, the elohim recapitulated, in a more advanced form, what was spiritually created in the first three Conditions of Consciousness. The three elements (fire, air, and water) and their related three lower kingdoms successively materialized, what had been only fire in the first becoming water in the third and so on. This materialization is described in Gen 2:4b–20.

Earth evolution was guided by the third or lowest order of the second threefold rank of the hierarchies known by their Hebrew title elohim (the Greek *exousiai* or the English *authorities*), appropriately called by Steiner the "Spirits of Form." At all levels the hierarchies truly reflected what came from above so that the highest levels were indeed involved through the agency of the respective lower levels.

In the earliest stage of Earth evolution, the Polarian, the earth was of an enormous size, made up only of fire or heat but containing all that became our present solar system. The second stage, the Hyperborean, was a period of densification and shrinking, and the sun separated from the rest to provide the higher spirits an abode, leaving the lower beings a denser home. In the third stage, the Lemurian, the moon also separated, taking the densest materialization with it, along with eloha-Yahweh, the primary guiding spirit in the formation of the earth. The formation of the other planets from the original fireball is beyond the scope of this overview. Only after the separation of both the sun and the moon could human beings descend to the earth, but

---

[340] Steiner, *Genesis*, 34 (lect. 3).

their form was grotesque and comprised as yet nothing solid. Not until Gen 3:17 was there an "Adam." But even this Adam was not yet in the material state of the one who became the single male ancestor of humanity, but was still only in preparatory spiritual form, in the process of descending into matter. The Adam who became the first material ancestor of humanity is the one who first appears in 4:25.[341] The progressive densification prior to that time had resulted in no bones of a human being (as distinguished from those animals that most nearly approached the human).

The physical, etheric, and astral bodies of human beings were progressively bestowed during Earth evolution in the first three Epochs (but nothing solid). Thus, in the third, that of Lemuria, human beings were huge in dimension (not unrelated to the "giants" or "mighty men of old" in Gen 6:4). Through the passions and desires of their astral bodies, and the fluidity of their denser etheric and physical bodies, they were able to control the elements, and their uncontrolled passions brought about mighty catastrophes of fire that eventually destroyed ancient Lemuria. The account of the fall of the human astral body is given in Genesis 3, where we witness the transition, after the "deep sleep" period (2:21) intervening between Lemuria and Atlantis, from the fluid to the earliest solid condition of humanity, as in Adam. The human being was originally androgynous, both male and female (1:27 and 5:2).[342]

THE FALL

The separation of the androgynous human being into different sexes (Gen 2:18–25) came toward the end of Lemuria, corresponding with the fall. As yet, the human being had no indwelling Ego, hence, like an animal, no consciousness of sin. But from what would have been the rank of an archangel, Lucifer, meaning light bearer, disobedient to the higher spirits, desired to bring the "light" of the "tree of knowledge" to

---

[341] That Gen 4:25 is when Adam finally, for the first time, succeeded in incarnating on earth in a material form is the position I have taken in Smith, *Soul's Long Journey*, 86–99.
[342] See n. 127.

the human being. The account of this fall of the human being and the archangel Lucifer is given in Genesis 3. By virtue of this, the human being's astral body was no longer pure but rather infected by "original sin," a sin invested in it through the Luciferic spirits before it even became a responsible being conscious of sin.

Prior to this time, the human being dwelled in the bosom of the gods and rather fully perceived their presence and divine guidance. Death was unknown, for consciousness was uninterrupted. But by virtue of this fall, the human being was severed from the "tree of life" (Gen 3:24) and began to experience pain, suffering, toil, and death (3:16–19). Only at this point did a human being's consciousness leave it periodically in the phenomena of both sleep and death. Its continuity did not cease, but rather only its consciousness. It was here, through the infection of the astral body and consequent infections of the etheric and physical bodies in turn, that karma and reincarnation began. Through the divine virginal wisdom, however, the governing spiritual powers had anticipated the infection of the human astral body and consequently also of its etheric body and had held back from the incarnating human being the higher element of its etheric body. Thus the higher etheric body of the original Adam did not descend until, ages later, the virginal wisdom caused it to descend as the pure and unspoiled, primal etheric body of the Nathan-Jesus child in Luke's Gospel.[343] When Luke's teacher, Paul, spoke of the first and second Adam, it is this of which he spoke (Rom 5:14 and 1 Cor 15:45–49).

By the time of this Eden event, the fall of Genesis 3, the sun, moon, and other planets had separated from the earth, leaving it far smaller than at the outset of the Polarian Epoch of Earth evolution. However, it was still larger than at present, and much of its water content was still in the form of vapor. Mists largely enshrouded the earth during the Atlantean Epoch. The Nephilim (Gen 6:4) were still large (i.e., 1 Enoch 7:2 speaks of them as "giants" whose height was

---

[343] See the discussion later in this section about how the Nathan-Jesus child of Luke's Gospel and the Solomon-Jesus child of Matthew's Gospel become one, Jesus of Nazareth, in Luke's account of the incident in Jesus' twelfth year (2:41–51).

"three thousand cubits," or about 4,500 feet), though not very solid, suggestive of clouds or mist-beings.[344]

Progressively from the time of the fall until the Christ event, and even until the present for a humanity that continues to misapprehend and miss the fullness of Christ, the consciousness of the human being darkened. The gods (God) "hid their face" more and more through the Atlantean Epoch even until now. This was experienced by Moses as the fading splendor (2 Cor 3:7,13), by the prophets as the loss of spiritual seeing, hearing, and understanding (Isa 6:9–13), and by the people of Israel first as the encroaching shades of Sheol and ultimately as the end of prophecy.

The separation from the gods in the form of loss of divine consciousness brought about an increase in wickedness (Gen 6:5). The fifth of the seven Atlantean eras (or ages) is called that of the Shemites, the ancestors of the Semitic race of the Post-Atlantean Epoch. The exalted leader of those who came to be called Shemites was head of the sun oracle, or sun mysteries. He was known as Manu, who is called Noah in the Bible, and he brought it about that certain advanced individuals, seven in number (Gen 6:10,18; 7:7), should be fashioned to lead Atlantean civilization into the next Epoch. Atlantis was eventually brought to an end by violent earthquake and volcanic activity, causing it to subside and become the floor of the ocean named for it. Plato speaks of the unnavigable mud from this subsidence west of the "Pillars of Hercules" (Gibraltar) (Timaeus 25c–d). Prior to the final cataclysms, however, the floods were increasingly menacing, brought about by the condensation of the ancient mists as the earth condensed, along with massive glacial melt caused by the increasing

---

[344] The Hebrew term *nephilim* derives from the root *npl*, which means "to fall" (Richard S. Hess, "Nephilim," *Anchor Bible Dictionary* 4:1072) or "the fallen ones" (Ronald S. Hendel, "Of Demigods and the Deluge: Toward an Interpretation of Genesis 6:1–4," *Journal of Biblical Literature* 106 [1987]: 22). The same *npl* root is found in the Greek word *nephelē*, meaning "cloud." The term *nephilim* "touches on common ground with Greek and other mythologies"; Robert Alter, *The Five Books of Moses: A Translation with Commentary* (New York: W. W. Norton, 2004), 39. I take the two meanings to be related in describing the descent of the human being from the spiritual to the mineralized earthly realm as described earlier in this work.

sunlight through the decreasing mists. Eventually, the mists were so thin that the sun became visible to the human being's eyes, and it was even possible for a rainbow to be seen (Gen 9:13).

The human being in its evolution had expelled, one by one, the various animal natures that hardened into the animal kingdom. However, some residue of the astral nature of each animal remained within the human being, so that when Noah took, metaphorically, into the ark the animals of all kinds, he was taking into the Post-Atlantean Epoch the human being filled with animal nature of all kinds, which would have to be purified over time. "When the [human being] emerged from the Flood of Atlantis, the proportions of [the human] physical body corresponded to" the measures 300 x 50 x 30 given for Noah's ark (Gen 6:15).[345] This was the ark of the first covenant (Gen 9:8–10).[346]

The disappearance of Atlantis actually covered a long period of time, but the final events were approximately ten to twelve thousand years ago, coinciding with the end of the last great ice age and the first archaeologically established appearance of humanity in the areas of the biblical account. The migrations from Atlantis were much more extensive and complex than can presently be indicated, but it was the Noah migration that established the principal lines of the human passage into the Post-Atlantean Epoch.

Human etheric and astral bodies extended far beyond the physical body in Atlantean times. Being without an indwelling Ego, and thus not yet possessed of any degree of intellect, the human being was endowed, instead, with incredible memory. That memory was a function of the etheric body and included the experiences of one's

---

[345] Rudolf Steiner, *Occult Signs and Symbols* (trans. Sarah Kurland, with emendations by Gilbert Church; Hudson, N.Y.: Anthroposophic Press, 1972), 14 (CW 101, lect. 1, September 13, 1907), 15–21 (lect. 2, September 14, 1907).

[346] According to Nahum Sarna (*The JPS Torah Commentary: Genesis* [Philadelphia: Jewish Publication Society, 1989], 52), "This vessel [the ark], significantly, is called *tevah*. This key word recurs seven times here in the instructions for building the ark and seven times again in connection with the subsidence of the waters in [Gen] 8:1–14. Yet *tevah*, in the sense of an ark, appears again in the Bible only in connection with the salvation of the baby Moses, in Exodus 2:3–5." The Hebrew term for ark in Exod 25:10 and later is *aron*; Nahum Sarna, *The JPS Torah Commentary: Exodus* (Philadelphia: Jewish Publication Society, 1991), 159.

ancestors for long periods of time through the blood connection. The biblical reckoning of generations prior to Abraham was different from subsequent times in that it counted as a single generation all those generations through which the memory was carried by the blood connection—being thus known by the name of the eponymous ancestor, the first of the line bearing that name.

Gradually over time the etheric and astral bodies condensed ever further into the physical body so that today they are nearly coterminous. Because it was through the portion of these less dense bodies not yet integrated into the physical that perception of spiritual beings was possible, this capability dwindled away with the passage of time, but the myths of old are real experiences of the human being of Atlantean times, given of course in allegorical form. Today's disinclination toward these myths corresponds to the inclination to interpret the biblical allegorical myths according to their vulgar meaning, but the deeper truths will not be attained in this manner, however much historical fact may be conveniently woven within them. It is the deeper truth and not the few surface facts that the purveyors intended.

So complete were the memories of ancient times that there was no need to write anything down. Only as this capacity faded did the necessity for writing arise around 3000 B.C.E. But as the human etheric body drew ever more within the physical, thus losing memory and perception within the spiritual world, the intellect correspondingly grew, albeit still in a most primitive state. All the time, hardening was proceeding as the material world came more and more into the human being's focus, and interest in the spiritual faded away.

Cultural Ages of the Post-Atlantean Epoch

With the final submergence of Atlantis, humanity entered the fifth of seven major Epochs of its Condition of Consciousness known as Earth evolution. While the duration of each of those Epochs prior to our Fifth may have varied in length from ours and from each other, the influence of the heavenly bodies on human evolution during the present Epoch has long been recognized by significant chapters of humanity.

One way that anthroposophy recognizes the influence of these heavenly bodies is through what it calls *cultural eras*. The parameters of such eras are prescribed by the stars so that their definition depends upon, and their comprehension presumes, some understanding in that sphere. Ancient and pre-modern history abounds in star symbolism. It flourishes within the biblical canon,[347] among early Jewish and Christian writers such as Philo, Clement of Alexandria, and Origen,[348] and within the earliest high Gothic cathedral.[349] Yet its significance remains relatively obscure in most areas of serious biblical scholarship. One would do well to contemplate the Lord's words to Abraham: "And he brought him outside and said, 'Look toward heaven, and number the stars, if you are able to number them.' Then he said to him, 'So shall your descendants be'" (Gen 15:5). According to Steiner this passage means that Abraham's descendants "would resemble the constellations of stars in heaven" and therefore refers "not to the quantity of Abraham's descendants but to their relationships."[350] In compliance with that promise the twelve tribes of Israel, the twelve sons of Ishmael (1 Chr 1:29–31), and Christ's selection of twelve disciples all reflected that pattern. The clear suggestion here is that the stars which Abraham was to count were the twelve constellations visible in the ecliptic belt known as the zodiac, or animal circle. One immediately senses a connection with the manifold animal nature (i.e., wild animals, Mark 1:13) that indwelled the human being, the original ark in the Noah metaphor, the Noah transition from Atlantean to Post-Atlantean civilization.

---

[347] Illustrative of both the zodiac or "twelve stars" and the "seven stars," see Gen 1:14; 15:5; 37:9; Job 26:10–11; 38:31–33; Prov 8:27; 9:1; Isa 13:10; 40:12; Rev 12:1; 22:1–2; see also Enoch 80:7.

[348] Jean Daniélou, *Primitive Christian Symbols* (trans. Donald Attwater; London: Burns & Oates, 1964), 124–35, http://www.archive.org/details/primitivechristi009995mbp.

[349] According to Serge Helfrich ("History of Gothic Architecture," http://www.xs4all. nl/~helfrich/gothic/architecture.html), "The cathedral at Chartres, built between 1194 and 1260, is considered to be the first manifestation of 'High Gothic' style."

[350] Steiner, *According to Matthew*, 71 (lect. 4), 191 (lect. 11). In giving such interpretation, Steiner was actually referring to those later passages that said, essentially, "I will multiply your descendants as the stars in heaven" (e.g., Gen 22:17; 26:4).

Through what is called the precession of the equinoxes, the sun traverses through all twelve of the zodiacal signs over the course of 25,920 years, the average length of each of the twelve zodiacal signs being thus 2,160 years.[351] The beginning of a zodiacal sign is determined by the date that the sun first rises in that sign at the vernal equinox. The twelve signs thus produced are known as "astrological ages" and they comprise the following:

Aquarius	23,546 – 21,386 B.C.E.
Capricorn	21,386 – 19,226
Sagittarius	19,226 – 17,066
Scorpio	17,066 – 14,906
Libra	14,906 – 12,746
Virgo	12,746 – 10,586
Leo	10,586 – 8426
Cancer	8426 – 6266
Gemini	6266 – 4106
Taurus	4106 – 1946
Aries	1946 B.C.E. – 215 C.E.
Pisces	215 – 2375
Aquarius	2375 – 4535

There is, however, a time lag of 1,199 years from the beginning of an astrological age till the beginning of its cultural age so that the parameters of the cultural ages of the Post-Atlantean Epoch are as follows:

---

[351] The number given for the full cycle is sometimes slightly more and sometimes slightly less than 25,920 but the difference is always *de minimis*.

CULTURAL AGE	DATES	CIVILIZATION
Cancer	7227 – 5067 B.C.E.	Indian
Gemini	5067 – 2907	Persian
Taurus	2907 – 747	Chaldo-Egyptian
Aries	747 B.C.E. – 1414 C.E.	Greco-Roman
Pisces	1414 – 3574	European
Aquarius	3574 – 5734	Russian-Slavonic
Capricorn	5734 – 7894	American

Steiner explained that this time lag is due to the fact that the influences from each such constellation must work for that period of time before they begin to manifest in human culture. And in 1909 he explained that there is a special relationship between the time spirits (the *archai* in the hierarchical structure) and the planetary sphere of venus.[352] Many decades later Robert Powell identified a remarkable phenomenon in the heavens, the venus pentagram, in which venus traces out a five-pointed star pattern within the full zodiacal circle in 1,199 years.[353]

The commencement of the cultural age of Aries in 747 B.C.E. is historically attested as part of the calendar reform carried out by King Nabonassar of Babylon, being when he began his reign, and the date "was utilized by the entire astronomy and chronology of antiquity."[354] Such utilization was confirmed by Ptolemy.[355] As noted earlier, the year the seraphim appeared to Isaiah (Isaiah 6) was 742 B.C.E. The traditional date for the founding of Rome was April 21, 753 B.C.E.

---

[352] Rudolf Steiner, *The Spiritual Hierarchies and the Physical World: Zodiac, Planets, and Cosmos* (trans. René M. Querido and Jann Gates; CW 110; Great Barrington, Mass.: SteinerBooks, 2008), 89.

[353] Robert Powell, *Hermetic Astrology* (2 vols.; Kinsau, West Germany: Hermetika, 1987), 1:58–63. The venus pentagram is portrayed graphically in chart I-19 in Smith, *Burning Bush*, but Powell's work gives its complex explanation.

[354] Hugo Winckler, *Die babylonische Kultur in ihren Beziehungen zur Unsrigen: Ein Vortrag* (Leipzig: J. C. Hinrichs, 1902), 36, quoted in Powell, *Hermetic Astrology*, 1:56.

[355] Ptolemy, *Almagest III*, cited by Powell, *Hermetic Astrology*, 1:56.

With this digression in explanation of the cultural eras or ages we return to the previous narrative.

The advanced Atlanteans led by Noah (Manu) went first to an area near Ireland and then overland to settle in an area of central Asia. Post-Atlantean evolution also comprises seven divisions described above as "cultural eras," of which we are now in the fifth. The first two were prehistoric, being the Ancient Indian (emanating from Manu) and then, "from the east" (Gen 11:2), the Ancient Persian, led by one prehistoric Zarathustra. These were followed by the Chaldo-Egyptian, Greco-Roman, and the present Germanic. Still in the future will be the Slavic and finally the Anglo-American. As indicated, each era lasts 2,160 years, and is known from the predominant evolutionary impulse of its time.[356] These seven cultural eras are reflected in the "churches" whose "angels" are addressed in the seven "letters" of the Apocalypse. The characteristics of each era can be readily detected in the light of anthroposophical insight. The most obvious is probably the third, the Chaldo-Egyptian, the age of the Balaam and Balak events (Numbers 22 and 24), the giving of the manna, the writing by Moses of the commandments on the stone, and the giving of the "new name ... which no one knows except him who receives it" (Rev 2:12–17). It was Steiner who gave meaning to the "new name" passage that appears again in Rev 19:12–13 and is implicit also in 3:12.[357]

The Ancient Indians under Manu and his seven holy rishis were a people who looked backward at the spiritual world, seeing reality

---

[356] The historical period and the third cultural era, the Chaldo-Egyptian, commenced about the same time so that at present something less than two and one half such ages, reflected in both scripture and artifact, can be seen as follows:

Taurus (the bull)	2907 – 747 B.C.E.
Aries (the ram, or lamb)	747 B.C.E. – 1414 C.E.
Pisces (the two fish)	1414 – 3574 C.E.

The age of the bull came to an end almost precisely at the time of Isaiah's vision (Isaiah 6), the Lamb of God (the Christ) came in the age of the lamb, and our *fifth* cultural age is that of the two fish that Christ looked out to see in the feeding of the *five* thousand.

[357] See n. 77.

there and maya (illusion) in the tangible world.[358] With the transition to the times of Ancient Persia, the human being began to turn its attention to the outer world, but under the leadership of Zarathustra it was able to see there the manifestation of the spirit. Zarathustra ("shining star") could see the Spirit of the descending Christ in the sun's aura, which he thus called Ahura Mazda, or Ormuzd ("great aura"). As its antithesis, he spoke of Ahriman, the evil being who hides the reality of the spirit existing in all creation and leads human beings to think of materiality as the ultimate reality. This Zarathustra lived many earthly lives between then and the incarnation of Christ, including one as the great Babylonian teacher of the Hebrew prophets known as Zarathas or Zoroaster (or Zarathustra). The Matthew Gospel, via the Essenes, reflects what Zarathustra taught.[359]

Approximately 1900 B.C.E. we come to Abraham. He became the ancestor of, among others, and from the biblical standpoint most significantly, the Hebrew people. Steiner attributed this to the special nature of his physical brain, calling him "the great organizer of the world-phenomena according to number and measure ... [the] person who, out of all mankind, was ... selected to be the first man to survey the outer physical world and to discover the unity in it ... the father of arithmetic." From Abraham such nature was thence conveyed through physical heredity.[360] In this light it is then not surprising to read of Yahweh's challenging him to "number the stars" and telling him that his descendants will be like them (Gen 15:5), namely, twelvefold, in the zodiacal structure. The unfolding of that structure in the Genesis account takes us through the patriarchal era and into Egyptian slavery.

---

[358] It is this looking backward at the spiritual world after the Ancient Indians had come over into the Post-Atlantean Epoch that is the basis of the admonition in the letter to the angel of the "church in Ephesus," the first cultural age in the new Epoch (Rev 2:4–5). The first love that had been abandoned was the desire to experience the sensate consciousness, the desire that occasioned the fall. Once the fall had commenced, the mission of humanity was to master the physical world and then ultimately to regain what had been lost in that process, an expanding consciousness again in the spiritual realm that would lead humanity back into that realm.

[359] See p. 116.

[360] Steiner, "The Gospels."

The Exodus 2 story of Moses' birth and training is a cryptic account of his initiation into the mysteries, first those of Egypt and later those of the Chaldeans through his father-in-law, Reuel or Jethro. Of paramount importance is what we read in Exodus 3, the account of the burning bush. We are here dealing with the descent of the Ego, the "I Am," to its dwelling place within the earthly human being. The Ego of each of the lower three kingdoms (animal, plant, and mineral) dwells in higher worlds and not on earth.[361] Further, the Ego that belongs to those kingdoms is not an individual one but collective. The human Ego has dwelled on earth at least from Atlantean times, but only as a highly immature creation and even then not as an individual Ego.[362] Rather, it commenced as a group Ego, so that human beings thought of themselves, not as individuals, but only as members of a tribe or clan united by blood kinship with some common ancestor, for the blood was the only entry port for the Ego into the human being. The Hebrews' ascription of themselves as children of Abraham, Isaac, and Jacob reflects this tribal unity, which of course was broken down further into individual tribes and clans. Ever so gradually over time the Ego approached the individual human being. But it was Moses to whom the essential revelation of this development was given by eloha-Yahweh. Moses was first shown that the Ego, though purified between lives from its impure astral body by the fire that is commonly called "purgatory," is not consumed thereby. The Ego is the "burning bush which is not consumed." Later, upon asking the name of Yahweh, Moses is told, "I Am the I Am" (Exod 3:14).[363]

This answer puzzles most people, which is why this verse has been the subject of endless commentary. The difficulty it presents to scholars begins with its translation. As K. J. Cronin put it, "The great majority of those who have translated Exodus 3:14 have agreed on at least one point, which is that the Hebrew word *ehyeh* as it occurs in this verse

---

[361] See p. 44 and n. 79.

[362] The gradual penetration of the human being's three bodies and entry into individual consciousness is described by Steiner in *Influence of Spiritual Beings*, 71 (lect. 4). See also Smith, *Burning Bush*, 402–3 and chart I–35.

[363] See n. 78.

derives from the verb-root *hayah*, meaning 'to be'. This single point of agreement is also where the consensus all but ends."[364] The many translations are quite varied as to what connects the two "I Am's," but I have found none that uses the simple "the." Many of the translations are footnoted with an indication of uncertainty.[365] All of them seem to comport with the concept of a two-tiered universe in which this "I Am" exists in the heavens and is making those below aware of its omnipotence. It is hard to garner from them any idea that this is the descending Christ revealing to Moses that the I Am, in both its higher and lower aspects, is entering into human evolution on earth. Steiner is clear—and the overall account of the progressive descent of the Christ and the evolution of human consciousness as described herein suggest—that "I am the I am" is the ancient and true meaning.

We are told that the people were fed by manna in the wilderness (Exod 16:4, 16, 31–36). That this manna was spiritual or super-sensible food is indicated (Exod 16:4; 1 Cor 10:3; John 6:31–39). According to Steiner, manna is the same as the Vedic Sanskrit word *manas*, which he westernized as Spirit Self, the first stage of the spirit of a human being,[366] that part of the astral body that has been brought under the control of the Ego, or I Am.[367] Spirit Self is the term applicable to the stage of spirituality that the human being will attain when its Ego has become the complete master of its astral body—a development still far in the future for all but those very few who are able to attain to a state of initiation and developed clairvoyance (as contrasted with atavistic clairvoyance, which is a remnant of old consciousness to be either overcome or converted). *Manas* is the next

---

[364] K. J. Cronin, "The Name of God as Revealed in Exodus 3:14: An Explanation of Its Meaning," http://www.exodus-314.com/part-i/exodus-314-in-early-translations.html.

[365] Among the translations are: "I Am who I Am"; "I Am that I Am"; "I Am what I Am"; "I Am or I will be what I will be"; "I Am he who is"; "I Am who I Am and What I Am, and I will be what I will be"; and "I Am the eternal God."

[366] See the chart on p. 183 depicting the sevenfold and ninefold human being.

[367] Steiner, *Gospel of St. John*, 108 (lect. 6); idem, *Theosophy of the Rosicrucian* (trans. M. Cotterell and D. S. Osmond; 2d ed.; London: Rudolf Steiner Press, 1966), 25 (CW 99, lect. 2); idem, *Outline of Esoteric Science*, 50 (ch. 2); idem, *Bhagavad Gita and the West*, 23–24.

state above the Ego in the sevenfold and ninefold characterizations of the human being. It represented a special form of spiritual leadership (i.e., spiritual food; 1 Cor 10:3) given to the people in the wilderness. Moses lived in the third cultural era, the Chaldo-Egyptian, and thus this manna is described in the letter to the angel of the third church, as is the "new name ... which no one knows except him who receives it" (Rev 2:17). As Steiner points out, the only name that meets that criterion is the name "I" or "I Am," for no one can speak that except in reference to oneself.[368]

The "I Am" thus introduced for the first time to Moses appears through the prophets (for instance, "I am He, I am the first, and I am the last," Isa 48:12b), then through the heights of John's Gospel, and finally in this and other passages of his Apocalypse.

Incarnation of Christ

Paul says that Christ died at "the right time," and the Baptist proclaimed that "the time is fulfilled." These proclamations are full of meaning. From the time of the fall until the Mystery of Golgotha, the human being had been in uninterrupted descent into materiality and mineralization. This had progressed to the point of no return. Had humanity hardened further, salvation from its hardened state would have been irretrievable. The divine powers had foreseen this, and the descent of the Christ from highest heaven to the sun and then downward to incarnation had been prepared over the millennia. A special people had to be set apart to consummate the preparation of the three bodies that could provide an earthly temple for the searing forces of the incarnating Christ Spirit. They were indeed set apart, a "chosen people" for that mission. Upon the entry of the Christ Spirit into Jesus of Nazareth at his baptism, that mission was accomplished, though Paul recognized and agonized over the fact that his people would be among the last to come to this realization. In fact, all racial, national, and other such prideful distinctions must fade away commensurate with the degree to which humanity takes the Christ into itself.

---

[368] See n. 77.

The nativity is both magnificent and complex. Matthew and Luke each present a version, but scholars have noted that the two versions conflict with one another in many particulars,[369] some irreconcilable,[370] if they purport to describe the birth of the same child. Steiner explained that they describe the births of two different children who become one when the Ego of the child born in Matthew's Gospel leaves its three bodies and enters into the previously egoless three bodies of the child in Luke's Gospel when the latter is twelve years old.[371] A complete account is beyond our present undertaking.[372]

That there was an expectation of a messiah could be laid in some instances to the hopes and rumors that sprang quickly to life in those days. But in other quarters, such as among those who kept alive a semblance of the teachings of the ancient Zarathustra, the magi, there was a deeper expectation.[373] They were able to perceive in the etheric realm their ancient master descending toward another incarnation. Apparently they referred to his descending soul and spirit as his "star"

---

[369] Raymond E. Brown, *The Birth of the Messiah: A Commentary on the Infancy Narratives in the Gospels of Matthew and Luke* (2d ed.; Anchor Bible Reference Library; New York: Doubleday, 1993), 33–37; Edward Reaugh Smith, *The Incredible Births of Jesus* (Hudson, N.Y.: Anthroposophic Press, 1998), 32–36.

[370] Brown, *Birth of the Messiah*, 36: "Indeed, close analysis of the infancy narratives makes it unlikely that either account is completely historical"; Smith, *Incredible Births*, 36, lists four conflicts that are certainly irreconcilable and others that are most likely so.

[371] Starting from the anthroposophical base given by Steiner, Bernard Nesfield-Cookson (*The Mystery of the Two Jesus Children and the Descent of the Spirit of the Sun* [London: Temple Lodge, 2005], 45–68) reviews Christian apocryphal gospels, Gnostic texts, and the Dead Sea Scrolls, all of which he suggests point to the two Jesus children. Plates 13–15 of his book present three works of Renaissance art which he reasons depict the two Jesus children; they are: Raphael, *Madonna del Duca di Terranuova* (Dahlem Gallery, Berlin), which also includes a third child, John the Baptist; Ambrogio Bergognone, *Twelve-year-old Jesus in the Temple* (Museo di Sant' Ambrogio, Milan); Defendente Ferrari, *Twelve-year-old Jesus in the Temple* (State Gallery, Stuttgart).

[372] For a more complete account see Smith, *Burning Bush*, 33–86 and the lectures of Steiner upon which it is based: *According to Luke*; *Gospel of St. Matthew*; and "The Gospels." See also Smith, *Incredible Births*.

[373] It has been suggested that the Nag Hammadi text the *Apocalypse of Adam* is an Essene text reflecting such an expectation. See pp. 105–6.

(Matt 2:2),[374] and so it is reported in Matthew's Gospel, which opens with a genealogy about the preparation of the three bodies, each in fourteen generations (1:17), of the Jesus child into which this wisest individuality would be born again. He is known as the Solomon-Jesus child, having descended from David's son Solomon (1:6).

Luke gives a quite different genealogy, and places it differently. Instead of positioning it before the birth of the child, Luke places it much later, between the baptism of Jesus and his temptations. Unlike Matthew's Gospel, Luke traces Jesus' descent through David's son Nathan (3:31). And instead of tracing Jesus' ancestry back only as far as Abraham, Luke traces it back through Adam to God (3:38). Luke traces the Nathan-Jesus child's lineage back to God because this child and Adam shared the same etheric body, a body brought with them at birth from the spiritual realm. Recall that the elohim had created the human, not on earth, but in the spiritual realm (Gen 1:26–27). Through their divine wisdom the elohim anticipated the fall, that is, the descent into materiality of the astral body that occurred after Lucifer enticed the as yet egoless human to want to experience what it observed down below in the physical body on earth. This desire contaminated or infected, if you will, the human astral body, which the Bible calls the tree of knowledge (2:17; 3:3–7, 22). The elohim further realized that the infected astral body would eventually infect the etheric body, which the Bible calls the tree of life (3:22–24). In order to preserve a pure etheric body unaffected by "original sin" and the "fall," the elohim held back from Adam a part of the undescended etheric body of the first human couple, Adam and his wife. The etheric body so held back was provided by eloha-Yahweh to this Nathan-Jesus child and his very young mother. The child had no need for an Ego during his first twelve years, the pure etheric body being sufficient as a provisional Ego for that period of time. The child was completely unsophisticated, naive to worldly ways, but having a divine love of, and compassion for, all creatures.

---

[374] It was this Zarathustra who, during the Ancient Persian cultural age, had perceived the descending Christ in the sun's aura and called it the Ahura Mazda, the Great Aura, and whose own name meant lustrous, radiant, or shining star.

So we have two Jesus children, the Luke child having been born long enough after the Matthew child to avoid the slaughter of the innocents described in Matthew's Gospel and the Matthew child having been saved from it by his family's flight to Egypt.

Only one incident is described in the life of either child prior to the baptism at thirty years of age. That incident is the one in the temple when the Nathan-Jesus child was twelve years old. The two Jesus families were friendly neighbors in the small community of Nazareth. By the time the Nathan-Jesus was twelve years of age, his mother and the father of the Solomon-Jesus had both died. The father of the Nathan-Jesus child took the mother of the Solomon-Jesus child and her surviving children (Mark 6:3) into his home, combining their families.

About this time, in a phenomenon known to the ancient initiates, the Zarathustra Ego had left the bodies of the Solomon-Jesus child (which then withered and died) and entered into the theretofore egoless bodies of the pure Nathan-Jesus child. This critical transition, as the child's wisdom in the temple demonstrated (Luke 2:46–47), is what so baffled his parents, for up till then the Nathan-Jesus child had shown a divine relationship to all of God's creatures but was totally unsophisticated in an earthly sense. It is from the time when the Solomon-Jesus child's Ego entered the Nathan-Jesus child until he was thirty years old that this individual could properly be known as Jesus of Nazareth.

Then, at the time of his baptism, as all four gospels relate in the descent of the dove and the heavenly pronouncement of divine Sonship, the descending Christ Spirit entered into Jesus as the Zarathustra Ego sacrificially withdrew, so that during the three-year ministry this individual is properly known as Jesus Christ.

The Christ Spirit, having lit on Jesus, had to enter fully into his three bodies. This is immediately described in Matthew and Luke as the three temptations (Matt 4:1–11; Luke 4:1–13).[375]

---

[375] Mark condenses the account of Christ's entry into Jesus' three bodies to the astral body, which he calls "wild beasts" (1:13), an appropriate designation of the astral nature that each must struggle to perfect.

So the Gospels of Matthew and Luke each give their respective version of the years that precede Jesus' ministry. More accurately it should be said that each gives an aspect, an essential aspect, rather than a full version. The two apparently conflicting gospel accounts must be addressed as a unity because neither is adequate standing alone, inasmuch as they tell of the births of two different children. In two thousand years no other account has been able to so fully reconcile and magnify the two gospel accounts, for the assumption that they tell of the birth of a single child has only led to increasing doubt about their historical accuracy.

Now what has been said above relates just to the first part of what Steiner calls the Mystery of Golgotha, which in its fullness is the Christ event on the stage of world history. Its fullness was not known in the ancient mysteries, but that there was a descending Christ was perceived, and its fullness was revealed to some early Christians who passed it down. But that knowledge was fully lost to Christendom by the fourth century. Only with the wisdom that came to light through such as Steiner has it again become possible to comprehend what these gospels are telling.

The Authenticity of the Secret Gospel of Mark:

The Current Challengers

Since the Secret Gospel of Mark is integral to this book's argument, we close Book Three with a reply to the recent allegations by Stephen Carlson and Peter Jeffery that Morton Smith, the discoverer of this manuscript, forged it himself. As I noted in the opening chapter of Book One, in the summer of 2003, Charles Hedrick pressed the New Testament guild to end the stalemate on the issue of this gospel's authenticity, noting that the longstanding suspicions against Smith remained unsubstantiated. Hedrick's call had the opposite effect to what he intended. Less than two years later, on May 9, 2005, Carlson announced on his blog that his paper "Identifying the Hand of Secret Mark" had been accepted for presentation in program unit Paleographical Studies in the Ancient Near East at the SBL convention in Philadelphia that November.[376] The hand it purported to identify, in a very roundabout manner, was Smith's. On an Internet discussion group on May 16, 2005, one of Carlson's supporters wrote to him, "Scott G. Brown has written a book defending the authenticity of Secret Mark." Carlson immediately replied, "I've read the book. I think that it will become obsolete in about five or six months."[377] That time frame pointed to the publication date for his own book, *The Gospel Hoax*, which was launched in the exhibit hall of the same SBL meeting in order to capitalize on the hype surrounding his presentation. Ironically, in the intervening years Carlson himself has been taken rather effectively to task on every point he makes in his book, whereas he has failed to obsolete Brown's book or even knock a dent in its arguments.

---

[376] Stephen C. Carlson, "My SBL Paper Proposal Accepted," *Hypotyposeis*, posted May 9, 2005, http://www.hypotyposeis.org/weblog/2005/05/my-sbl-paper-proposal-accepted.html.
[377] Stephen C. Carlson, e-mail to crosstalk2 mailing list, May 16, 2005, http://groups.yahoo.com/group/crosstalk2/message/18968.

Although Carlson's book is the more famous of the allegations against Smith, the greater diversity of issues in Carlson's book prompts me to look first at Jeffery's *The Secret Gospel of Mark Unveiled*.

Jeffery's Book

Jeffery's argument that the *Letter to Theodore* is a modern forgery, most likely by Smith, revolves around two principal contentions. First, the letter describes Secret Mark as a reading for baptism that, in terms of its implicit theology, does not fit anywhere in the history of the liturgy of the Alexandrian church. Second, the letter's two gospel quotations depict a kind of homosexual relationship between Jesus and the young man that was standard in Smith's milieu but not in that of Jesus or Mark. If the sexual mores of ancient Athens prevailed in Jesus' Palestine and Mark's Alexandria, then the normal same-sex relationship was between an older, amorous, yet basically bisexual lover and his passive but selective teenage beloved. In Secret Mark, however, the two men are close in age, the relationship is egalitarian, and the younger one is the pursuer.[378]

First Point—An Anachronistic Reading for Baptism

On his first point, Jeffery writes to an academic audience that is largely predisposed to accept his premise. I was surprised to learn from Brown that the scholars who had opined on the matter had almost unanimously agreed with Smith that the incident in Secret Mark describes some type of baptismal event. Brown states to me in an e-mail on April 21, 2009, "I think I'm the only person who argues for a non-cultic interpretation in which the longer gospel is interpreted allegorically in the context of the transmission of the secret gnostic tradition." The position I take supports Brown's conclusion that the incident in the letter is not baptismal.

---

[378] Jeffery, *Unveiled*. Jeffery's first point occupies the first ninety pages, chs. 1–4. The rest of his text, chs. 5–11, are devoted to the second.

Jeffery does not make any arguments based on the physical manuscript or its handwriting. His book is predominantly involved with
Smith's interpretation and its implications, arguing that they are not
historically plausible. That approach is fundamentally mistaken. As
Brown demonstrates in a detailed review of Jeffery's book, "Jeffery
has confused Morton Smith's misinterpretation of the letter with the
letter itself." Brown makes a cogent point: "Anyone who argues that
Smith forged this text is bound to believe that it basically means what
Smith claimed it meant, for the story of a forger who misunderstood
his own proof text is a really hard sell." So Jeffery is bound to suppose
that the Secret Gospel depicts Jesus baptizing the young man. But
Jeffery does not mention an inconvenient fact: Smith's baptismal
interpretation "did not originate with Smith. It was suggested to
him by Cyril C. Richardson, a professor of church history at Union
Theological Seminary who was in attendance when Smith announced
his discovery of the manuscript at the 1960 meeting of the Society of
Biblical Literature (SBL)."[379] Even more problematic is the fact that,
as Brown further notes, "Richardson himself ultimately adopted an
entirely different interpretation of the letter and the gospel quotations
after realizing some of the problems with his baptismal interpretation, including the fact that the great mysteries"—the term used
in the letter to describe the setting in which this gospel was read—
"could not denote baptism because Clement explicitly dissociated
these mysteries from baptism in *Strom.* 5.11.70.7–71.1."[380] Rather,
as Brown elaborates, in Clement's writings the great mysteries are
theological mysteries about God and his realm that were taught to
the most advanced students as secrets concealed within the scriptures.

---

[379] Scott G. Brown, essay review of Peter Jeffery, *The Secret Gospel of Mark Unveiled*,
Review of Biblical Literature (September 15, 2007): 21, http://www.bookreviews.org/
pdf/5627_5944.pdf. Jeffery's responses are on his website: "The Secret Gospel of Mark
Unveiled: Reply to Scott G. Brown," Peter Jeffery's Home Page, http://www.music.princeton.
edu/~jeffery/replytobrown.pdf; http://music.princeton.edu/~jeffery/Review_of_Biblical_
Literature-Jeffery_reply_to_Brown.pdf.

[380] Brown, review of Jeffery, 22, citing Cyril C. Richardson, review of Morton Smith,
Clement of Alexandria and a Secret Gospel of Mark and *The Secret Gospel*, *Theological Studies*
35 (1974): 574–76.

So the actual situation is that Smith fundamentally misinterpreted his own find, and he did so in language apt to trouble many readers, especially the conjectural snippets about physical union that were not part of his main argument and that he made no later effort to defend. But his interpretation is irrelevant, except perhaps to show his innocence.

While I concur with Brown's conclusion that the incident depicted was not baptismal, and also with his rationale based upon Clement's three uses of the phrase "the great mysteries" in his *Stromateis*, my main reason for concurring with his conclusion is not one he addresses. It has to do with the Secret Gospel text itself. There is widespread recognition that it depicts a version of the Lazarus event. The Secret Mark version involves two events, the resuscitation and then, six days later, Jesus teaching the youth the mystery of the kingdom of God. John's account presents both aspects as a single event, the raising. Smith construed the raising portion of Secret Mark as a miracle and focused upon the nature and meaning of the later teaching event. The dichotomy of Secret Mark's version lends itself to the controversial interpretation of Smith and to the differing views of the scholars who have wrestled with its issues. Were it not for this dual nature these issues would not have arisen. Nothing in John's account gives any basis for thinking that a baptism was involved. This is important if John's version is the more reliable.

However, since I agree with Brown's conclusions and supporting rationale to the effect that the text of Secret Mark does not describe a baptismal event, I refer the reader to Brown's published review of Jeffery's book.

SECOND POINT—GAY IN THE WRONG WAY

Brown labels his review of Jeffery's second point "The Gay Gospel Hypothesis (Once More)."[381] Brown's review effectively rebuts Jeffery's contention, point by point, obviating the need for laborious repetition beyond brief illustration below.

---

[381] Brown, review of Jeffery, 23. The phrase "The Gay Gospel Hypothesis," as it referred to critics of Morton Smith's discovery, first appeared in Brown, "Question of Motive," 353, prior to Jeffery's book.

On this second point, Jeffery's book is a study in how to read into spiritual language meanings of the most prurient sort. He says at the outset that he proposes to see in the language of the Secret Gospel "humorous double entendre,"[382] but one senses that his interpretation of the letter tends to veer from the humorous to the scandalous, for he endeavors to unveil the most imaginative and lurid sexual innuendos. The book presumes moral depravity to be the essence of Smith's character and intent—a harsh judgment upon one generally deemed a scholar of high order.

Jeffery says his second point about homosexuality provides a simpler basis for judgment than the issue of early liturgical history. The letter, he says, is a "cento [i.e., patchwork] of words and phrases from the canonical gospels and other ancient writings, carefully structured to create the impression that Jesus practiced homosexuality."[383] His opening salvo refers to Mark's fleeing youth (Mark 14:51–52), noting that he was *naked*. It sets the tone for the segue that follows: "In fact, by slightly shifting the translation of a single word, we can read the entire Secret Gospel addition as an account of Jesus rejecting a woman in order to help an anguished young man 'come out of the closet' for his first (homo)sexual experience":

> And they come into Bethany, and a certain woman whose brother had died was there. And coming, she *bent down to kiss* [*prosekynēse;* italics added] Jesus and says to him, "Son of David, have mercy on me." But the disciples rebuked her. And Jesus, being angered, went off with her into the garden where the tomb was, and straightway a great cry was heard from the tomb. And going near Jesus rolled away the stone from the door of the tomb. And straightway, going in where the youth was, he stretched forth his hand and raised him, seizing his hand. But the youth, looking upon him, loved him and began to beseech him that he might be with him. And going out of the tomb they came into the house of the youth, for he was rich.[384]

---

[382] Jeffery, *Unveiled*, 93.
[383] Jeffery, *Unveiled*, 91.
[384] Jeffery, *Unveiled*, 92 (the italics and bracketed addition are Jeffery's).

Jeffery says that "in the mid-twentieth century it was thought that the word [*prosekynēse*] was related etymologically to the notion of kissing, as one might kiss an idol," thus, "bent down to kiss," which has the advantage of "making a coherent narrative out of what had been a sequence of perplexing events." He then explains what this retranslation clarifies: "For example, the anger of Jesus and the rebukes of the disciples would be particularly understandable if the Secret Evangelist was an English speaker who wanted to imply that, while 'coming, she bent down to kiss Jesus,' the woman was 'coming' in the slang English sense—that is, 'experiencing sexual orgasm.'"[385]

Jeffery thinks the Secret Gospel's use of the word "hand(s)" ("stretched forth his hand and raised him, seizing his hand") expresses sexual activity—a rather surprising inference given that hands are used in virtually every human activity, including very sacred ones. But he sees mischief in the imagery here: "The pointless duplication of hands is a *sure sign* that something's afoot" (emphasis mine). He rightly acknowledges that Mark often describes Jesus' use of his hands (1:31, 41; 5:23, 41; 6:2; 7:32; 8:22, 23, 25; 9:27; 10:16). But language that is sacred in the canonical gospel becomes prurient in Secret Mark, at least in Jeffery's eyes. He thinks that Secret Mark's hand references have been "repositioned to suggest homosexuality … in at least three ways," all of which stretch credulity too far to merit repetition here, but they permit Jeffery to emphasize the *nakedness* [*sic*] of the youth during the evening of instruction. After six days, the youth *comes* to Jesus "in the dark of night, minimally clothed … [and] finds out who Jesus really is."[386]

With reference to all of this, Jeffery asks, "Was the Secret Evangelist a twentieth-century American bent on teasing us? Or am I, a product of mid-twentieth-century American schoolyard culture, misreading an ancient text through prurient eyes?" Good question. And one, he says, that "will haunt us for the rest of this book."[387] The above is a taste of all that follows. His arguments succeed only in showing how much

---

[385] Jeffery, *Unveiled*, 92–93.
[386] Jeffery, *Unveiled*, 93, 94–95.
[387] Jeffery, *Unveiled*, 93.

ingenuity is needed to characterize this story as an anachronistic tale of homosexual desire. Those wanting a more extensive treatment can turn to Brown's review.

FORGERY AND THE BURDEN OF PROOF

Forgery is everywhere within the modern Western world considered a crime, one involving moral turpitude. The lay mind naturally tends to consider that a person of bad character who is charged with a crime is probably guilty. But the wisdom of the courts prohibits the prosecution from introducing evidence of the bad character of the defendant unless and until the defendant has introduced evidence of his or her own good character. No scholar to my knowledge has attempted to support the authenticity of Smith's find by introducing evidence of his good character.

That Jeffery approaches his subject matter in criminal investigation mode seems clear. Chapter one is introductory, but the book's conclusions are clearly telegraphed by the moral depravity of Smith that it implies. Even before we get to chapter one, we find the acknowledgments concluded with "And I pray for the late Morton Smith—may God rest his anguished soul." Of course there is nothing wrong or even unusual about stating a book's conclusions at the outset. However, it does point to the criteria upon which judgment is predicated. Chapter one gives some relevant history but does so in a way that places Smith as a suspect at the outset. Chapter two gives some worthy history of the treatment of the matter. But its tenor is suggested by the condition of "read[ing] the Mar Saba document with the suspicions of a profiler," terminology related to criminal detection. That would lead, he suggests, to a consideration of "the secretive initiation liturgies in the church of Alexandria, where the Secret Gospel was read."[388]

One cannot be convicted of forgery so long as there is any reasonable doubt about guilt. A jury in a criminal case must be charged that it can arrive at a guilty verdict only if it is convinced of guilt

---

[388] Jeffery, *Unveiled*, 54.

beyond a reasonable doubt. Most scholars who have dealt with the issue have given Secret Mark the benefit of the doubt. The point is that the most its detractors can do is raise doubt, but that doubt is almost always associated with suspicion based largely on inadmissible evidence, defamatory in nature, of Smith's character without which doubt could hardly arise, let alone proof of guilt beyond a reasonable doubt. Jeffery himself laments that "Almost all the discussion has been focused on the Secret Gospel and its relationship to canonical Mark."[389] Yet this is really the primary, if not the only, area of relevance.[390] In this regard obviously a physical examination of the document is highly relevant. Smith's detractors put the onus upon him to have produced the document for examination. The evidence shows that shortly after Smith published his books the document was made unavailable by circumstances beyond Smith's control. In any event it is the responsibility of those who claim Smith is a forger to produce the document for examination, and, other than Quentin Quesnell, there is no showing that any of his antagonists made any serious effort to do so.

No antagonist has produced any evidence that Smith ever intentionally and knowingly deceived another person in any manner, criminal or otherwise, outside of the allegations regarding his discovery itself. In other words, there is no evidence of prior criminal acts upon which to conclude beyond a reasonable doubt that he acted to deceive by forging Secret Mark. It is irrelevant that he might have had the skills to do so, a point demonstrated later to be in considerable doubt in spite of his admitted scholarship.[391] There must be evidence that he did. Aside from physical examination of the document itself, the issue must be decided from the content of the document itself in its relationship with the work of Clement and the content of canonical Mark. Whatever doubt may remain must relate to the lack of the

---

[389] Jeffery, *Unveiled*, 42.

[390] Meyer, *Secret Gospels*, 115: "Instead of using the fragments to formulate conjectures about the historical Jesus, after the manner of Smith, we may rather interpret the fragments within the redactional history of the Markan tradition"; cf. 119.

[391] Scott G. Brown, "The Question of Ability in the Case against Morton Smith" (unpublished).

physical document, but this doubt can in no way establish forgery, nor is its absence evidence of forgery.

The real foundation of Jeffery's case is Smith's own mistaken interpretation of what he found and Jeffery's inadmissible, personal judgment that Smith was morally depraved.

Carlson's Book

As a teenager in the mid-1980s, Carlson noticed the reference to Secret Mark in *Holy Blood, Holy Grail*. His idea that it was a fake first arose when he read an article by Andrew Criddle in 1995. But Carlson was stirred to debunk Secret Mark as a Morton Smith forgery by three events in 2003, only one of which, the triptych headed by Hedrick's "Stalemate in the Academy" article, dealt specifically with Secret Mark. Moreover, Carlson was encouraged to publish a book by three professors and one publisher. Two of those professors, Mark Goodacre, assistant professor of religion at Duke University, and Larry Hurtado, professor in the divinity school at New College, University of Edinburgh, wrote back-cover plaudits for the book. Hurtado wrote the foreword in which he all but pronounces the issue of Secret Mark's authenticity resolved in the negative by Carlson's "persuasive, decisive, practically unanswerable" text. While obviously doubting that such could be done, he did leave room for refutation "in at least an equally detailed and thorough manner."[392] Hurtado invites Carlson's reader to inspect all that has been set forth against the claim of Smith forgery. I suggest that the defense case is even more "detailed and thorough" and, moreover, is even more "persuasive, decisive, practically unanswerable" than Carlson's work.

But Hurtado errs on one point. He puts the burden on the defendant (Smith) rather than the prosecutor (Carlson) in this case. It is upon Carlson that the burden of proof lies. His is the burden of persuasion.

---

[392] Larry W. Hurtado, foreword to Stephen C. Carlson, *The Gospel Hoax: Morton Smith's Invention of Secret Mark* (Waco, Tex.: Baylor University Press, 2005), xii.

THE STANDARD OF PROOF

Anyone claiming forgery, a criminal act involving moral turpitude, has the burden of proof so that any uncertainty on the matter must be resolved in favor of the defendant, Morton Smith in this case. It would be naive to think that all minds require the same level of proof on the issue of forgery by Smith. Everyone comes to it with certain biases to begin with. Nevertheless, it is well for each to reflect upon the pertinent wisdom that has evolved on the matter within our judicial system. Over many centuries the courts of law have established rules pertaining to the required burden of proof. We should first bear in mind that the ancient practice, more or less sanctioned in those earlier times, of writing pseudonymously has no relevance in modern laws on forgery, at least on our issue.

Three distinct levels of proof are generally recognized. The first is proof by a "preponderance of the evidence." This is the level required in civil cases (not involving fraud). The middle level is that required, for instance, in federal tax matters where the government is not seeking a criminal conviction but collection of the civil fraud penalty. In such cases the standard is "clear and convincing" proof. The third level applicable in virtually all criminal fraud cases is proof "beyond a reasonable doubt."

At issue in Carlson's *The Gospel Hoax* is forgery by Smith. Forgery and fraud are blood related, forgery being just a specific type of fraud, requiring the same level of proof. Carlson's own website recognizes this.[393]

Which standard should apply to our question? Morton Smith is dead. And while some have criticized belated attempts to label Smith a forger when he is no longer alive to defend himself, it is true that one cannot be convicted of a crime postmortem. But if we consider the present issue one of civil fraud, is the standard thus lessened? Some cases have held that the standard should still be the

---

[393] Stephen C. Carlson, "Legal Definitions of Forgery and Fraud," *Hypotyposeis*, posted February 25, 2004, http://www.hypotyposeis.org/weblog/2004/02/legal-definitions-of-forgery-and-fraud.html.

same.[394] What we have just been discussing relates to the different levels of proof applicable in arriving at a verdict. Few parties who lose any lawsuit feel that the right verdict has been rendered. So, what we've been saying must be held by each individual reader in mind in determining what level he or she will require. Certainly there are those, like the losers in lawsuits, that will not be convinced no matter the level of proof. At the very least, however, it is hoped that consideration will only be given to evidence that is admissible under the general civil standard developed by our courts over the centuries under the common law applicable in our society. Carlson's allegation of forgery by Smith must be supported by the "preponderance" of that evidence, and the "burden of persuasion" is upon him and not upon those who would defend Smith.

Finally, we should not be misled by Carlson's clever effort, recognized by Hurtado, to escape this burden of proof by virtue of the premise that the document is a "hoax."[395] Let us be clear, the alleged hoax in this case requires a forgery. Carlson's position is that this technicality excuses him from meeting the stiff "beyond a reasonable doubt" burden of proof applicable in *criminal* cases. He speaks of the "crime of cheating" and "criminal forgery done to defraud."[396] Carlson attempts to escape this heaviest burden by claiming that the document was forged only to embarrass other scholars, as if professional embarrassment to reputable scholars would not have been damage equivalent to Smith's own monetary gain. But even where "consideration" or "monetary gain" would be required, that gain can

---

[394] For the burden of proof in cases of insurance fraud, see Financial Ombudsman Service, "Aspects of Insurance Fraud," *Ombudsman News* 41 (November 2004), http://www.financial-ombudsman.org.uk/publications/ombudsman-news/41/41_aspects _ins.htm, which reads in pertinent part: "An allegation of fraud should not be made lightly. The burden of proof is on the insurer, if it suspects that fraud has taken place. Strictly speaking, the civil standard of proof 'on the balance of probabilities' applies. However, some courts have acknowledged that stronger evidence than this is usually required, which has the practical effect of raising the burden of proof to a degree more akin to the criminal standard of 'beyond reasonable doubt.'"

[395] Carlson, *Gospel Hoax*, 78–79; Hurtado, foreword to *Gospel Hoax*, xii.

[396] Carlson, *Gospel Hoax*, 79.

be minimal, and who can say that Smith got nothing for his own publication whether in immediate royalties or from other professional gain or enhancement? Nevertheless, if intentional damage to others, such as professional embarrassment, is not the equivalent to monetary gain to self in *criminal* cases, it would seem to be sufficient in *civil* cases, at least morally, where the center of judgments must lie in this case. Should Carlson's position excuse him from the lesser standard applicable in *civil* cases? He does not appear to make that claim. And even if he were now to successfully make that claim, he would not be excused from the need to rebut positive evidence that Smith did not forge the letter.

In any case, let us proceed to marshal the various points of evidence that Carlson has advanced and consider how they stand up against the evidence adduced in defense of Smith's alleged discovery.

THE CARLSON ISSUES

Carlson's case for forgery by Smith consists essentially of the thirteen issues listed below (the page references are to where in his book he raises the issue).

1. The original is not available for investigation (*Gospel Hoax*, 13)
2. The letter in question is the only evidence of the existence of Secret Mark (*Hoax*, 1, 49)
3. Smith was well prepared to write Secret Mark (*Hoax*, 8, 74)
4. The year 1958 was an unsettling time for Smith (*Hoax*, 8, 79–80)
5. Smith displayed a pre-1958 interest in Clement and other relevant subjects (*Hoax*, 8–9)
6. The Voss edition could have been purchased by Smith on the used book market (*Hoax*, 45)
7. Clement didn't write the letter (*Hoax*, 54–64)
8. The 1940 novel *The Mystery of Mar Saba* could have inspired Smith to forge Secret Mark (*Hoax*, 19, 79)
9. Smith's dedication of his book to "the one who knows" is a clue that he forged the letter (*Hoax*, 79)

10. The Secret Gospel, the manuscript, and the letter belong to the twentieth century (*Hoax*, xvii, 23–72)
11. The Madiotes—bald swindler clue (*Hoax*, 42–47)
12. The Morton Salt clue (*Hoax*, 58–64)
13. Andrew Criddle's argument that the letter is too Clementine to be by Clement (*Hoax*, 50–54)

Following discussion of these thirteen points we will consider various ongoing developments.

RESPONSES TO CARLSON'S ISSUES

1. The original is not available for investigation

This issue is of interest to all parties. Both sides of this controversy hope that the document will eventually be produced for expert examination. Guy Stroumsa established that it continued to reside at the Mar Saba library undisturbed until 1976 (this is a period of eighteen years from the time of its discovery), at which time a Greek Orthodox monk brought it to the Patriarchate library in Jerusalem but he refused to let it be taken to the Israeli police for a professional examination. Although a librarian removed the manuscript pages from the Voss book prior to photographing them, despite repeated requests, Western scholars have not been permitted to see them since 1983.[397] Recently, a Greek paleographer named Agamemnon Tselikas searched the Patriarchate library in Jerusalem for the manuscript and failed to find it. The library considers the issue closed.

Clearly Smith never at any time had the right to control the document so as to be able to produce it for expert examination, nor did he ever take any action to prevent any interested party from examining it.[398] Absent Smith's affirmative obstruction of any such effort, the mere absence of physical examination of the document is not evidence of forgery. Moreover, the burden is on the one alleging

---

[397] Brown, *Mark's Other Gospel*, 25–26; Stroumsa, "Comments."
[398] Brown, *Mark's Other Gospel*, 36.

forgery to produce the document and have it examined. The fact that Carlson came on the scene too late to produce and examine the document neither excuses him from that burden nor permits him to place the responsibility for it on Smith, particularly at a time when Smith is no longer alive to make any such effort.

2. The letter in question is the only evidence of the existence of Secret Mark

Carlson's point is well raised, though it is only the absence of an item of evidence that if produced would tend to corroborate Smith's claim, not evidence of a forgery by him. Smith himself recognized the point Carlson makes and gave a plausible explanation for the lack of any prior evidence of the letter's existence.[399] His four-page discussion includes the statement, "There are a number of examples of texts that have survived for a thousand years without being cited...."[400] Very pertinent are his following comments: "We know that a collection of Clement's letters did exist in the Monastery of Mar Saba during the eighth century. Three passages from them were quoted by a writer called John of Damascus, who worked there from 716 to 749. Since no trace of Clement's letters is found anywhere else, it seems probable that our letter did come from this collection. It certainly came from some collection; that is proved by its heading, 'From the letters of Clement.' John of Damascus cites a 'twenty-first letter,' so there must have been at least that many in his collection; probably there were more."[401]

General Nature of Issues Three through Nine

Notably, at the end of his chapter two, having recounted a few "known fakes" that he calls "parallels," Carlson admits, "These parallels

---

[399] Smith, *Secret Gospel*, 143–47; see also Smith, *Clement*, 287, and its argument that such absence in the period before Smith's discovery is more in keeping with Clementine authorship than with forgery, for a forgery can serve no purpose unless people know of its existence.

[400] Smith, *Secret Gospel*, 145.

[401] Smith, *Secret Gospel*, 143–44.

between *Secret Mark* and known fakes may be grounds for suspicion but are not proof."[402] Very true.

His statement would apply to each of his seven issues numbered 3 through 9. Each is an attempt to arouse suspicion. To what extent can suspicion substitute for evidence? Are circumstances that raise suspicion themselves circumstantial evidence upon which a prosecution can be based? In general the answer to both should be no, as Carlson's point rightly recognizes. But in fairness, can we leave it at that? Where do suspicious circumstances themselves become circumstantial evidence?

A case before the Supreme Court of Canada (whose common laws derive from the common law of England, as do ours in the United States) involved a challenge to the validity of a will where the challengers introduced evidence of suspicious circumstances bearing upon whether the will was executed under undue influence. Justice Sopinka stated, "Suspicious circumstances may be raised by (1) circumstances surrounding the preparation of the will, (2) circumstances tending to call into question the capacity of the testator, or (3) circumstances tending to show that the free will of the testator was overborne by acts of coercion or fraud." Earlier he had said that such "evidence must, however, be scrutinized in accordance with the gravity of the suspicion.... The extent of the proof required is proportionate to the gravity of the suspicion and the degree of suspicion varies with the circumstances of each case."[403] It should be noted that this was a civil proceeding. While it spoke of the possibility of the instrument having resulted from fraud, it was not aimed at determining the guilt or innocence of a defendant, as in a forgery case where the burden of proof is likely to be heavier. But at the very least the ruling indicates that circumstances giving rise to suspicion can only be considered in relation to evidence that explains or contradicts the otherwise suspicious character of the alleged circumstances. Nothing Carlson presents by way of such circumstance is free from countervailing evidence, usually overwhelmingly so.

---

[402] Carlson, *Gospel Hoax*, 20.
[403] Vout v. Hay, 2 S.C.R. 876 (1995), http://scc.lexum.org/en/1995/1995scr2-876/1995scr2-876.html.

3. Smith was well prepared to write Secret Mark

Any question of Smith's ability to have done what Carson accuses him of doing would only be relevant to show that he did not do it. An affirmative showing of ability is not even a suspicious circumstance, let alone evidence of forgery. But it has been affirmatively shown that Smith did not have the requisite ability.[404]

The following is from Roy Kotansky, a scholar who knew and worked closely with Smith on transcription projects:

> I am a scholar of magic, and though I did my Ph.D. on magic at Chicago (1988) under Dieter Betz, I asked Morton Smith, a longtime colleague and friend, to be my principal reader, outside of Chicago. My work, on the magical lamellae, has long since been published in a Cologne papyrological series. As a managing editor of Betz's *Greek Magical Papyri in Translation*, years ago, I also read, and critiqued, all of the contributors' translations, including those of Morton Smith. What strikes me most about the issue of forgery with SM, is not that Morton would have done this at all (he wouldn't have, of course), but rather that he COULD NOT have done it: his Greek, though very good, was not that of a true papyrologist (or philologist); his translations of the big sections of PGM XIII did not always appreciate the subtleties and nuances of the text's idioms, I believe, and he seemed very appreciative of my corrections, at that time. He certainly could not have produced either the Greek cursive script of the Mar Saba ms., nor its gram- matical text, as we have it. There are few up to this sort of task.... He would never forge, nor could he. I was with him once at the Getty Museum examining magical gemstones in the collection in the '80s, and many times I had to gently correct his misreadings of

---

[404] Scott G. Brown, "Reply to Stephen Carlson," *Expository Times* 117 (2006): 148; idem, "Question of Ability"; Allan J. Pantuck and Scott G. Brown, "Morton Smith as M. Madiotes: Stephen Carlson's Attribution of *Secret Mark* to a Bald Swindler," *Journal for the Study of the Historical Jesus* 6 (2008): 112–16, noting errors in Smith's transcription of the names Madiotes and Anobos in his entry for MS 22 in his catalog of Mar Saba's manuscripts; see also the professional handwriting analysis by Venetia Anastasopoulou in "Ongoing Developments," below.

rather obvious readings. Morton was not a palaeographer/epigraphist, nor a papyrologist. I don't think that he read these kinds of Greek texts very well.[405]

I witnessed Scott Brown's discovery of one item of evidence that shows beyond the shadow of a doubt that Smith could not have been the Secret Gospel's author. The item is described by Brown in his "The Question of Ability." We were both in attendance at the same seminar in New York City in March 2007. While in the city we met at the library at the Jewish Theological Seminary (JTS) where Brown was examining the annotations that Smith had written inside the books that now comprise its Morton Smith collection. Well I recall his returning to our table with Smith's copy of C. H. Dodd's *Historical Tradition in the Fourth Gospel*.[406] On page 249, Dodd had noted, "Among these topographical notes [in John's Gospel] there are three which refer to the work of John the Baptist," which he identified as John 1:28 ("This took place in Bethany beyond the Jordan, where John was baptizing"), 10:40 ("He went away again across the Jordan to the place where John at first baptized, and there he remained"), and 3:23 ("John also was baptizing at Aenon near Salim, because there was much water there . . ."—this was located in Judea, west of the Jordan). Dodd continues, "Taking x.40 to be a mere back reference to i.28, we have two distinct statements regarding the scene of the Baptist's activity at two separate periods of his life."

Starting opposite the reference to 10:40, Smith had written in the margin, "This ∴ is Bethany. So the journey back was from Bethany to Bethany?! Some mix up here."

This comment shows us the moment when Smith first realized that there were two places called Bethany involved in the raising of Lazarus: it was no earlier than 1963, five years after his work at Mar Saba. This is interesting in itself, for the forger of a gospel pericope based on this narrative would surely know this fact about the raising of Lazarus.

---

[405] Roy Kotansky, e-mail to Scott Brown, August 17, 2006.
[406] C. H. Dodd, *Historical Tradition in the Fourth Gospel* (Cambridge: Cambridge University Press, 1963).

But more importantly, it shows Smith's ignorance of a fundamental fact about Secret Mark, namely, that its own account of the raising of the young man is set in this other Bethany east of the Jordan as Brown had demonstrated in 2003."[407]

What Brown has made clear is that there was a Bethany in Perea, as suggested by John 1:28 ("in Bethany beyond the Jordan, where John was baptizing"). Its location was plausibly shown by Rami Khouri in his 2005 article in the *Biblical Archaeology Review*.[408] Immediately following it was Brown's companion article.[409] The two tend to corroborate each other's conclusions that indeed there was a Bethany beyond Jordan, and indeed Secret Mark's description of the journey to Jerusalem had integrity within itself. Clearly Secret Mark has the youth being raised and instructed in the mystery of the kingdom of God in this Bethany on the east side of the Jordan.

Smith could not have written Secret Mark when he did not even understand the geographical setting the story so clearly describes.

4. The year 1958 was an unsettling time for Smith

In his search for clues Carlson conceives the notion that 1958 was a moment when Smith's life was at a low ebb and he needed some stimulant to his career. The perpetration of a hoax on the academy would be a perfect solution, so Carlson suggests: "These were unsettling times for Smith, however; he was denied tenure at Brown in 1955 and was a visiting professor at Drew before securing a position at Columbia in 1957 where he would spend the rest of his career."[410]

Carlson's point here is that the time of Smith's discovery was "a vulnerable point in Smith's life when few people of importance

---

[407] Scott G. Brown, "Bethany beyond the Jordan: John 1:28 and the Longer Gospel of Mark," *Revue Biblique* 110 (2003): 497–516.

[408] Rami Khouri, "Where John Baptized: Bethany beyond the Jordan," *Biblical Archaeology Review* 31, no. 1 (January/February 2005): 34–43.

[409] Scott G. Brown, "The Secret Gospel of Mark: Is It Real? And Does It Identify 'Bethany beyond the Jordan'?" *Biblical Archaeology Review* 31, no. 1 (January/February 2005): 44–49, 60–61.

[410] Carlson, *Gospel Hoax*, 8.

appreciated his abilities."[411] This description of Smith's situation is an inference—a guess—which may be compared to what Smith's eminent peers were actually saying about him around this time. Here is what Erwin Goodenough, professor of the history of religion at Yale, had to say:[412] "He is the only young man I know, that is, who gives promise of being a great scholar in the religions of the Roman world in the tradition of G. F. Moore. For his mind is as critical and constructive as his equipment is fabulous";[413] "As a scholar he is sound as a rock, and he has a high standing indeed in his field. I know no American of his age more likely to come into the great succession of scholars in Classics and Early Christianity than he is. In our field, mine very close to his, we often disagree, but I know no one in the world whose approval I had rather have, and it hurts when he, often caustically, refuses it";[414] and again, "He has tremendous scholarly range, acute critical powers, and impressive productivity."[415]

Allan Pantuck, presently on the medical faculty of UCLA, sensing a bum rap against his former religion professor, undertook an investigation of Smith's archives and, as he expected, found many exculpatory documents. Sensitive of the proprietary interests of JTS he opted to present them by PowerPoint at the pro and con panel on Secret Mark at the 2008 SBL convention. Among Pantuck's exhibits were correspondence Smith had with others, the contents of which confute Carlson's guesses about Smith's career anxieties. We learn, for instance, that although it is true that Smith's contract was not renewed at Brown in 1955, as a junior assistant professor he had not yet been considered for tenure, and his letters demonstrate that he was neither overly intent on staying there nor distraught by the denial, the reasons for which had nothing to do with his scholarly competence. In fact, Smith himself believed that he was dismissed by his department's chair, who was intimidated by Smith's acumen

---

[411] Carlson, *Gospel Hoax*, 79–80.
[412] Provided to me by Allan Pantuck.
[413] Letter dated March 29, 1955, to Alastair Cameron.
[414] Letter dated December 15, 1959, from Erwin Goodenough to Richard Morris.
[415] Letter dated October 20, 1959, to Norman Malcolm.

rather than unimpressed with him. Smith acknowledged his need for employment but only as a prerequisite to eating, for teaching kept him from more cerebral pursuits that he had in mind. Moreover, as even Carlson recognizes, well before Smith went to Mar Saba in 1958 he had secured a faculty position at Columbia that eventually led to tenure and employment for the rest of his life. Carlson himself acknowledges that "this motive ... was overtaken by events," citing Smith's employment in 1957 as well as other academic successes well before his 1973 publications.[416]

Carlson ignores another serious problem. Smith had become tenured before he announced his discovery late in 1960, a fact not mentioned by Carlson. Since one of the things that can terminate one's tenure is action that reflects moral turpitude, such as forgery, why, if Smith had originally forged the document to help his career, would he then publish it after his career was safely established and thereby run the risk of losing it?

5. Smith displayed a pre-1958 interest in Clement and other relevant subjects

Still under the general rubric of item 3 above, "For such a life-time discovery, no one could have been better prepared for Secret Mark than Morton Smith," Carlson states that "Smith's publications before the summer of 1958 exhibited his [Smith's] erudition in a wide range of subjects relevant to Secret Mark." He notes four. First, Smith "published a detailed analysis of Vincent Taylor's commentary on the Gospel of Mark" in 1955. Second, Smith "had both an intimate knowledge of monastic libraries with their eighteenth-century Greek texts and a fine grasp of patristic letter transmission"; this is demonstrated by the fact that he published two articles on Isidore of Pelusium (mid-fifth century) in 1956 and 1958. Third, "While at Drew [1956–1957], Smith also became interested in an early third-century heresiological text" by Hippolytus "that includes a description of the Carpocratians." And fourth, "Smith's interest in

---

[416] Carlson, *Gospel Hoax*, 80.

Clement of Alexandria became evident as early as [*sic*] March 1958 when he published an article ... that cited Clement of Alexandria four times."[417]

What stands out is how woefully inadequate these four things are for establishing the immense learning and technical ability that would have been essential to produce this document. As stated above, even if Smith did have the ability, it would not be evidence that it was applied fraudulently. Moreover, extensive evidence is given herein that he did not have the unique ability such a forgery would have demanded.

6. The Voss edition could have been purchased by Smith on the used book market

It was Quesnell who had suggested that the book containing the disputed manuscript written into its endpapers could have been carried into the Mar Saba library at any time between 1936 and when Smith was there in 1958.[418] Quesnell noted that the 1646 Voss edition in question was one of the 191 books that Smith found in 1958 that were not in the 1910 catalog.[419] However, in 1910 there were between fifty and sixty monks living at Mar Saba. By 1958 only thirteen monks lived there, yet Smith found 489 books in the tower library alone (there are actually two libraries, one in the great tower, and a second in a room over the porch of the new church). So it is possible that someone smuggled the Voss edition into the monastery. But it is doubtful that Smith smuggled in over three hundred books. It seems far more likely that the 1910 catalog was simply incomplete. Smith's own 1958 catalog included information on only 76 of the 96 books containing manuscript material that he found in 1958 (he

---

[417] Carlson, *Gospel Hoax*, 8–9, 107 n. 9.

[418] The 1936 date is used because that was the year that Stählin published volume 4 of his critical edition of the works of Clement, in which there is an index of most of the words contained in Clement's works. This index is discussed below in item 13 related to Criddle's analysis.

[419] Quentin Quesnell, "The Mar Saba Clementine: A Question of Evidence," *Catholic Biblical Quarterly* 37 (1975): 56.

didn't describe 20 liturgical MSS). To even call the 1910 catalog a catalog is to make it sound much more impressive than it probably was. Smith describes it as a list consisting only of seven single-sided pages—hardly, it seems, a formal, official Patriarchal accounting of its library holdings.[420]

In lieu of offering evidence that Smith had acquired a copy of Voss prior to visiting the Mar Saba library, Carlson devotes a paragraph to suggesting that copies were available on the used-book market (though at substantial cost) and that Smith had the resources to buy a copy. There is no indication that Carlson attempted to determine if Smith had purchased such a copy. He merely speculated that Smith could have done so.

But this is another case where Carlson's imagination erred. In his PowerPoint presentation at the 2008 SBL panel, Pantuck presented evidence showing that Smith was unacquainted with the Mar Saba Voss book prior to his visit to the monastery. Pantuck's comments were extemporaneous, so I later asked him for an explanation. The next two paragraphs comprise the essence of what he said.

The Mar Saba Voss book was missing its first few pages, including the title page with publication information. Carlson and a supporter of his named Stephen Goranson suggested that Smith bought the Voss book in advance and deliberately removed these pages to hide any evidence of where Smith bought it or to use the front pages as "practice sheets."[421] Smith wrote that he had photographed the first extant page (page 2) and the last page to compare these to known editions of Voss in order to date the volume. Pantuck found Smith's photograph at JTS. In his presentation, Pantuck displayed a slide with Smith's photograph on the left side. On the right side was a photograph Pantuck made of page 2 of the Voss book from the Union Theological Seminary (UTS). Pantuck is familiar with the labeling system Smith used in marking manuscripts from monasteries.

---

[420] See Morton Smith, "Monasteries and Their Manuscripts," *Archaeology* 13 (1960): 172–77.

[421] See the posts by Carlson and Goranson to the Yahoo Group textual criticism, archived on The Secret Gospel of Mark Homepage, http://www-user.uni-bremen.de/~wie/Secret/discussion-hoax.html.

The markings on Smith's photograph applied that system, including identifying the manuscript ("Smith 65") in the upper corner with his catalog number and with tiny labels at the bottom indicating where photographed ("Mar Saba"). The UTS library "keeps a dated record of when users accessed books, and their records show Smith was there in February, 1959." The current library-loaned card reflects this, though made from library records after Smith's 1959 visit. UTS acquired the volume in 1848, but Smith was the first one to check it out.[422]

Except with respect to the issue of forgery, the date of the particular Voss edition is irrelevant. The first edition was in 1646 and the second was in 1680. As it turns out the letter was dated in the eighteenth century, later than both editions. A forger though would need to have known the date of the book beforehand to make sure that he faked a writing of a later date than the date of the book. The fact that Smith went to UTS in 1959 shows that he didn't know the date of the edition he discovered in 1958. While the date turned out to be irrelevant, as a bit of minutia it fit Smith's meticulous personality to track it down. Notably, he didn't bother to do that, however, until he had been back in New York for six months and had already filed for copyright protection of his translation two months earlier.[423]

7. Clement didn't write the letter

Within this specific context, Carlson is arguing, not that Smith in particular forged the letter, but that Clement did not write it.[424] Aside from the one thing on which all parties agree, namely, the desirability of having the document itself examined, this is the most legitimate issue that Carlson addresses, for the issue of Clement's authorship remains even if it is conceded that Smith did not forge the letter.

In *Mark's Other Gospel*, Brown names "eleven well-informed scholars who have given *reasons* to deny Clement's authorship of the *Letter to Theodore*" and then proceeds to respond to every argument

---

[422] Pantuck and Brown, "Morton Smith as M. Madiotes," 107 n. 4.

[423] Pantuck, e-mail to author, April 16, 2009.

[424] Carlson, *Gospel Hoax*, 54–64.

that had been advanced prior to 2003.[425] Brown paid primary attention to Charles E. Murgia and Quentin Quesnell, but also addressed
scholars such as Jacob Neusner, whose attacks on Smith were entirely
personal, retributive, and vindictive.[426]

On the subject of Clement's authorship Carlson tends to assert
rather than demonstrate, which makes it difficult to evaluate the claims
he makes. Fortunately, the shortcomings in Carlson's presentation
were exposed by Brown's careful analysis and discussion, issue by issue,
in an article published in 2008.[427] Brown's listing of the issues are:[428]

1. A private letter of Clement would not include a *sphragis* or the
   words "in Alexandria."[429]
2. Clement would not need to quote the gospel excerpts in order
   to prove that they do not contain the troubling words that
   Theodore had asked about.
3. Clement would not quote the gospel excerpts so accurately.
4. The letter's tradition about Mark is unlike authentic patristic
   traditions.
5. The *Letter to Theodore* contradicts Clement's use of salt as a
   metaphor.

In each case, Brown examines the available evidence of Clement's
writings and early traditions about Mark to determine whether

---

[425] Brown, *Mark's Other Gospel*, 23. He suggests that the "list might be overstated," since
some of the scholars he names could not formulate clear reasons to reject the letter's
authenticity.

[426] Brown, *Mark's Other Gospel*, 39–47.

[427] Scott G. Brown, "*The Letter to Theodore*: Stephen Carlson's Case against Clement's
Authorship," *Journal of Early Christian Studies* 16 (2008): 535–72.

[428] Brown's listing omits two issues that he had covered elsewhere, namely, A. H. Criddle's statistical argument, which Brown addressed in *Mark's Other Gospel*, 54–57, and
Carlson's alleged Morton Salt anachronism, which Brown addressed in his article "Factualizing the Folklore: Stephen Carlson's Case against Morton Smith," *Harvard Theological
Review* 99 (2006): 291–327.

[429] Carlson, following Murgia, uses the term *sphragis*, which he defines as a "seal of
authenticity," which he further defines for his purposes as "a textual device that authors
sometimes use to identify themselves" (*Gospel Hoax*, 54). A major part of Carlson's work
focuses upon the idea that he has ferreted out such devices Smith allegedly planted as
clues to his own identity as the perpetrator of a hoax upon the academy.

Carlson's characterizations of what is wrong with the letter have merit. On each point Brown undoes Carlson's argument and shows that the letter actually agrees with Clement's modus operandi or with the early traditions about the evangelist Mark. Insofar as Brown has demonstrated his points with remarkable strength of argument and citation of evidence, he has enhanced the probability that the letter came originally from Clement's hand.

In concluding, Brown says, "In most cases, the very things that Carlson asserts are uncharacteristic of Clement or of an authentic ancient letter are precisely what one might expect of a real letter by Clement.... In the remaining cases, the significant omissions in Carlson's presentation of the evidence create a false impression that the letter differs from Clement.[430]

In the interest of brevity the reader is referred to Brown's article.

8. The 1940 novel *The Mystery of Mar Saba* could have inspired Smith to forge Secret Mark

The discussion turns melodramatic as Carlson relates how James H. Hunter's "popular evangelical thriller, *The Mystery of Mar Saba*, originally published in 1940" could conceivably have inspired Smith to forge his discovery.[431]

Hunter's fictional spy story is set in the late 1930s when Nazi military designs for Europe had become ominous and their implementation imminent. Hitler's agents imprison a Greek-born British scholar named Yphantis in Mar Saba and, threatening harm to his sister in Berlin, coerce him to forge an ancient letter of the gospel character Nicodemus. The document declares that he (Nicodemus) and Joseph of Arimathea had arrived at the tomb of Jesus early on the Sabbath and found the stone rolled away, so they buried the precious body in a different sepulchre—a revelation that disproves the Easter narrative. The Nazi behind the scheme then engineers the document's discovery by a leading British scholar, confident that the announcement of

---

[430] Brown, "*Letter to Theodore*," 569.
[431] James Hogg Hunter, *The Mystery of Mar Saba* (New York: Evangelical, 1940).

this discovery, shortly before an important speech by Hitler, would deaden the moral fiber of Britain, paralyzing its ability to withstand an imminent attack. Through hair-rising episodes, interspersed with saintly romance, our manly evangelical hero converts the beautiful sister, rescues her and her hapless brother, exposes the fraud at the last minute, and confounds the Nazi scheme.[432]

The parallels, striking in a few respects, are superficial. The evangelical thrust of the book—painfully sermonizing throughout—is so foreign to what is widely known about Smith's nature and attitudes that it is hard to imagine he would have given it the time of day.

It seems most unlikely Smith ever even knew of the book. In his early life as a student, apparently late in the year 1940 (whether or not before Hunter's book was published is unclear), he went "to Jerusalem on a traveling fellowship from Harvard Divinity School [and] got stuck there when the Mediterranean was closed by the war." He had started work on a doctorate in philosophy at the Hebrew University. His first trip to Mar Saba was apparently in 1941 and did not develop through his own initiative. The Greek Archimandrite Father Kyriakos said to him, "After the Christmas season I shall go down to Mar Saba for a few days. You must come, too." He went to Mar Saba early in 1941.[433]

He didn't return to the States until 1944, but continued working on his doctorate, which he received from the Hebrew University in 1948.[434] Thereafter he completed a Th.D. degree at Harvard and started his academic career at Drew and Brown with a brief hiatus before accepting his long-term position at Columbia in 1957. He was in a part of the world where access to Hunter's book seems virtually impossible for several years after its publication. In short, it is not likely he ever knew about Hunter's book. Carlson said Smith's library

---

[432] An excellent two-page summary of the book is provided in Brown, *Mark's Other Gospel*, 57–58.

[433] Smith states that his return to Mar Saba was in 1941 when he was twenty-six (*Secret Gospel*, 1). He was born in 1915. It seems almost certain that it was after the 1940 Christmas that he was invited to go to Mar Saba.

[434] Cohen, "In Memoriam," 279.

by the time of his death in 1991 numbered to ten thousand volumes, but Carlson says nothing about Hunter's book being in it,[435] and the evidence indicates that the book was not there.[436]

Brown shows how Hunter's book is not of a character to have likely drawn Smith's attention or interest, and points out that it was not till 2001 that a scholar, Philip Jenkins, called attention to the novel, thinking that its story sounded familiar. The matter having thus been raised, Robert M. Price then "transform[ed] this novel into incriminating evidence against Smith by seriously misrepresenting its plot."[437]

Carlson subsequently included the book as a point of suspicion, elaborating upon its perceived similarity to Smith's discovery.[438] What Carlson doesn't explain is why in spite of the supposed similarity and all the controversy that had surrounded Smith's discovery, no one drew attention to this book's supposed relevance until ten years after Smith had died. If Hunter's book had been so popular that Smith was likely to have read it, as Carlson suggests, how did it go unnoticed for so long, especially among all the conservative opponents who were viscerally appalled by Smith's publications?

In a court of law such a parallel would not be admitted as relevant evidence without at the very least some showing that Smith had been aware of the book before 1958. No critic of Smith's discovery, Carlson included, has come forward with any evidence to show that Smith knew of it during that time frame, and what is in evidence shows how unlikely it is he was aware of it. Parallels are not proof, as Carlson himself noted with specific reference to this novel and some other of his asserted parallels.[439]

In short, the idea that Smith's knowledge of this book is a legitimate consideration should be abandoned. It is the type of speculation that one resorts to when no solid evidence is available.

---

[435] Carlson, *Gospel Hoax*, 45.
[436] See n. 509.
[437] Brown, *Mark's Other Gospel*, 57–59.
[438] Carlson, *Gospel Hoax*, 19–20.
[439] Carlson, *Gospel Hoax*, 20.

9. Smith's dedication of his book to "the one who knows" is a clue
   that he forged the letter

The dedication page of Smith's popular version, *The Secret Gospel*, says simply, "FOR THE ONE WHO KNOWS." Like many of us, Carlson wonders who this dedicatee might be and what this person knows. Hoping that it could be a forger's clue, Carlson turns to Smith's scholarly book, *Clement of Alexandria and a Secret Gospel of Mark*, and notes that Smith dedicated it to the late A. D. (Arthur Darby) Nock, who thought the letter was an ancient forgery. Does the one dedication illuminate the other?

Let's consider who Nock was. It is said that he was widely regarded as the leading authority on the history of religion, had become a full professor at Harvard at age 28 upon his arrival from Cambridge in England in 1930, and had an immense reputation as a scholar with an encyclopedic memory and an extraordinary range of knowledge such that he was consulted by experts even outside his field. Added to all that, he was said to have been "a warm man" and "a joyful and generous friend" who "did many, many kind things that no one ever knew about." Unfortunately, Dr. Nock stunned the academic world when he died prematurely on January 11, 1963, at a mere sixty years of age.[440]

Obviously Smith had an immense regard for Nock and for his knowledge. In a fascinating way, in chapter four of *The Secret Gospel* Smith describes his initial presentation of his discovery to Professors Erwin Goodenough of Yale and A. D. Nock of Harvard. Smith paints a captivating word picture of each, describing them as "great scholars whom it was my good fortune to know well" and "a remarkable pair, the opposite extremes of the English character." Smith describes Goodenough as being disposed favorably toward "a hidden, potentially mystical side in early Christianity." By contrast, "one of the major campaigns of [Nock's] scholarly career had been

[440] Michael Lerner, "Arthur Darby Nock Dies at Sixty: Religion Historian's Death Stuns Academic World," *Harvard Crimson*, January 14, 1963, http://www.thecrimson.com/article/1963/1/14/arthur-darby-nock-dies-at-sixty/.

the refutation of attempts to explain the Christian sacraments from the mystery religions. Consequently he was predisposed against a discovery that threatened to reveal an esoteric element at the root of Christianity."[441]

The following paragraph in which Smith describes Nock's reaction to his discovery is instructive for what follows:

I didn't tell him about the text. I just said, "I have a surprise for you: look at this," and handed him the photographs. (I hope no student ever does that to me!) He passed the test brilliantly. I can still hear him muttering as he bent over the pages, "Ha, Clement! A fragment of a letter, no less. Congratulations! ... The Carpocratians! I say, this may be important. (My God, this hand is cursive!) 'Carnal and bodily sins' ... 'slaves of servile desires' ... Yes, yes, that's what he'd say; that's the language.... This stuff on Mark is excellent. Just what Clement would say; of course he'd defend the Alexandrian position; look at Swete on Mark for that, still the best collection.... What's this, a 'more spiritual Gospel'?... 'Hierophantic teaching of the Lord'?... Well ... it does sound like Clement ... I suppose he would use the mystery language; they all borrowed it later.... 'Foul demons' ... 'devising destruction' ... blasphemous and carnal doctrine,' that rings true again.... Yes, now we get the quotations.... That's an odd text of Proverbs, you must look that up ... Good heavens, a Gospel quotation! Oh no, this is too much! No, my dear boy, this can't be genuine. It must be something medieval; fourth or fifth century, perhaps. They made up all sorts of stuff in the fifth century. That's where this will come from; it's not an ancient *flosculum*. But, I say, it is exciting. You must do it up in an article for the [*Harvard Theological*] *Review* [noting that Nock was its editor].[442]

As Smith writes in *Clement*, Nock imagined a fourth- or fifth-century author forging this letter as a "mystification for the sake of

---

[441] Smith, *Secret Gospel*, 23–25.
[442] Smith, *Secret Gospel*, 24–25.

mystification."[443] This origin would have been in keeping with his general resistance to the esoteric in early Christianity.

What, if anything, has this opinion to do with the dedication of *The Secret Gospel* to "the one who knows"? Was this dedication a hint by Smith that he had forged the book, as Carlson suggests?

Absolutely nothing has been shown to indicate that Professor Nock ever said or even suspected that Smith forged the *Letter to Theodore*. What he did suspect was that the letter originated with someone other than Clement in the fourth or fifth century. Nock's initial impression was that the text was worthy of an article in *Harvard Theological Review*, and his subsequent comments on Smith's analysis (quoted by Smith in his scholarly edition) show that Nock continued to consider the document to be a real ancient letter. The present tense of Smith's dedication to "the one who knows" is inconsistent with Nock as the dedicatee of *The Secret Gospel*, since he was long deceased when the book was written.

The language of Smith's dedications can hardly raise any legitimate suspicion, let alone function as evidence on its own. Since there is no demonstrable connection between the two dedications, and since it would make little sense for Smith to dedicate two books on the same subject to the same person in the same year, it makes more sense to suppose that Smith's dedication of his scholarly book to Nock is an honest and fitting tribute to an individual he greatly admired, and his mysterious dedication of his popular book is incapable of proving anything that we might try to read into it.

10. The Secret Gospel, the manuscript, and the letter belong to the twentieth century

The title of this issue is descriptive of the content of Carlson's chapter three, "The Modernity of the Mar Saba Manuscript," chapter four, "The Modernity of *Theodore*," and chapter five, "The Modernity of *Secret Mark*," except for those aspects of these three chapters addressed under items 11, 12, and 13 that follow.

---

[443] Smith, *Clement*, 88 n. 1.

Two Carlson arguments are being addressed under this issue 10. The first is that the letter, being homoerotic, is a product of the 1950s. The second, which in a sense subsumes the first, is that the manuscript's origin before 1958 cannot be established.

Carlson writes, "Both books, *Secret Gospel* and *Clement*, expound an interpretation of *Secret Mark* **that took Smith years to develop**."[444] That statement alone disproves Carlson's claim that Smith forged the *Letter to Theodore*. For if Smith forged this text, he must have determined what he intended it to represent in order to create it and therefore would not need to spend any time, let alone several years, developing an interpretation after this. We've shown elsewhere that Smith didn't understand the document well enough to have forged it. Now Carlson is saying that he didn't even have a theory about what it represents when he created it. Had he forged the letter, he would have possessed his own theory about it in 1958. But if Smith didn't forge the letter, it isn't a homoerotic product of the 1950s, and its prior existence is shown. What remains to be proved? Both of Carlson's arguments fail.

Pious reactions to Smith's 1973 publications honed in on his tentative suggestion that the nighttime concourse involved physical symbolism of spiritual union, often transforming this conjecture into the essence of his interpretation of the Secret Gospel as an easy means of discrediting both. In an article published in the *Journal of Biblical Literature*, Brown credits the vindictive writings of Jacob Neusner in the 1990s, following Smith's death, with elaborating the so-called "gay gospel hypothesis" as Smith's motive for forgery.[445] Brown argues cogently that Smith's motive was not to establish Jesus as a homosexual. Brown's only reference to Carlson on this particular hypothesis dealt with Carlson's argument that "Smith devised [the letter] in part to influence the way people interpret" the mysterious youth in Mark 14:51–52.[446] Nevertheless, Carlson responded, "the 'Gay Gospel Hypothesis' ... is not the position I set out in my

---

[444] Carlson, *Gospel Hoax*, 11 (bold emphasis added).
[445] Brown, "Question of Motive," 354.
[446] Brown, "Question of Motive," 372–73. Carlson's argument is found in *Gospel Hoax*, 70.

book, *The Gospel Hoax*."[447] One might legitimately inquire, What is *the position* Carlson sets out? for he shotgunned an assortment of arguments, no one of which can stand alone as convincing proof and most of which are merely "could be's." But that the gay gospel hypothesis is one of the significant positions Carlson utilized is clear from his preface and chapter five.[448] I refer the reader to Brown's article controverting homoeroticism as Smith's motive.

As one born in 1932, I suggest that Carlson's premise that the letter's homoerotic aspect is more characteristic of the 1950s than it is of the time of Clement of Alexandria could only come from one who did not live through the 1950s. There was little similarity in regard to American sexual customs between the 1950s and what began in the 1960s (the decade in which I presume Carlson was born). The sexual revolution was not a phenomenon of the 1950s. Back then overt sex was not as prevalent in the culture as it has become since the 1960s. The term gay did not become predominantly associated in the public mind with homosexuality until the sexual revolution of the 1960s.[449] It is the cultural setting of the latter third of the twentieth century, Carlson's part, not that of Smith's life from 1915 up through 1958, that fits Carlson's scheme. The colloquial idiom "spent the night with (someone)," which Carlson uses to translate Secret Mark's "and he remained with him that night," was far more common as a euphemism for having sex during Carlson's time than it was before him. Even Carlson does not claim that the euphemistic meaning was entrenched before 1965.[450]

But even if the sexual mores of the 1950s had been the same as those in later decades, that would not justify giving a carnal interpretation to a passage that, as the letter states, was supposed to be read in a spiritual way. Neglect of the deeply spiritual and esoteric nature

---

[447] Stephen C. Carlson, "Brown on Smith's Motives (pt. 2)," *Hypotyposeis*, posted July 25, 2006, http://www.hypotyposeis.org/weblog/2006/07/brown-on-smiths-motives-pt-2.html.
[448] Carlson, *Gospel Hoax*, xvii, 65–72.
[449] George Chauncey, *Why Marriage? The History Shaping Today's Debate Over Gay Equality* (New York: Basic Books, 2004), 24–35; idem, *Gay New York: Gender, Urban Culture, and the Making of the Gay Male World, 1890–1940* (New York: Basic Books, 1994), 20; Lillian Faderman, *Odd Girls and Twilight Lovers: A History of Lesbian Life in Twentieth-Century America* (New York: Columbia University Press, 1991), 194–201.
[450] Carlson, *Gospel Hoax*, 65–71.

of some passages of scripture is the reason that symbolic passages such as Mark 14:51–52 have presented such a hermeneutical challenge for so many scholars.[451] Language of that sort is more characteristic of Secret Mark. So, disregarding Smith's erroneous interpretation, if there are interpretations of Secret Mark that render a deep spiritual meaning, then Carlson's characterization of the 1950s, assuming *arguendo* that it were right, would have probative force only for those who were unable to allow a deeper spiritual meaning, one reflecting the reality of initiation into higher realms of spiritual comprehension by those who were special disciples of Christ. Basically Carlson's case rests upon the premise that the language in the letter, that is, a slightly clad young man who remained with Jesus that night, can only mean that they had sexual relations. It clearly could have meant something entirely different, as is the strong contention herein and of most scholars who have considered the document.

There is a similarity between the youth who "began to beseech [beg] him that he might be with him" (*Letter to Theodore* III.5) and the Gerasene demoniac who "begged him that he might be with him" (Mark 5:18). And others besides the youth in Secret Mark have stayed with Jesus at night. Andrew and an unnamed disciple (widely considered to be "the disciple whom Jesus loved"), the first two of Jesus' disciples according to John, "saw where [Jesus] was staying; and they stayed with him," presumably overnight (John 1:39).[452]

But the deepest insight into being with Jesus at night should be garnered from the Nicodemus incident in John 3. We are told that Nicodemus came to Jesus *by night*. And Jesus there taught him. Nicodemus's instruction at night in the kingdom of God is for the same purpose as that in Secret Mark. Steiner spoke of this: "We are told that Nicodemus came to Jesus 'by night;' this means that he received outside of the physical body what Christ-Jesus had to communicate to him. 'By night' means that when he makes use of his spiritual senses, he

---

[451] See Book Two, ch. 3, "Mark's Fleeing Youth."

[452] John explains that they stayed with Jesus because "it was about the tenth hour." The "tenth hour" means 4:00 p.m., the day starting at 6:00 a.m.; Brown, *Gospel according to John*, 1:75.

comes to Christ-Jesus. Just as in their conversation about the fig-tree, Nathaniel and Christ-Jesus understood one another as initiates, so too a faculty of understanding is indicated here also."[453]

Turning to the second of his arguments under this issue, Carlson minimizes Smith's efforts to document the manuscript but says, "Nevertheless, Smith did consult experts, so any conclusion that the manuscript may not be authentic must go beyond merely pointing out the inadequacies of the initial examination"; therefore, "New reasons for doubting the apparent origin of the hand have to be developed."[454]

He then lists three such reasons. First, upon careful analysis the handwriting itself negates an eighteenth-century origin. Second, "the manuscript's provenance cannot be traced back before 1958," meaning that a twentieth-century origin is possible. Third, another manuscript at Mar Saba is from the same hand as the letter and Smith identified that hand as that of a twentieth-century individual.

The first and third reasons are shown later herein to be devoid of merit. The second reason has been disposed of under the preceding issues. For instance, that the Voss book the letter was written in could have been carried into the Mar Saba library by Smith was disposed of in issue 6. Not addressed there, however, is Carlson's contention that, of the ten books in the tower library that Smith listed as bearing manuscript material, the Voss book was the only one that was not printed in Venice.[455] Carlson sees this as suspicious, but his contention is wrong. Carlson limited his investigation to those books in Smith's published inventory. However, Pantuck's investigation of Smith's archives revealed that Smith found and photographed at least one other volume containing manuscript material, a book published in Leipzig in 1768.[456]

In his chapter four, Carlson contends that the *Letter to Theodore* is not a personal letter from Clement's lifetime.[457] Carlson cites several

---

[453] Steiner, *Gospel of St. John*, 90–91 (lect. 5).

[454] Carlson, *Gospel Hoax*, 25.

[455] Carlson, *Gospel Hoax*, 39.

[456] See Pantuck and Brown, "Morton Smith as M. Madiotes," 116 n. 28.

[457] Carlson, *Gospel Hoax*, 54–58.

elements in the letter that he contends indicate it was not written by Clement. The points Carlson raises are countered by two detailed articles published in tandem in 2008 in the *Journal of Early Christian Studies*, the first by Brown and the second by Jeff Jay.[458] Brown lists these seriatim in his rebuttal article (bold numbers inserted in brackets to identify separate issues are mine):

> Most of the [arguments in *Gospel Hoax*, 54–58] stem from the premise that modern forgeries of ancient letters convey authenticating information to their intended modern readers that would be unnecessary to convey to the stated (fictional) addressee(s). In this case, [1] the letter's opening remarks about the Carpocratians constitute a *sphragis* or literary seal of authenticity which would be unnecessary in an authentic letter of a private nature. [2] The letter's specification that Mark bequeathed his longer [secret] gospel to the church "in Alexandria" ... is likewise unnecessary for its named addressee, who, having written to Clement, would know where Clement is residing, but is necessary for a modern reader. Furthermore, [3] the real Clement would have no need to reproduce two excerpts from the longer gospel in order to answer Theodore's questions about it, [4] nor would Clement need to describe precisely where these passages occur within Mark's narrative. Clement would simply have asserted that Mark's longer gospel did not contain the disturbing phrases that Theodore inquired about.... [5] The distinctly Markan character of the gospel excerpts is also problematic because it implies that Clement quoted this gospel pericope more accurately than normal. [6] And the letter's tradition about the evangelist Mark inexplicably shares the modern gospel scholar's preoccupation with literary composition, but differs from undisputed early traditions about Mark, "which are tantalizingly brief and usually stress the role of Mark's memory,... not his note-taking ability."[459]

---

[458] Brown, "*Letter to Theodore*"; Jay, "Epistolary Framework."
[459] Brown, "*Letter to Theodore*," 537.

Carlson is inviting his readers to put themselves in Clement's shoes, to imagine whether Clement would do things such as these that seem odd to us. Brown's response, by contrast, invites us to look at what Clement actually did do in similar circumstances. Ironically, Brown demonstrates that the anomalies that Carlson perceives are actually so consistent with Clement's modus operandi as to be precisely what one would expect in a real letter from Clement dealing with such a request; they thus support the letter's authenticity.

While Brown's article addresses the points raised by Carlson issue by issue, Jay's article looks at the facts of letter writing in the second and third centuries and shows, contrary to Carlson's "modernity" arguments, that the letter accords with the conventions of letters of Clement's day. Indeed, Jay demonstrates that the *Letter to Theodore* fits an identifiable genre of letter that was used to combat the unauthorized distribution of literary works that were not intended (or ready) for publication. Jay was the first to identify this genre, although he does not note that fact in his article. After extensively analyzing examples of this genre of ancient letter, he concludes, "The letter to Theodore is plausible in light of letter writing in the late second or early third century and has tight generic coherence in form, content, and function. The account offered here can thereby become one part of a cumulative argument for authenticity." While recognizing that some will concede that the letter is not a forgery by Smith only if and when the manuscript itself can be examined, he continues: "But those who argue the letter is a twentieth century forgery must now allow that the forger had a solid knowledge of epistolography, ancient practices of composition and transmission, and the ability to weave a letter with fine generic texture, in addition to previously recognized competency in patristics, eighteenth-century Greek paleography, Markan literary techniques, and tremendous insight into the psychology and art of deception. Those developing theories of forgery must thus posit a forger whose breadth of knowledge is becoming, we may say, superhuman."[460]

---

[460] Jay, "Epistolary Framework," 596–97.

11.   The Madiotes—bald swindler clue

The cover of *The Gospel Hoax* displays a magnifying glass casting its focus upon a manuscript, suggesting the tale of how a master sleuth (Carlson) uncovered a clue that identifies the villainous Professor Smith as the perpetrator of a gospel hoax.[461] Our Sherlock's clue is a pipe dream.

For simplicity, I will follow Carlson in calling the *Letter to Theodore* (MS 65) *Theodore.*

Carlson advances, as we have seen, several "what if" or "could be" situations in support of his contention that the manuscript "could well be a fake." But recognizing that the mere "possibility [of] a modern fake" is not sufficient to "establish when or by whom" this cunning was perpetrated, Carlson affirms that all is well "because Smith's writings contain previously unnoticed evidence that answers this question." This other evidence emerges, he says, from a careful inspection of a manuscript identified as MS 22 in conjunction with *Theodore* (MS 65).[462]

Like the three pages of MS 65, MS 22 consists of Greek handwriting on a blank endpage of a printed book in the tower library at Mar Saba. The binding of this book was reinforced in the eighteenth century using pages from several much older manuscripts. Smith included a photograph of MS 22 in his book *The Secret Gospel* to illustrate both that old manuscripts were available to the monks in the eighteenth century and that monks sometimes used the endpages of printed books as writing material in that century because paper was scarce.

Carlson reasoned that Smith had actually used his photograph of MS 22 to plant a clue to the identity of the author of *Theodore,* namely, Smith himself. Carlson recognizes that, for a hoaxer, the "psychological payoff depends on [the hoax's] eventual disclosure," and thus it is "not uncommon for the hoaxer to plant deliberate ... clues."[463] Carlson notes that MS 22 contains "three different handwrit-

---

[461] The words "master sleuth" come from Mark Goodacre's back-cover endorsement.

[462] Carlson, *Gospel Hoax,* 41–42.

[463] Carlson, *Gospel Hoax,* 16; see also discussion in item 12, below.

ing styles." The first one, *he says*, was from the same hand as *Theodore* because both hands look the same, both hands used a narrower pen nib compared to the other hands on MS 22, and this first hand had "blunt ends and the 'forger's tremor'" that *he concluded* was also true of *Theodore*. Carlson finds it "interesting" that Smith's catalog dates this first hand not to the eighteenth century but to the twentieth.

Carlson tells us that Smith had attributed this first hand to a certain *M. Madiotes*, who lacked a religious title and thus appeared to be a visitor to Mar Saba. Of the name Madiotes, Carlson says: "While the name superficially appears Greek with the [*otes*] suffix of many Greek surnames, such a surname cannot be found at all in the current Greek telephone directory available online. Rather, the name is a pseudonym built on the root [*mad*—]. Few modern Greek words begin with [*mad*—], but one of them is the verb [*mado*], which literally means 'to lose hair' and has a figurative meaning of 'to swindle.'"[464] Carlson notes what he takes to be the following similarities of this Madiotes to Smith himself: he belongs to the twentieth century; his given name begins with the letter "M"; and he bears "a pseudonymous surname that means either 'baldy' or 'swindler'" (Smith himself was bald).

Carlson further notes that Smith deduced several qualifications that the writer of the letter probably had, and points out that Smith also had these qualifications, thus further indicating that Smith was describing himself as the writer. These qualifications are not in the least unusual for any scholar doing the type of scholarly work Smith was doing.[465]

Our sleuth's next point is simply unintelligible. "If this is a cleverly disguised confession claiming credit for penning the manuscript, it is still important to probe whether it is a false confession." Please tell me what that means. Carlson claims that Smith forged the document in order to dupe other scholars and planted a clue in it as a confession of his own authorship. Carlson now says that it is important to determine if the confession itself is false. Why on earth would Smith plant

---

[464] Carlson, *Gospel Hoax*, 43 (Latin letters replace Greek).
[465] Carlson, *Gospel Hoax*, 44.

a confession in the document if the confession was false to begin with? If he planted a confession to make people think he wrote the letter when he didn't write it, his confession thus being false, then Carlson's case claiming that Smith wrote it simply goes out the window. It is hard to find anything meaningful in that paragraph and the one that follows,[466] and the one that follows that is where he talks about Smith having had the money to buy a copy of the Voss book (see item 6).

In the rest of his chapter three Carlson attempts to show similarities between Smith's handwriting and that in *Theodore*. He concludes: "The manuscript is not what it appears to be. Instead of being scribed by an eighteenth-century monk at Mar Saba, the evidence shows that it was penned by an imitator whom Smith identified with a pseudonym that means 'baldy' or 'swindler,' and a description that uncannily resembles Smith himself. Moreover, Smith's own handwriting exhibits several of the idiosyncrasies of the scribe of the *Secret Mark* manuscript, and therefore confirms the veracity of Smith's concealed claim of credit."[467]

In order to evaluate the Madiotes argument, let us review its three main points:

1. The topmost handwriting in Smith's published photograph of MS 22 is identical to the handwriting of *Theodore* (MS 65).
2. Although an eighteenth-century hand, Smith's catalog of Mar Saba's manuscripts ascribed the topmost handwriting of MS 22 to a twentieth-century individual named *M. Madiotes*.
3. The name *Madiotes* is a made-up name based on a root that means "baldy" and "swindler," a deliberate clue pointing to Smith himself.

The issues are a bit technical and complex, but Carlson's position in all three points has been completely dismembered by Allan Pantuck and Scott G. Brown in their article "Morton Smith as M. Madiotes" published in *Journal for the Study of the Historical Jesus* (*JSHJ*).

---

[466] Carlson, *Gospel Hoax*, 44–45.
[467] Carlson, *Gospel Hoax*, 47.

Brown thoroughly disproved Carlson's first contention, that the topmost handwriting on MS 22 is the same as the handwriting of MS 65, by a systematic comparison in the *JSHJ* article as well as in earlier articles. Carlson recognized that both writers use several of the same letterforms (which is not at all unusual for writers of the same period), but Brown demonstrated that they rarely connect the same letters together in the same way, and the writer of the top hand of MS 22 had no idea when and how to use accents, in contrast to the correct use of accents by the scribe of MS 65. So we are dealing not only with different scribes, but with very different levels of literacy.

On the second point, Carlson's inference that Smith attributed the topmost, eighteenth-century handwriting of MS 22 to a twentieth-century person named Madiotes is also mistaken. According to Smith's catalog entry for MS 22, M. Madiotes is the first of three monks whose handwriting appears on the page that Smith photographed from MS 22, so Carlson inferred that the top handwriting belongs to Madiotes. He was wrong. Carlson was working with the published photograph, which was heavily cropped down the right side in order to center on the old manuscripts that Smith found within the binding. But as Pantuck demonstrated, the original photograph, which Pantuck found in Smith's archive, reveals five different hands on this page, and the handwriting of Madiotes appears to be limited to a very faint signature, which appears directly under the top handwriting and upside down in relation to it. The top hand from the eighteenth century was not that of Madiotes at all.

Although these two errors are both fatal on their own, Pantuck discovered an additional error in Carlson's argument which pertains to his third point, the spelling of Madiotes. Carlson's argument that Madiotes is a pseudonym rests upon the precise spelling of the name *Madiotes*, which he found in Smith's catalog. Carlson could not find that surname in the Greek phonebook. However, Smith kept an offprint of the published catalog, into which he made corrections to errors made by the person who translated his English notes into Greek. Smith indicated that the spelling *Madiotes* (as well as that of the third name, *Anobos*) was incorrect, and should be *Madeotas*. Further, on careful inspection of the photograph,

Pantuck determined that Smith himself was probably incorrect and that the faint signature actually reads *M. Modestos*, Modestos being a common name of monks at this monastery. Indeed, according to Smith's catalog, a twentieth-century monk named Modestos had signed the other side of the same page of MS 22 in 1916. Every aspect of the Madiotes argument is rooted in a mistake.

The fact that this argument relies entirely on misinformation should not be surprising, given its inherent implausibility. One wonders how many of those who accepted Carlson's position on this really stopped to ponder how likely anyone would be to describe himself as either bald or a swindler. While baldness is a noticeable feature, it is fairly common and hardly the first adjective one would be expected to use in describing oneself. And the premise that Smith would describe himself as a swindler is implausible, as any self-respecting person would likely find the appellation repugnant. Moreover, this word hardly accords with the premise of a hoax, which is merely to fool people rather than swindle them out of their money. At the very outset there is an element of the preposterous in this theory that should have put an objective reader on the alert. Carlson never suggests any pattern in Smith's life indicating deceptiveness or dishonesty. Fortunately, many scholars have been highly skeptical and given Smith the benefit of the doubt. But it is most appropriate that one of Smith's former students, coauthor of the *JSHJ* article, has seen fit to rehabilitate his late professor by dedicating the article to the memory of his name.

12. The Morton Salt clue

Carlson's hunt for clues connecting the manuscript to Smith did not end with the mistaken Madiotes discovery. He also probed the letter's salt metaphor for a concealed Smith confession. This decision likely required considerably less imagination. Salt is one of life's absolute necessities, and from our childhood many of us have lived with the name of the dominant brand, Morton Salt. In a conversation about Morton Smith, the name Morton Salt might even come out just by slip of the tongue. The imagination required here is how to fashion a clue stemming from that most obvious similarity. For that is Carlson's method: unlike a detective, who starts with a crime scene, identifies objective clues amid the evidence, and then follows them back to a suspect, Carlson starts with a suspect, finds features in the evidence that could, with research and ingenuity, be construed as clues left behind by that suspect, and then uses these clues as evidence for a crime scene. This inversion of the scientific method stems from his discovery that hoaxers cannot resist leaving clues to their deception: "Now that I knew what to look for and where to look for it, all I had to do was to find it."[468] This is what we find him doing on pages 58–64 of *The Gospel Hoax.*[469]

The Morton Salt argument concerns the letter's metaphor "For the true things, being mixed with inventions, are falsified, so that, as the saying goes, even the salt loses its savor" (I.13–15). Carlson begins with the postulate that this salt metaphor "involves mixing an adulterant with salt and spoiling its taste," which "presupposes salt-making technology that did not exist in Clement's place and time." The letter's salt metaphor also "presumes that the letter's recipient [Theodore] would have appreciated the adulteration of salt as a problem," which (whether or not true) Carlson argues would not have been the case. That is because the process of adulterating salt through mixing requires salt that is "free-flowing, but free-flowing salt is a modern invention." This invention occurred in 1911, when "a chemist at the Morton Salt Company" devised a way to combine salt crystals with an anti-caking agent that prevents salt from clumping by "draw[ing] moisture from the air," so that "When it rains it pours." The letter's salt metaphor would be meaningless before that invention. Ergo, the passage in the letter about salt having lost its savor through mixture could not have been written before the twentieth century. Carlson parlays all of this into a progression of ideas, first

---

[468] Carlson, *Gospel Hoax*, xviii.

[469] Carlson's "un-Clementine" argument about salt losing its flavor (Matt 5:13; Luke 14:34) in *Gospel Hoax*, 58–60 is based upon his misquoting John Ferguson's translation of Clement's *Stromateis* I.8.41.3–4 and therefore does not need to be addressed. Even Carlson seems to set it aside on p. 60.

that of free-flowing salt, which triggers the thought of Morton Salt, which then easily morphs into the name Morton Smith as his putative clue to the authorship of the letter.[470]

Carlson's assumption that the saying in the letter presupposes the physical mixing of salt with another material that constitutes an impurity is not self-evidently true. The salt imagery is metaphorical, and "salt" is a term having a great depth of esoteric meaning, something that Clement seems to have been far more attuned to than Carlson.[471] One of such mind might speak of salt as being "truth" or "purity" so that one's truthfulness is sullied by even once being untruthful. In this context Clement is describing the effect that Carpocrates' additions had on the Secret Gospel (cf. II.8–9). Hence, Brown argues, the salt in this saying refers metaphorically to the inherent value and sanctity of the Secret Gospel, and the loss of its savor refers to the complete loss of this sanctity and value through the addition of falsifications. The text itself says nothing about actual salt losing its taste by being mixed with material impurities, and Carlson does not explain why we should suppose that this is implied.[472] If we agree with Brown, Carlson's whole laborious argument goes down the drain.

Even if we accept Carlson's unexplained premise, Kyle Smith has shown that the conclusions drawn from this premise are erroneous. Smith picks the meat from every bone of Carlson's case on this issue, with extensive discussion of the evidence. He concluded that the metaphor is neither anachronistic nor inconsistent with Clement's known references to salt.[473]

Carlson's blogged response to this paper fails to address all of Kyle Smith's points and, in concluding, attempts to lead the reader away

---

[470] Carlson, *Gospel Hoax*, 60–61.

[471] See the many references to these meanings in the deeply esoteric work of the Egyptologist R. A. Schwaller de Lubicz, *The Temple of Man: Apet of the South at Luxor* (trans. Deborah Lawlor and Robert Lawlor; Rochester, Vt.: Inner Traditions, 1998). See its index under "salt." The classical three elements of alchemy are salt, sulfur, and mercury, and from the first salt has had a rich presence in the Bible.

[472] Brown, "Factualizing the Folklore," 307–8.

[473] Kyle Smith, "'Mixed with Inventions': Salt and Metaphor in Secret Mark," The Secret Gospel of Mark Homepage, http://www-user.uni-bremen.de/~wie/Secret/SALT-PAPER.rtf.

from the larger issues: "In Sum, I am glad that K. Smith agrees with me that *Secret Mark* is Morton Smith's hoax" and "that his vetting of the salt metaphor ... has not diluted the strength (or flavor) of this aspect of the case in the *Gospel Hoax*."[474] What Carlson fails to note is that while K. Smith leans to the idea, early on, that the letter is a hoax, he does so only conditionally upon each of Carlson's points being confirmed after careful examination, and he purports to thoroughly examine only the salt metaphor, about which he is clear that Carlson has failed on all aspects of his argument.

The Goldsmith Clue

Finally, Carlson brings in Jeremiah for another clue. This one is not based upon anything in the letter, but rather upon some of the commentary Smith wrote in his more scholarly work. While discussing the letter's salt saying, Smith suggests that it might contain a "recollection" of Jer 10:14. Because Clement read the Old Testament in Greek, Smith quoted this verse from the most common Greek translation (the Septuagint), where it appears at 28:17. Carlson supplies this English translation: "every person is made dull from knowledge ... because they have cast false things, there is no breath in them." Carlson could see no valid parallel in these words to the letter's salt metaphor or to the original saying about salt losing its savor in Matt 5:13, so he looked up the part that Smith omitted using ellipses. It reads, "every goldsmith is confounded because of his graven images" (Carlson's translation). Intent on finding a clue, Carlson focused on the word *goldsmith*, which, at least in English translation, contains the word *smith* within it. And so Carlson has found not only a clue to his suspect's given name in the letter (*Morton* Salt), but also a concealed reference to his surname in Smith's commentary on the salt metaphor (gold*smith*). Construed as a clue, the missing words are a cleverly hidden self-condemnation: "*Secret Mark* is not just a corruption of

[474] Stephen C. Carlson, "Kyle Smith's Critique of *Gospel Hoax*," *Hypotyposeis*, posted December 23, 2005, http://www.hypotyposeis.org/weblog/2005/12/kyle-smiths-critique-of-gospel-hoax.html.

the gospel of Mark but a graven image that will confound its own smith: Morton Smith."[475]

I expect the normal reader will find this reasoning baffling in the extreme. It is unnecessary for us to demonstrate, as Brown has done, that Carlson's justification for seeking Smith's actual meaning in the ellipsis of the words he quoted is based on Carlson's oversight of the notation "(and ff.)," which Smith used to indicate that he had the *next* verse in Jeremiah in mind as well.[476] For any argument that treats Smith's commentary as containing intricately veiled allegorical confessions is already assuming the very thing such "discoveries" are intended to prove.

The remarkable thing about the alleged Morton Salt–goldsmith confession is how abstruse and convoluted the whole thing is. Recall that the premise of a hoaxer leaving self-incriminating clues in his handiwork is based on the raison d'être of a hoax—the emotional payoff that comes from the deception being uncovered. In hindsight, the self-incriminating clues must be indubitable for the hoaxer to receive credit for duping so many people. That is certainly not the case here. It is bad enough that the hoax hypothesis requires us to assume that Smith somehow calculated his clues so that they would remain undetected for as long as he wished to work in a university. Can we really believe that he thought anyone could follow the same arbitrary (and sometimes erroneous) steps in reasoning needed to "discover" these veiled references to himself and that, following their exposure, others would think them indubitable? What these highly contrived hoax arguments really show us is how much difficulty Carlson had finding a way to connect Smith to the manuscript.

13. Andrew Criddle's argument that the letter is too Clementine to be by Clement

In 1995 Andrew H. Criddle published a statistical study suggesting that the *Letter to Theodore* was a deliberate imitation of Clement's

---

[475] Carlson, *Gospel Hoax*, 62–63.
[476] Brown, "Factualizing," 311–13.

style.[477] Carlson says it was this article that first raised his own suspicions about the letter.

Criddle's analysis examined whether or not the relationship (ratio) between *two classes of words* found in the *Letter to Theodore* is essentially the same as that ratio within the body of Clement's undisputed works. The *first class of words* comprises all those words that are *found only one time* in the body of Clement's undisputed works. The *second class of words* comprises words *not found* in the body of Clement's undisputed works (these are called "new words"). Criddle had determined, based upon a study of Clement's undisputed works, that the letter should include five words from the *first class* for every eight words from the *second class*. What Criddle found in the letter were nine words from the *first class* and four from the *second class*. In other words, there were too few "new words" in the letter. Criddle did not base his judgment just on this ratio comparison, but added in the fact that several of the *first class* words in the letter were rare among Patristic writers, which suggests an effort to look distinctively Clementine. Criddle concluded that the letter was written by someone who was trying too hard to make it look like Clement's work.

Carlson's contention that the letter is "too Clementine" for Clement relies entirely upon Criddle's 1995 article.[478] Carlson introduced into the discussion the Greek phrase *hapax legomena* to describe the *first class* of words, those used only one time in the body of Clement's undisputed works. In doing so he creates confusion at the outset by defining it as "vocabulary words found only in *Theodore* but not anywhere else in the previously recognized works of Clement."[479]

The fallibility of Criddle's test is revealed by Brown in his 2008 article in the *Journal of Early Christian Studies*. Passing along information from Pantuck, Brown reports that two statisticians had

---

[477] Andrew H. Criddle, "On the Mar Saba Letter Attributed to Clement of Alexandria," *Journal of Early Christian Studies* 3 (1995): 215–20.

[478] Carlson, *Gospel Hoax*, 50–54.

[479] Carlson, *Gospel Hoax*, 50.

previously applied the same statistical analysis to seven poems by, or attributed to, Shakespeare in order to test its validity.[480] It "correctly identified the writer of only three out of seven poems tested" and "would have excluded at least two of the four undisputed poems of Shakespeare" that had been used as controls.[481] These statisticians concluded that such analyses are unreliable when they focus only on words used once before and words not previously used, adding, "there is no consistent trend toward an excess or deficiency of new words."[482] Hence, as Brown put it, "Criddle did not show that this letter of Clement is more like Clement than Clement ever is."[483]

Brown also had observed that Criddle's hypothesis that the author of the letter tried to sound like Clement by using words that were rarely used by other Patristic authors is implausible, for it would require the forger to keep checking the corpora of the other church fathers. That would be a very laborious thing to do prior to the computer age. He further noted that "Criddle has not proven that this author did for the most part use words that are not found in other patristic writers: Criddle merely inferred this conclusion, by way of generalization, from the fact that six of the thirteen words isolated by his model are rare in patristic writings"; much more would have been required to support Criddle's conclusion.[484]

Whatever his personal feelings are about Secret Mark, Criddle does appear candid and transparent in his dialogues on his work.[485] In 1999 he posted his "Secret Mark—Further Comments" on the Internet in recognition of several mentions of his published paper in

---

[480] Brown is referring to Ronald Thisted and Bradley Efron, "Did Shakespeare Write a Newly-Discovered Poem?" *Biometrika* 74 (1987): 445–55.

[481] Brown, *"Letter to Theodore,"* 536 n. 5. Brown initially addressed Criddle's study in his *Mark's Other Gospel,* 54–57.

[482] Thisted and Efron, "Shakespeare," 451.

[483] Brown, *Mark's Other Gospel,* 55.

[484] Brown, *Mark's Other Gospel,* 55. Additional criticisms of Criddle's methodology appear in Walter M. Shandruk, "Statistics and Hapax Legomena in the Mar Saba Letter," Thoughts on Antiquity, posted August 10, 2008, http://neonostalgia.com/weblog/?p=496.

[485] Criddle's personal feelings are probably obvious from his 1995 article and 1999 post (see n. 486), and it is notable that he has been listed as a "guest blogger" on Carlson's *Hypotyposeis* blog site since August 2006.

discussions on Crosstalk.[486] He there says, "The precise level of statistical significance claimed for my results does, I agree, depend upon arguable decisions as to how to analyze the statistics ..." and "I agree that one should use this type of statistical argument with caution...." He seems to be suggesting, if I read him fairly, that it is merely one thing, when accompanied by others, that can give rise to suspicion, while recognizing its weakness as proof or even as admissible evidence.

By contrast, Carlson expresses no uncertainty about the utility of Criddle's statistical analysis or its correct interpretation as evidence that the letter is too much like Clement. What Carlson does question is whether anyone could have forged a letter like this without the benefit of a concordance. He decides that the true author must have utilized the first and only index of Clement's vocabulary, which Otto Stählin published in 1936.[487] Carlson had already noted that Smith's personal library, now housed at JTS, contains a copy of this index together with the three volumes of Stählin's critical text of Clement's writings.[488]

But here Carlson's reasoning works against him, for there is compelling evidence that Smith first utilized these books in his research after his stay at Mar Saba. Pantuck examined the notations that Smith made inside his own copies of these books. They show him modifying Stählin's critical text in light of more recent scholarship and "studying and counting vocabulary words and charting out the rhythms of Clement's verses."[489] Here we see Smith doing the research that would be required either to forge the letter before 1958 or to authenticate it after 1958 (he would not need to do this research twice). So it is very significant that the academic literature Smith noted in the margins includes dates. The earliest study is from 1896, and the most recent ones are from 1959. Those latter studies indicate that he was in fact doing this research after his visit to Mar Saba, not in preparation for that visit. Pantuck also noted that Smith owned some critical texts of Clement that were published in 1960,

---

[486] Andrew H. Criddle, "Secret Mark—Further Comments," The Secret Gospel of Mark Homepage, http://www-user.uni-bremen.de/~wie/Secret/Criddle-Feb99.html.
[487] Carlson, *Gospel Hoax*, 53–54.
[488] Carlson, *Gospel Hoax*, 45–46.
[489] Pantuck, e-mail to author, May 5, 2009.

namely, *Clement d'Alexandrie, Le Pédagogue*, Livre 1, by Henri Irénée Marrou and Marguerite Harl, and the second volume of Stählin's critical edition.[490] These further corroborate Smith's account of when he did this research. The images on the following pages, which show three annotations dated 1959 and the publication dates on the two critical editions, are from Pantuck's PowerPoint presentation during the panel on Secret Mark at the 2008 SBL convention in Boston.

Ongoing Developments

Three new and essentially contemporaneous developments came to light in April, 2010. They are the professional handwriting analysis comparing MS 65 to Morton Smith's Greek handwriting by Greek questioned document examiner Venetia Anastasopoulou, the publication of the full text of a letter written for Carlson by English questioned document examiner Julie C. Edison, and an article by Francis Watson arguing for forgery and some responses to that article.

THE PROFESSIONAL HANDWRITING ANALYSIS BY
VENETIA ANASTASOPOULOU

On April 16, 2010, the *Biblical Archaeology Review* announced on the Internet that the Greek handwriting expert it had commissioned "to compare the handwriting in which the Clement letter was written with Greek handwriting known to be Smith's" had submitted her written opinion, a copy of which was made immediately available. A more complete announcement followed in *BAR*'s next published edition.[491]

---

[490] The JTS call numbers are BR65.C6 P314 1960 and BR65.C54 1960, respectively.

[491] Venetia Anastasopoulou, "Experts [*sic*] Report Handwriting Examination," Biblical Archaeology Review, http://www.bib-arch.org/pdf/secret-mark-analysis.pdf. The report was commissioned by the editor of *Biblical Archaeology Review*; see "Handwriting Experts Weigh In on 'Secret Mark,'" *Biblical Archaeology Review* 36, no. 3 (May/June 2010): 18, 79; and "Did Morton Smith Forge 'Secret Mark'? A Handwriting Expert Weighs In," Biblical Archaeology Review (April 2010), http://www.bib-arch.org/e-features/secret-mark-handwriting-analysis.asp.

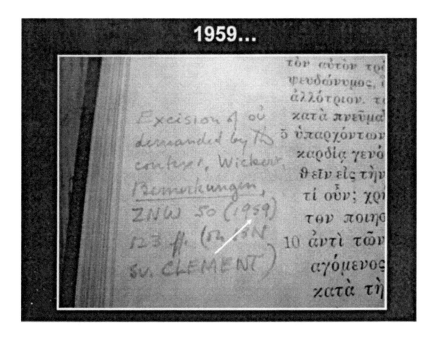

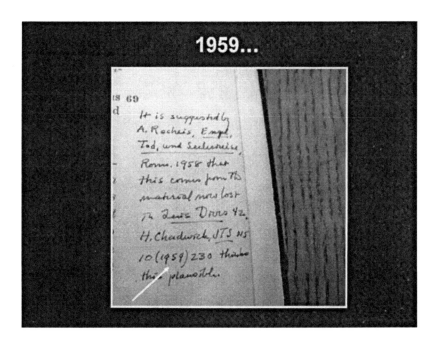

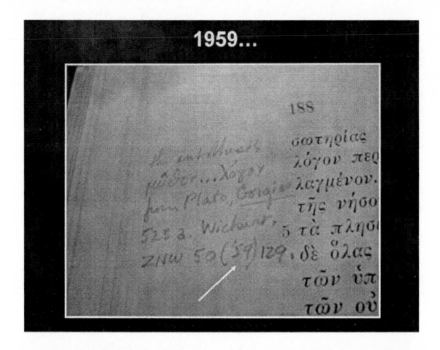

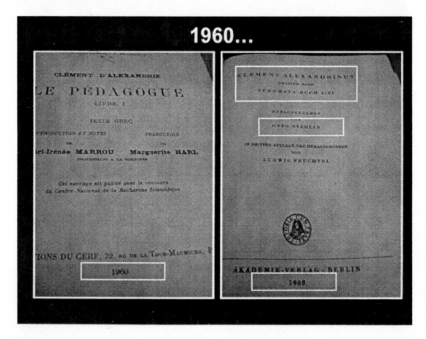

Anastasopoulou's thirty-nine-page report described the documents she examined, being the three pages in the *Letter to Theodore* (Q1, Q2, and Q3) and several documents containing Morton Smith's known handwriting in both Greek and his native English (K1–K27). Her professional opinion was that "the writers of ... Q1, Q2 an[d] Q3 and Morton Smith's handwriting on ... K1–K27, are most probably not the same. Therefore it is highly probable that Morton Smith could not have simulated the [*Letter to Theodore*]." She considers Smith's proficiency in Greek writing to be like that of a schoolboy, far inferior to the dexterous and complex handwriting displayed in MS 65.

In a subsequent paper Anastasopoulou addressed the question of whether MS 65 reveals any indications of forgery. After listing the various signs of suspicious and genuine writing that document examiners look for, she stated, "The Secret Mark letter, as written in detail in my analysis report, is written in a natural and spontaneous way and in my opinion, does not have such indications so to make us think of a suspicious writing."[492] Her expert opinion flatly contradicts Carlson's analysis, which purported to disclose several indications of forgery in the handwriting.

Carlson has not replied to Anastasopoulou's report, although *BAR* posted responses by Jeffery and Brown in the Scholar's Study section of their website. Writing before *BAR* commissioned her second paper, Jeffery conceded that the first report "does raise the bar for those who argue that Smith penned the Mar Saba document in his own hand (a claim I never made myself)." Jeffery seems to distance himself from Carlson's claim that Smith forged the document himself. He continues, however, to maintain the modernity of the document and specifically raises the possibility that Smith might have had a Greek accomplice capable of writing the letter.[493] Brown considers that

---

[492] Venetia Anastasopoulou, "Can a Document in Itself Reveal a Forgery?" Biblical Archaeology Review (July 22, 2010), http://www.bib-arch.org/scholars-study/secret-mark-handwriting-document-reveal-forgery.asp.

[493] Peter Jeffery, "Response to Handwriting Analysis," Biblical Archaeology Review (April 19, 2010), http://www.bib-arch.org/scholars-study/secret-mark-handwriting-response-jeffery.asp.

possibility in his own reply, which discusses the larger implications that Anastasopoulou's observations about the handwriting of MS 65 have for the question of forgery. Surveying the secondary literature on questioned document examination, Brown shows that the particular set of writing features that she observed in this document (internal consistency, complicated style, excellent rhythm, fluency, freedom, and artistic flair) is "extremely unlikely" to appear in a forged document. As Anastasopoulou herself noted, these features indicate that the writing was done quickly and unconsciously, which is the opposite of how a forgery is produced. Brown concludes, "Since this is a very difficult and skilful eighteenth-century Greek monastic hand, quite unlike Greek writing of the twentieth century, we may infer that this document was most likely penned by a Greek monk in the eighteenth century."[494]

CARLSON'S MISUSE OF JULIE C. EDISON'S LETTER

On April 14, 2010, Timo S. Paananen presented, on his Salainen evankelista blog site, an article entitled "Stephen Carlson's Questionable Questioned Document Examination," written as a guest post by Brown and Pantuck.[495]

After noting that Carlson has no training or experience in handwriting comparison and questioned document examination, and pointing to the fact that he incorrectly identified another document as both a forgery and an example of the same handwriting in MS 65, the authors

---

[494] Scott G. Brown, "My Thoughts on the Reports by Venetia Anastasopoulou," Biblical Archaeology Review (January 24, 2011), http://www.bib-arch.org/scholars-study/secret-mark-handwriting-response-brown.asp.

[495] Scott G. Brown and Allan J. Pantuck, "Stephen Carlson's Questionable Questioned Document Examination," Salainen evankelista, posted April 14, 2010, http://salainenevankelista. blogspot.com/2010/04/stephen-carlsons-questionable.html; reposted on The Secret Gospel of Mark Homepage, http://www-user.uni-bremen.de/~wie/Secret/Pantuck-Brown-2010. pdf. Paananen is a Finnish doctoral student at the University of Helsinki whose 2009 master's thesis critiques Carlson's methodology. See his "A Conspiracy of the Secret Evangelist: Recent Debate concerning Clement of Alexandria's Letter to Theodore," Salainen evankelista, http://salainenevankelista.blogspot.com/2009/06/masters-thesis-conspiracy-of-secret.html.

write, "It is surprising that his ability to detect forgery has gone unquestioned by so many readers of his book *The Gospel Hoax*. The most likely reason for this is Carlson's appeals to a professional document examiner named Julie C. Edison, who advised him and wrote a letter assessing his methods." They cite two websites at which he quoted portions of her letter to him dated May 6, 2005. These excerpts, and the manner in which Carlson introduced them, convey the impression that Edison independently studied the document herself, fully concurred with his methods, and supported his conclusions. Out of curiosity, Brown and Pantuck contacted Edison herself, to learn her opinion firsthand. To their surprise, she revealed that she spent only one afternoon considering this document, that Carlson showed her only the halftone reproductions of Smith's black-and-white photographs (halftone images are not adequate for questioned document examination because they distort the details when magnified), and that Edison acknowledged in her letter that she is not competent to examine Greek documents. She also offered a fundamental criticism of Carlson's methodology that Carlson excised from her report when he published it (claiming to be omitting background information).[496]

When Paananen posted the article by Brown and Pantuck, he extended to Carlson, out of a principle of benevolence, an invitation "to write a response, an explanation for what appears to be an attempt to selectively present facts that support his theories while suppressing others that might call these theories into question."

Among the visitor responses, generally critical of Carlson, Paananen writes on April 16, 2010, that "Stephen Carlson left a comment on Philip Harland's [blog] Religions of the Ancient Mediterranean." The pertinent portion of it reads:

It is hardly damaging. Brown and Pantuck have misunderstood a fairly standard disclaimer and used [it] to attack a position I have not espoused. All the disclaimer says, rightly, is that without a sample from

---

[496] Carlson published Edison's report on the Yahoo Group textual criticism (http://groups.yahoo.com/group/textualcriticism/message/1224) and on his blog *Hypotyposeis* (http://www.hypotyposeis.org/weblog/2005/11/some-initial-reviews-and-second.html).

the person [who] is supposed to have written it, it cannot be shown to be forgery "solely on the basis of forensic document examination." My book, of course, does not make that claim and more cautiously states that the examination raises a question of its genuineness.

It would have been better had Carlson just admitted that his handwriting analysis in *The Gospel Hoax* was methodically flawed due to the absence of known standards of comparison written by the person whose handwriting appears in MS 65. He is certainly not defending his analysis with this statement, nor is it clear that he has justified his representations about the part Julie C. Edison played in validating his method and his competence.

THE FRANCIS WATSON ARTICLE

The April 2010 issue of the *Journal of Theological Studies* included an article by Francis Watson, University of Durham, entitled "Beyond Suspicion: On the Authorship of the Mar Saba Letter and the Secret Gospel of Mark."[497] It was countered, point by point, beginning April 18, 2010, by an anonymous author on the Synoptic Solutions blog.[498]

Watson's article came out before the publication of Anastasopoulou's opinion, which, as Jeffery conceded, "does raise the bar for those who argue that Smith penned the Mar Saba document in his own hand," a claim Jeffery clearly is not making, but Watson is.[499] In fact, Watson's position is that he has shown Smith's forgery *beyond a reasonable doubt*, which he purports to do "on the basis of the internal evidence of the Clementine letter, read against the double background of the undisputed work of Clement (and Mark) on the one hand, and

---

[497] Francis Watson, "Beyond Suspicion: On the Authorship of the Mar Saba Letter and the Secret Gospel of Mark," *Journal of Theological Studies* 61 (2010): 128–70.

[498] Synoptic Solutions, "A Critique of Watson," http://synopticsolutions.blogspot.com/search/label/A%20Critique%20of%20Watson. In order to read the replies, click on the links that say "Read the rest."

[499] Peter Jeffery, "Response to Handwriting Analysis," *Biblical Archaeology Review* (April 19, 2010), http://www.bib-arch.org/scholars-study/secret-mark-handwriting-response-jeffery.asp.

Smith's own work on the other."[500] Beyond a reasonable doubt is quite a high standard. Can he be serious? His task is monumental in the sense that he is relying entirely upon circumstantial evidence without so much as a nod to any of the positive evidence that Smith could not, and did not, forge the letter.

Regarding the first half of Watson's efforts, those related to comparison of the contents of the letter to the undisputed work of Clement, I'm reminded of the classic saying that one can prove anything by the Bible through skillful selection of passages, especially when, as in Watson's efforts, one looks only at literary works without a broad contextual basis of comparison. The anonymous respondent has taken Watson to task on these comparisons and their accuracy and significance. Watson admits that the comparisons he gives in his first section "do not as yet amount to a *proof*" that Smith forged the letter.[501] What strikes me in section two is Watson's statement, "The authentic Secret Mark [as per Clement's instruction to Theodore] is only slightly less prurient than the falsified one."[502] Watson is here not straying far from Jeffery in starting with the assumption that Secret Mark portrays an immoral, homosexual encounter fashioned by the degenerate thinking of a dishonest scholar, and largely on the basis of that assumption concluding that the real purpose of the letter is "to disclose the existence and content of the Secret Gospel, not to respond appropriately to Theodore."[503] Like Jeffery, no thought is given to the deeper spiritual meaning of nakedness and its relationship to an initiation into the mysteries, a subject fully explored elsewhere herein but wholly ignored by Watson's approach.[504]

Later, in item 3 of his section two, Watson adopts Carlson's Morton Salt clue as Smith's "forger's signature," a point that has been thoroughly discredited with respect to Carlson's argumentation.[505]

---

[500] Watson, "Beyond Suspicion," 131.
[501] Watson, "Beyond Suspicion," 144.
[502] Watson, "Beyond Suspicion," 147.
[503] Watson, "Beyond Suspicion," 148.
[504] See pp. 160–61.
[505] Watson, "Beyond Suspicion," 152–55.

Watson takes a different approach, connecting Smith's given name to the Greek verb *mōranthēnai*, which means "lose its savor." The anonymous respondent rightly replies that Watson can make this connection to Smith only by arbitrarily ignoring the four letters that are not part of the name Morton (*alpha, nu, alpha, iota*) and by changing the *th* sound of *theta* to simple *t* (and the *ā* sound of *eta* to the *ə* sound in *mòr-t^ən*).

Watson concludes his article with a ten-page presentation of the asserted similarities between Smith's *The Secret Gospel* and Hunter's *The Mystery of Mar Saba* (see Carlson issue no. 8).[506] The anonymous respondent comments that Watson offers "nothing very new to the discussion" except his discovery of two one-sentence parallels between Hunter's novel and Smith's *The Secret Gospel* which, "at best … raise the suspicion that Smith could have read Hunter's novel," but "suspicions and insinuations do not make a case for forgery" without further evidence.[507] Allan J. Pantuck, in a further response posted on the BAR website, recognizes the parallels as "provocative," but illustrates with several quite extraordinary examples how life sometimes very closely imitates art by pure coincidence. Pantuck also disproves Watson's allegations that secret Mark confirms an idiosyncratic theory about the relationship between the Gospels of Mark and John that Smith held in 1955.[508]

Save for inferences from the asserted similarities, there is no evidence that Smith was ever aware of Hunter's book. It was not in his personal library at the time of his death.[509] Remarkable coincidences may be a

---

[506] Watson, "Beyond Suspicion," 161–70.

[507] For the two one-sentence parallels, see Watson, "Beyond Suspicion," 165–66.

[508] Allan J. Pantuck, "Solving the *Mysterion* of Morton Smith and the Secret Gospel of Mark," Biblical Archaeology Review (February 20, 2011), http://www.bib-arch.org/scholars-study/secret-mark-handwriting-response-pantuck.asp.

[509] Pantuck, e-mail to author, May 11, 2010: "I've now had a chance to look into this a little. I spoke with Smith's research assistant who took care of Smith's books after he died. He tells me that only Smith's academic books went to JTS. However, he organized and sold, according to Smith's wishes, all the non-academic books to Ideal Books in NY. The owner of Ideal Books had previously inventoried and valued the entire book collection for Smith. Anyway, Smith's assistant says that the Hunter book was not in Smith's collection, and that Smith never mentioned it to him."

basis for suspicion of forgery, but they should never be considered themselves as evidence of forgery.[510]

The Verdict

Pending recovery of the original manuscript for examination, the evidence is in. Based upon any of the generally recognized standards of proof, the challengers have failed to carry their burden of proof that Morton Smith forged the *Letter to Theodore*. On the contrary, the evidence affirmatively shows that the letter was not written by Smith.

Postscript

An additional rumination on the possibility that Luke knew something similar to Mark's source for the Lazarus story is posted on my website. See http://www.bibleandanthroposophy.com/Smith/main/anthroposophy.html and click on *Temple Sleep Rumination.*

---

[510] Consider the Wikipedia article, "Futility, or the Wreck of the Titan," for a real-life tragedy that seemed to reenact an earlier work of fiction.

Bibliography

Albanese, Catherine L. "Introduction: Awash in a Sea of Metaphysics." *Journal of the American Academy of Religion* 75 (2007): 582–88.

———. *A Republic of Mind and Spirit: A Cultural History of American Metaphysical Religion.* New Haven: Yale University Press, 2007.

Alter, Robert. *The Five Books of Moses: A Translation with Commentary.* New York: W. W. Norton, 2004.

Anastasopoulou, Venetia. "Can a Document in Itself Reveal a Forgery?" Biblical Archaeology Review (July 22, 2010), http://www.bib-arch.org/scholars-study/secret-mark-handwriting-document-reveal-forgery.asp.

———. "Experts [*sic*] Report Handwriting Examination." Biblical Archaeology Review, http://www.bib-arch.org/pdf/secret-mark-analysis.pdf.

Armstrong, John. *The Paradise Myth.* London: Oxford University Press, 1969.

Baigent, Michael, Richard Leigh, and Henry Lincoln. *Holy Blood, Holy Grail.* New York: Dell Publishing, 1982.

Baltz, Frederick W. *Lazarus and the Fourth Gospel Community.* Lewiston, N.Y.: Mellen, 1996.

Barton, J. "Postexilic Hebrew Prophecy." Pages 489–95 in vol. 5 of *Anchor Bible Dictionary.* Edited by D. N. Freedman. 6 vols. New York: Doubleday, 1992.

Bauckham, Richard. "In Response to My Respondents: *Jesus and the Eyewitnesses* in Review." *Journal for the Study of the Historical Jesus* 6 (2008): 225–53.

———. *Jesus and the Eyewitnesses: The Gospels as Eyewitness Testimony.* Grand Rapids: Eerdmans, 2006.

———. "Response to the Respondents." *Nova et Vetera* 6 (2008): 529–42.

———. *The Testimony of the Beloved Disciple: Narrative, History, and Theology in the Gospel of John.* Grand Rapids: Baker Academic, 2007.

Beck, Roger. "The Mysteries of Mithras: A New Account of Their Genesis." *Journal of Roman Studies* 88 (1998): 115–28. http://www.jstor.org/stable/300807.

Biblical Archaeology Review. "Did Morton Smith Forge 'Secret Mark'? A Handwriting Expert Weighs In." Biblical Archaeology Review (April 2010), http://www.bib-arch.org/e-features/secret-mark-handwriting-analysis.asp.

———. "Handwriting Experts Weigh In on 'Secret Mark.'" *Biblical Archaeology Review* 36, no. 3 (May/June 2010): 18, 79.

Black, C. Clifton. "The First, Second, and Third Letters of John." Pages 363–469 in vol. 12 of *The New Interpreter's Bible*. Edited by Leander E. Keck. 12 vols. Nashville: Abingdon, 1998.

Blavatsky, Helena P. *The Secret Doctrine: The Synthesis of Science, Religion, and Philosophy*. London: Theosophical, 1888. Repr., Pasadena: Theosophical University Press, 1977.

Blenkinsopp, Joseph. "Introduction to the Pentateuch." Pages 305–18 in vol. 1 of *The New Interpreter's Bible*. Edited by Leander E. Keck. 12 vols. Nashville: Abingdon, 1994.

Bock, Emil. *The Apocalypse of St. John*. Edinburgh: Floris, 1957.

———. *The Three Years: The Life of Christ between Baptism and Ascension*. Edinburgh: Floris, 1955.

Boer, Esther A. de. *The Gospel of Mary: Beyond a Gnostic and a Biblical Mary Magdalene*. New York: T&T Clark, 2004.

———. "Mary Magdalene and the Disciple Jesus Loved." *Lectio difficilior* 1 (2000), http://www.lectio.unibe.ch/00_1/m-forum.htm.

Boyce, Mary. *Zoroastrianism: Its Antiquity and Constant Vigour*. Costa Mesa, Calif.: Mazda, 1992.

Brown, Raymond E. *The Birth of the Messiah: A Commentary on the Infancy Narratives in the Gospels of Matthew and Luke*. 2d ed. Anchor Bible Reference Library. New York: Doubleday, 1993.

———. *The Death of the Messiah: From Gethsemane to the Grave: A Commentary on the Passion Narratives in the Four Gospels*. 2 vols. New York: Doubleday, 1994.

———. *The Epistles of John*. Anchor Bible 30. Garden City, N.Y.: Doubleday, 1982.

———. *The Gospel according to John: Introduction, Translation, and Notes*. 2 vols. Anchor Bible 29–29A. Garden City, N.Y.: Doubleday, 1966–1970.

Brown, Scott G. "Bethany beyond the Jordan: John 1:28 and the Longer Gospel of Mark." *Revue Biblique* 110 (2003): 497–516.

———. Essay Review of Peter Jeffery, *The Secret Gospel of Mark Unveiled*. *Review of Biblical Literature* (September 15, 2007), http://www.bookreviews.org/pdf/5627_5944.pdf.

———. "Factualizing the Folklore: Stephen Carlson's Case against Morton Smith." *Harvard Theological Review* 99 (2006): 291–327.

———. "The *Letter to Theodore*: Stephen Carlson's Case against Clement's Authorship." *Journal of Early Christian Studies* 16 (2008): 535–72.

———. "Mark 11:1–12:12: A Triple Intercalation?" *Catholic Biblical Quarterly* 64 (2002): 78–89.

———. *Mark's Other Gospel*. Waterloo, Ont.: Wilfrid Laurier University Press, 2005.

———. "My Thoughts on the Reports by Venetia Anastasopoulou." Biblical Archaeology Review (January 24, 2011), http://www.bib-arch.org/scholars-study/secret-mark-handwriting-response-brown.asp.

———. "On the Composition History of the Longer ('Secret') Gospel of Mark." *Journal of Biblical Literature* 122 (2003): 89–110.

———. "The Question of Motive in the Case against Morton Smith." *Journal of Biblical Literature* 125 (2006): 351–83.

———. "Reply to Stephen Carlson." *Expository Times* 117 (2006): 144–49.

———. "The Secret Gospel of Mark: Is It Real? And Does It Identify 'Bethany beyond the Jordan'?" *Biblical Archaeology Review* 31, no. 1 (January/February 2005): 44–49, 60–61.

Brown, Scott G., and Allan J. Pantuck. "Stephen Carlson's Questionable Questioned Document Examination." Salainen evankelista. Posted April 14, 2010. http://salainenevankelista.blogspot.com/2010/04/stephen-carlsons-questionable.html. Reposted on The Secret Gospel of Mark Homepage. http://www-user.uni-bremen.de/~wie/Secret/Pantuck-Brown-2010.pdf.

Bruce, F. F. *The Teacher of Righteousness in the Qumran Texts*. London: Tyndale, 1957. http://www.biblicalstudies.org.uk/pdf/qumran_bruce.pdf.

Bruns, J. Edgar. "Ananda: The Fourth Evangelist's Model for 'the Disciple Whom Jesus Loved'?" *Studies in Religion* 3 (1973): 236–43.

Bultmann, Rudolf. *The Gospel of John*. Translated by G. R. Beasley-Murray. Philadelphia: Westminster, 1971.

Carlson, Stephen C. *The Gospel Hoax: Morton Smith's Invention of Secret Mark*. Waco, Tex.: Baylor University Press, 2005.

Charlesworth, James H. *The Beloved Disciple: Whose Witness Validates the Gospel of John?* Valley Forge: Trinity Press International, 1995.

Chauncey, George. *Gay New York: Gender, Urban Culture, and the Making of the Gay Male World, 1890–1940*. New York: Basic Books, 1994.

———. *Why Marriage? The History Shaping Today's Debate Over Gay Equality*. New York: Basic Books, 2004.

Cohen, Shaye J. D. "In Memoriam Morton Smith." Pages 279–85 in *New Testament, Early Christianity, and Magic*. Vol. 2 of *Studies in the Cult of Yahweh*. Edited by Shaye J. D. Cohen. Leiden: Brill, 1996.

Collins, Adela Yarbro. *Mark: A Commentary*. Minneapolis: Fortress, 2007.

Criddle, Andrew H. "On the Mar Saba Letter Attributed to Clement of Alexandria." *Journal of Early Christian Studies* 3 (1995): 215–20.

Cullmann, Oscar. *The Johannine Circle*. Translated by J. Bowden. Philadelphia: Westminster, 1975.

Daniélou, Jean. *Primitive Christian Symbols*. Translated by Donald Attwater. London: Burns & Oates, 1964. http://www.archive.org/details/primitive christi009995mbp.

Dart, John. *Decoding Mark*. Harrisburg: Trinity Press International, 2003.

DeConick, April D., and Jarl Fossum. "Stripped before God: A New Interpretation of Logion 37 in the Gospel of Thomas." *Vigiliae christianae* 45 (1991): 123–50.

Derrett, J. Duncan M. "Fig Trees in the New Testament." *Heythrop Journal* 14 (1973): 249–65.

Distasi, Richard. *The Fleeing Youth: The Cosmic Principle of Christ* (2009), http://www.lulu.com/items/volume_67/6997000/6997588/6/print/6997588.pdf.

Dodd, C. H. *Historical Tradition in the Fourth Gospel*. Cambridge: Cambridge University Press, 1963.

Dunning, Benjamin H. "What Sort of Thing Is This Luminous Woman? Thinking Sexual Difference in *On the Origin of the World*." *Journal of Early Christian Studies* 17 (2009): 55–84.

Easton, Stewart C. *Rudolf Steiner: Herald of a New Epoch*. Hudson, N.Y.: Anthroposophic Press, 1980.

Ehrman, Bart D. *Misquoting Jesus: The Story behind Who Changed the Bible and Why*. New York: HarperCollins, 2005.

———. "Response to Charles Hedrick's Stalemate." *Journal of Early Christian Studies* 11 (2003): 155–63.

Eisler, Robert. *The Enigma of the Fourth Gospel: Its Author and Its Writer*. London: Methuen, 1938.

Esler, Philip F. "The Incident of the Withered Fig Tree in Mark 11: A New Source and Redactional Explanation." *Journal for the Study of the New Testament* 28 (2005): 41–67.

Faderman, Lillian. *Odd Girls and Twilight Lovers: A History of Lesbian Life in Twentieth-Century America*. New York: Columbia University Press, 1991.

Fitzmyer, Joseph A. *First Corinthians*. Anchor Bible 32. New Haven: Yale University Press, 2008.

Freedman, David Noel, ed. *The Anchor Bible Dictionary*. 6 vols. New York: Doubleday, 1992.

Griffith-Jones, Robin. *Beloved Disciple: The Misunderstood Legacy of Mary Magdalene, the Woman Closest to Jesus*. New York: HarperCollins, 2008.

Haren, Michael J. "The Naked Young Man: A Historian's Hypothesis on Mark 14,51–52." *Biblica* 79 (1998): 525–31. http://www.bsw.org/project/biblica/bibl79/Ani10.htm.

Hedrick, Charles W. *The Apocalypse of Adam*. Chico, Calif.: Scholars Press, 1980. Repr., Eugene, Oreg.: Wipf & Stock, 2005.

———. "The Secret Gospel of Mark: Stalemate in the Academy." *Journal of Early Christian Studies* 11 (2003): 133–45.

———, ed. *When Faith Meets Reason: Religion Scholars Reflect on Their Spiritual Journeys*. Santa Rosa, Calif.: Polebridge, 2008.

Hedrick, Charles W., and Nikolaos Olympiou. "Secret Mark: New Photographs, New Witnesses." *The Fourth R* 13, no. 5 (September/October 2000): 3–16.

Hedrick, Charles W., and Robert Hodgson Jr., eds. *Nag Hammadi, Gnosticism, and Early Christianity*. Peabody, Mass.: Hendrickson, 1986. Repr., Eugene, Oreg.: Wipf & Stock, 2005.

Hemleben, Johannes. *Rudolf Steiner: An Illustrated Biography*. Translated by Leo Twyman. London: Sophia Books, 2000.

Hendel, Ronald S. "Of Demigods and the Deluge: Toward an Interpretation of Genesis 6:1–4." *Journal of Biblical Literature* 106 (1987): 13–26.

Hindes, James H. Introduction to *Reading the Pictures of the Apocalypse*, by Rudolf Steiner. Great Barrington, Mass.: Anthroposophic Press, 1993.

Hunter, James Hogg. *The Mystery of Mar Saba*. New York: Evangelical, 1940.

Hurtado, Larry W. Foreword to *The Gospel Hoax: Morton Smith's Invention of Secret Mark*, by Stephen C. Carlson. Waco, Tex.: Baylor University Press, 2005.

Hypotyposeis. http://www.hypotyposeis.org.

Jay, Jeff. "A New Look at the Epistolary Framework of the *Secret Gospel of Mark*." *Journal of Early Christian Studies* 16 (2008): 573–97.

Jeffery, Peter. "Response to Handwriting Analysis." Biblical Archaeology Review (April 19, 2010), http://www.bib-arch.org/scholars-study/secret-mark-handwriting-response-jeffery.asp.

———. *The Secret Gospel of Mark Unveiled: Imagined Rituals of Sex, Death, and Madness in a Biblical Forgery*. New Haven: Yale University Press, 2007.

————. "The Secret Gospel of Mark Unveiled: Reply to Scott G. Brown." Peter Jeffery's Home Page. http://www.music.princeton.edu/jeffery/ replytobrown.pdf; http://music.princeton.edu/jeffery/Review_of_ Biblical_Literature-Jeffery_reply_to_Brown.pdf.

Jusino, Ramon K. "Mary Magdalene: Author of the Fourth Gospel?" http:// ramon_k_jusino.tripod.com/magdalene.html.

Key, Andrew F. "The Giving of Proper Names in the Old Testament." *Journal of Biblical Literature* 83 (1964): 55–59. http://www.jstor.org/ pss/3264907.

Khouri, Rami. "Where John Baptized: Bethany beyond the Jordan." *Biblical Archaeology Review* 31, no. 1 (January/February 2005): 34–43.

King, Karen L. *What Is Gnosticism?* Cambridge, Mass.: Belknap, 2003.

Klitenic, Sarah. "The Teacher of Righteousness and the End of Days." *Sources* 3 (Spring 1997), http://humanities.uchicago.edu/journals/jsjournal/klitenic. html.

Koester, Helmut. "Gnostic Sayings and Controversy Traditions in John 8:12–59." Pages 97–110 in *Nag Hammadi, Gnosticism, and Early Christianity*. Edited by C. W. Hedrick and R. Hodgson Jr. Peabody, Mass.: Hendrickson, 1986. Repr., Eugene, Oreg.: Wipf & Stock, 2005.

————. "History and Development of Mark's Gospel (From Mark to *Secret Mark* and 'Canonical' Mark)." Pages 35–57 in *Colloquy on New Testament Studies: A Time for Reappraisal and Fresh Approaches*. Edited by Bruce Corley. Macon, Ga.: Mercer University Press, 1983.

————. "Was Morton Smith a Great Thespian and I a Complete Fool?" *Biblical Archaeology Review* 35, no. 6 (November/December 2009): 54–58, 88.

König, Karl. *The Mystery of John and the Cycle of the Year*. N.p.: Camphill Books, 2000.

Kovacs, Judith L. "Concealment and Gnostic Exegesis: Clement of Alexandria's Interpretation of the Tabernacle." Pages 414–37 in *Studia Patristica: Papers Presented at the Twelfth International Conference on Patristic Studies Held in Oxford, 1995*. Studia patristica 31. Edited by Elizabeth A. Livingstone. Leuven: Peeters, 1997.

Kreyenbühl, Johannes. *Das Evangelium der Wahrheit: Neue Lösung der Johanneischen Frage*. 2 vols. Berlin: C. A. Schwetschke und Sohn, 1900, 1905.

Le Boulluec, Alain. "La Lettre sur l' 'Évangile secret' de Marc et le *Quis dives salvetur?* de Clément d'Alexandrie." *Apocrypha* 7 (1996): 27–41.

Léonard, J.-M. "Notule sur l'Évangile de Jean: Le disciple que Jésus aimait et Marie." *Études Théologiques et Religieuses* 58 (1983): 355–57.

Lerner, Michael. "Arthur Darby Nock Dies at Sixty: Religion Historian's Death Stuns Academic World." *Harvard Crimson*, January 14, 1963. http://www. thecrimson.com/article/1963/1/14/arthur-darby-nock-dies-at-sixty/.

Lissau, Rudi. *Rudolf Steiner: Life, Work, Inner Path and Social Initiatives.* Stroud, UK: Hawthorn, 1987.

Luttikhuizen, Gerard P. *Gnostic Revisions of Genesis Stories and Early Jesus Traditions.* Nag Hammadi and Manichaean Studies 58. Leiden: Brill, 2006.

Marcus, Joel. *Mark 8–16: A New Translation with Introduction and Commentary.* Anchor Bible 27A. New Haven: Yale University Press, 2009.

McCarter, P. Kyle, Jr. *I Samuel: A New Translation with Introduction, Notes, and Commentary.* Anchor Bible 8. Garden City, N.Y.: Doubleday, 1980.

Meyer, Marvin W. *The Ancient Mysteries: A Sourcebook: Sacred Texts of the Mystery Religions of the Ancient Mediterranean World.* New York: HarperCollins, 1987. Repr., Philadelphia: University of Pennsylvania Press, 1999.

———. *Secret Gospels: Essays on Thomas and the Secret Gospel of Mark.* Harrisburg: Trinity Press International, 2003.

Nesfield-Cookson, Bernard. *The Mystery of the Two Jesus Children and the Descent of the Spirit of the Sun.* London: Temple Lodge, 2005.

O'Day, Gail R. "The Gospel of John: Introduction, Commentary, and Reflections." Pages 491–865 in vol. 9 of *The New Interpreter's Bible.* Edited by Leander E. Keck. 12 vols. Nashville: Abingdon, 1995.

Paananen, Timo S. "A Conspiracy of the Secret Evangelist: Recent Debate concerning Clement of Alexandria's *Letter to Theodore.*" Salainen evankelista. http://salainenevankelista.blogspot.com/2009/06/masters-thesis-conspiracy-of-secret.html. English translation of "Salaisen evankelistan salaliitto: Uusin keskustelu Klemens Aleksandrialaisen kirjeestä Theodorokselle." Master's thesis, University of Helsinki, 2009. https://oa.doria.fi/bitstream/handle/10024/45340/salaisen.pdf?sequence=2.

Pagels, Elaine H. *Beyond Belief: The Secret Gospel of Thomas.* New York: Random House, 2003.

———. "Exegesis of Genesis 1 in Thomas and John." *Journal of Biblical Literature* 118 (1999): 477–96.

———. *The Gnostic Gospels.* New York: Random House, 1981.

Pantuck, Allan J. "Solving the *Mysterion* of Morton Smith and the Secret Gospel of Mark." Biblical Archaeology Review (February 20, 2011), http://www.bib-arch.org/scholars-study/secret-mark-handwriting-response-pantuck.asp.

Pantuck, Allan J., and Scott G. Brown. "Morton Smith as M. Madiotes: Stephen Carlson's Attribution of *Secret Mark* to a Bald Swindler." *Journal for the Study of the Historical Jesus* 6 (2008): 106–25.

Parrott, Douglas M. "The 13 Kingdoms of the Apocalypse of Adam: Origin, Meaning and Significance." *Novum Testamentum* 31 (1989): 67–87.

Perkins, Pheme. "The Gospel of Mark." Pages 507–733 in vol. 8 of *The New Interpreter's Bible*. Edited by Leander E. Keck. 12 vols. Nashville: Abingdon, 1996.

Phillips, J. *The Disciple Whom Jesus Loved*. 3d rev. ed. Kearney, Nebr.: Morris, 2004.

Powell, Robert. *Hermetic Astrology*. 2 vols. Kinsau, West Germany: Hermetika, 1987.

Prokofieff, Sergei O. *Eternal Individuality: Towards a Karmic Biography of Novalis*. London: Temple Lodge, 1992.

Querido, René M. Introduction to *The Book of Revelation and the Work of the Priest*, by Rudolf Steiner. London: Rudolf Steiner Press, 1998.

Quesnell, Quentin. "The Mar Saba Clementine: A Question of Evidence." *Catholic Biblical Quarterly* 37 (1975): 48–67.

Richardson, Cyril C. Review of Morton Smith, *Clement of Alexandria and a Secret Gospel of Mark* and *The Secret Gospel. Theological Studies* 35 (1974): 571–77.

Robinson, James M., ed. *The Nag Hammadi Library in English*. 3d rev. ed. San Francisco: HarperCollins, 1990.

Rose, Martin. "Names of God in the OT." Pages 1001–11 in vol. 4 of *Anchor Bible Dictionary*. Edited by D. N. Freedman. 6 vols. New York: Doubleday, 1992.

Salainen evankelista. http://salainenevankelista.blogspot.com/.

Sarna, Nahum. *The JPS Torah Commentary: Exodus*. Philadelphia: Jewish Publication Society, 1991.

———. *The JPS Torah Commentary: Genesis*. Philadelphia: Jewish Publication Society, 1989.

Sasson, Jack M. *Jonah: A New Translation with Introduction, Commentary, and Interpretations*. Anchor Bible 24B. New York: Doubleday, 1990.

Schenke, Hans-Martin. "The Function and Background of the Beloved Disciple in the Gospel of John." Pages 111–25 in *Nag Hammadi, Gnosticism, and Early Christianity*. Edited by C. W. Hedrick and R. Hodgson Jr. Peabody, Mass: Hendrickson, 1986.

Scholer, David M. *Nag Hammadi Bibliography, 1948–1969*. Leiden: Brill, 1971.

———. *Nag Hammadi Bibliography, 1970–1994*. New York: Brill, 1997.

Schwaller de Lubicz, R. A. *The Temple of Man: Apet of the South at Luxor.* Translated by Deborah Lawlor and Robert Lawlor. Rochester, Vt.: Inner Traditions, 1998.

Shandruk, Walter M. "Statistics and Hapax Legomena in the Mar Saba Letter." Thoughts on Antiquity. Posted August 10, 2008. http://neonostalgia. com/weblog/?p=496.

Shanks, Hershel. "Losing Faith: How Scholarship Affects Scholars." *Biblical Archaeology Review* 33, no. 2 (March/April 2007): 50–57.

Shepherd, A. P. *Rudolf Steiner: Scientist of the Invisible.* Rochester, Vt.: Inner Traditions, 1983. Reprint of *A Scientist of the Invisible: An Introduction to the Life and Work of Rudolf Steiner.* London: Hodder & Stoughton, 1954.

Simon, Uriel. *Jonah: The Traditional Hebrew Text with the New JPS Translation.* Translated by Lenn J. Schramm. Philadelphia: Jewish Publication Society, 1999.

Smith, Edward Reaugh. *The Burning Bush.* Vol. 1 of *Rudolf Steiner, Anthroposophy, and the Holy Scriptures.* Rev. ed. Great Barrington, Mass.: Anthroposophic Press, 2001.

———. *David's Question: "What Is Man?" (Psalm 8).* Vol. 2 of *Rudolf Steiner, Anthroposophy, and the Holy Scriptures.* Great Barrington, Mass.: Anthroposophic Press, 2001.

———. *The Disciple Whom Jesus Loved: Unveiling the Author of John's Gospel.* Great Barrington, Mass.: Anthroposophic Press, 2000.

———. *The Incredible Births of Jesus.* Hudson, N.Y.: Anthroposophic Press, 1998.

———. *The Soul's Long Journey: How the Bible Reveals Reincarnation.* Vol. 3 of *Rudolf Steiner, Anthroposophy, and the Holy Scriptures.* Great Barrington, Mass.: SteinerBooks, 2003.

Smith, Jonathan Z. *Drudgery Divine: On the Comparison of Early Christianities and the Religions of Late Antiquity.* Chicago: University of Chicago Press, 1990.

Smith, Kyle. "'Mixed with Inventions': Salt and Metaphor in Secret Mark." The Secret Gospel of Mark Homepage. http://www-user.uni-bremen. de/~wie/Secret/SALT-PAPER.rtf.

Smith, Morton. *Clement of Alexandria and a Secret Gospel of Mark.* Cambridge, Mass.: Harvard University Press, 1973.

———. *Jesus the Magician.* San Francisco: Harper & Row, 1978. Repr., New York: Barnes & Noble, 1993.

———. "Monasteries and Their Manuscripts." *Archaeology* 13 (1960): 172–77.

———. "On the Authenticity of the Mar Saba Letter of Clement." *Catholic Biblical Quarterly* 38 (1976): 196–99.

———. *The Secret Gospel: The Discovery and Interpretation of the Secret Gospel according to Mark.* New York: Harper & Row, 1973. Repr., Clearlake, Calif.: Dawn Horse, 1982.

———. *Studies in the Cult of Yahweh.* Edited by Shaye J. D. Cohen. 2 vols. Leiden: Brill, 1996.

Steiner, Rudolf. *According to Luke: The Gospel of Compassion and Love Revealed.* Translated by Catherine E. Creeger. Great Barrington, Mass.: SteinerBooks, 2001. (CW 114.)

———. *According to Matthew: The Gospel of Christ's Humanity.* Translated by Catherine E. Creeger. Great Barrington, Mass.: SteinerBooks, 2003. (CW 123.)

———. *The Apocalypse of St. John.* 4th ed. London: Rudolf Steiner Press, 1977. (CW 104.)

———. *At the Gates of Spiritual Science.* Translated by E. H. Goddard and C. Davy. 2d ed. London: Rudolf Steiner Press, 1986. (CW 95.)

———. *Autobiography: Chapters in the Course of My Life, 1861–1907.* Translated by Rita Stebbing. CW 28. Great Barrington, Mass.: SteinerBooks, 2006.

———. *Background to the Gospel of St. Mark.* Translated by E. H. Goddard and D. S. Osmond. Hudson, N.Y.: Anthroposophic Press, 1985. (CW 124.)

———. *The Bhagavad Gita and the West: The Esoteric Significance of the Bhagavad Gita and Its Relation to the Epistles of Paul.* Translated by Doris Bugbey, Lisa Monges, George Adams, and Mary Adams. CW 142/146. Great Barrington, Mass.: SteinerBooks, 2009.

———. *The Book of Revelation and the Work of the Priest.* Translated by J. Collis. London: Rudolf Steiner Press, 1998. (CW 346.)

———. *Christ and the Human Soul.* 4th ed. London: Rudolf Steiner Press, 1984. (CW 155.)

———. *The Christian Mystery.* Translated by James H. Hindes, Catherine E. Creeger, D. S. Osmond, and Christopher Bamford. Hudson, N.Y.: Anthroposophic Press, 1998. (CW 97.)

———. *Christianity as Mystical Fact and the Mysteries of Antiquity.* Translated by Andrew J. Welburn. CW 8. Great Barrington, Mass: SteinerBooks, 2006.

———. *The Concepts of Original Sin and Grace.* Translated by D. S. Osmond. 2d ed. London: Rudolf Steiner Press, 1973. (CW 127.)

———. *Correspondence and Documents, 1901–1925.* Edited by Joan M.

Thompson. Translated by Christian von Arnim and Ingrid von Arnim. London: Rudolf Steiner Press, 1988. (CW 262.)

——. *Cosmic Memory*. Translated by Karl E. Zimmer. Blauvelt, N.Y.: Rudolf Steiner Publications, 1959. (CW 11.)

——. *Deeper Secrets of Human History in the Light of the Gospel of St. Matthew*. Translated by D. S. Osmond and A. P. Shepherd. Rev. ed. London: Rudolf Steiner Press, 1957. (CW 117.)

——. *Egyptian Myths and Mysteries*. Translated by Norman Macbeth. Hudson, N.Y.: Anthroposophic Press, 1971. (CW 106.)

——. *The Festivals and Their Meaning*. Translated by M. Cotterell. 2d ed. London: Rudolf Steiner Press, 1992. (CW 102.)

——. *Festivals of the Seasons*. CW 156. London: Anthroposophical Publishing Co., 1928.

——. *The Fifth Gospel: From the Akashic Record*. Translated by A. R. Meuss, C. Davy, and D. S. Osmond. 3d ed. London: Rudolf Steiner Press, 1995. (CW 148.)

——. *Foundations of Esotericism*. Translated by Vera Compton-Burnett and Judith Compton-Burnett. London: Rudolf Steiner Press, 1983. (CW 93a.)

——. *From Jesus to Christ*. Translated by H. Collison and revised by C. Davy. London: Rudolf Steiner Press, 1973. (CW 131.)

——. *Genesis: Secrets of the Bible Story of Creation*. Translated by Dorothy Lenn and Owen Barfield. 2d ed. London: Rudolf Steiner Press, 1982. (CW 122.)

——. *The Gospel of St. John and Its Relation to the Other Gospels*. Translated by Samuel Lockwood and Loni Lockwood. 2d ed. Spring Valley, N.Y.: Anthroposophic Press, 1982. (CW 112.)

——. *The Gospel of St. John*. Rev. ed. New York: Anthroposophic Press, 1962. (CW 103.)

——. "The Gospel of St. John." Typescript at Rudolf Steiner Library, Ghent, N.Y. (CW 100.)

——. *The Gospel of St. Mark*. Edited by Stewart C. Easton. Translated by C. Mainzer. Hudson, N.Y.: Anthroposophic Press, 1986. (CW 139.)

——. *The Gospel of St. Matthew*. Translated by Catherine E. Creeger. Great Barrington, Mass: Anthroposophic Press, 2003. (CW 123.)

——. "The Gospels." Lecture, Stuttgart, November 14, 1909. Typescript at Rudolf Steiner Library, Ghent, N.Y. (CW 117.)

——. *How to Know Higher Worlds: A Modern Path of Initiation*. Translated by Christopher Bamford. Hudson, N.Y.: Anthroposophic Press, 1994. (CW 10.)

————. *The Influence of Spiritual Beings upon Man.* Spring Valley, N.Y.: Anthroposophic Press, 1961. (CW 102.)

————. *Isis Mary Sophia: Her Mission and Ours.* Great Barrington, Mass.: SteinerBooks, 2003. (CW 94.)

————. *The Last Address.* Translated by George Adams. London: Rudolf Steiner Press, 1967. (CW 238.)

————. *Mystery Centers.* Blauvelt, N.Y.: Garber Communications, 1989. (CW 232.)

————. *The Occult Movement in the Nineteenth Century and Its Relation to Modern Culture.* London: Rudolf Steiner Press, 1973. (CW 254.)

————. *An Occult Physiology.* London: Rudolf Steiner Press, 1951. (CW 128.)

————. *Occult Signs and Symbols.* Translated by Sarah Kurland, with emendations by Gilbert Church. Hudson, N.Y.: Anthroposophic Press, 1972. (CW 101.)

————. *An Outline of Esoteric Science.* Translated by Catherine E. Creeger. Great Barrington, Mass.: Anthroposophic Press, 1997. (CW 13.)

————. *Philosophy, Cosmology, and Religion.* Edited by Stewart C. Easton. Translated by Lisa Monges and Doris Bugbey and revised by Maria St. Goar. Spring Valley, N.Y.: Anthroposophic Press, 1984. (CW 25/215.)

————. *The Principle of Spiritual Economy.* Translated by Peter Mollenhauer. Hudson, N.Y.: Anthroposophic Press, 1986. (CW 109/111.)

————. *The Reappearance of Christ in the Etheric.* Translated by Barbara Betteridge, Diane Tatum, Ruth Pusch, Margaret de Ris, and Alice Wulsin. 2d ed. Spring Valley, N.Y.: Anthroposophic Press, 1983. (CW 118.)

————. *Rosicrucian Esotericism.* Translated by D. S. Osmond. Spring Valley, N.Y.: Anthroposophic Press, 1978. (CW 109/111.)

————. *The Spiritual Hierarchies and the Physical World: Zodiac, Planets, and Cosmos.* Translated by René M. Querido and Jann Gates. CW 110. Great Barrington, Mass.: SteinerBooks, 2008.

————. *The Sun Mystery and the Mystery of Death and Resurrection: Exoteric and Esoteric Christianity.* Translated by Catherine E. Creeger. CW 211. Great Barrington, Mass.: SteinerBooks, 2006.

————. *The Temple Legend.* Translated by John M. Wood. London: Rudolf Steiner Press, 1985. (CW 93.)

————. *Theosophy: An Introduction to the Spiritual Processes in Human Life and in the Cosmos.* Translated by Catherine E. Creeger. Hudson, N.Y.: Anthroposophic Press, 1994. (CW 9.)

———. *Theosophy of the Rosicrucian.* Translated by M. Cotterell and D. S. Osmond. 2d ed. London: Rudolf Steiner Press, 1966. (CW 99.)

———. *Turning Points in Spiritual History: Zarathustra, Hermes, Moses, Elijah, Buddha, Christ.* Translated by Walter F. Knox. Great Barrington, Mass.: SteinerBooks, 2007. (CW 60, 61.)

———. *Universe, Earth and Man.* London: Rudolf Steiner Press, 1987. (CW 105.)

———. "The Wisdom Contained in Ancient Documents and in the Gospels: The Event of the Christ." *Anthroposophic News Sheet* 5, no. 26 (June 27, 1937): 105–7; 5, no. 27 (July 4, 1937): 109–11; 5, no. 28 (July 11, 1937): 113–15; 5, no. 29 (July 18, 1937): 117–18. http://wn.rsarchive. org/Lectures/19101113p01.html. (CW 125.)

———. *Wonders of the World: Ordeals of the Soul, Revelations of the Spirit.* Translated by Dorothy Lenn and Owen Barfield. London: Rudolf Steiner Press, 1963. (CW 129.)

Stewart, Desmond. *The Foreigner.* London: Hamish Hamilton, 1981.

Stroumsa, Guy G. "Comments on Charles Hedrick's Article: A Testimony." *Journal of Early Christian Studies* 11 (2003): 147–53.

Tabor, James D. *The Jesus Dynasty: The Hidden History of Jesus, His Royal Family, and the Birth of Christianity.* New York: Simon & Schuster, 2006.

Teilhard de Chardin, Pierre. *The Phenomenon of Man.* 2d ed. New York: Harper Colophon, 1975.

Telford, William R. *The Barren Temple and the Withered Tree: A Redaction-Critical Analysis of the Cursing of the Fig-Tree in Mark's Gospel and Its Relation to the Cleansing of the Temple Tradition.* Sheffield: JSOT Press, 1980.

Theissen, Gerd. *The Gospels in Context: Social and Political History in the Synoptic Tradition.* Minneapolis: Fortress, 1991.

Thisted, Ronald, and Bradley Efron. "Did Shakespeare Write a Newly-Discovered Poem?" *Biometrika* 74 (1987): 445–55.

Thomassen, Einar. *The Spiritual Seed: The Church of the "Valentinians."* Nag Hammadi and Manichaean Studies 60. Leiden: Brill, 2006.

Tilborg, Sjef van. *Imaginative Love in John.* Leiden: Brill, 1993.

Trible, Phyllis. "The Book of Jonah." Pages 463–529 in vol. 7 of *The New Interpreter's Bible.* Edited by Leander E. Keck. 12 vols. Nashville: Abingdon, 1996.

———. *God and the Rhetoric of Sexuality.* Philadelphia: Fortress, 1978.

———. *Rhetorical Criticism: Context, Method, and the Book of Jonah.* Minneapolis: Fortress, 1994.

Ulansey, David. *The Origins of the Mithraic Mysteries.* New York: Oxford University Press, 1989.

Waetjen, Herman C. *The Gospel of the Beloved Disciple: A Work in Two Editions.* New York: T&T Clark, 2005.

Walker, N. "Fourth Gospel Authorship." Pages 599–603 in *Studia evangelica VI: Papers Presented to the Fourth International Congress on New Testament Studies Held at Oxford, 1969.* Edited by E. A. Livingstone. Berlin: Akademie-Verlag, 1973.

Watson, Francis. "Beyond Suspicion: On the Authorship of the Mar Saba Letter and the Secret Gospel of Mark." *Journal of Theological Studies* 61 (2010): 128–70.

Welburn, Andrew J. *The Beginnings of Christianity: Essene Mystery, Gnostic Revelation and the Christian Vision.* Edinburgh: Floris Books, 1991.

———. *The Book with Fourteen Seals: The Prophet Zarathustra and the Christ-Revelation.* London: Rudolf Steiner Press, 1991.

———. *From a Virgin Womb: The Apocalypse of Adam and the Virgin Birth.* Leiden: Brill, 2008.

———. "The Identity of the Archons in the 'Apocryphon Johannis.'" *Vigiliae christianae* 32 (1978): 241–54.

———. "Iranian Prophetology and the Birth of the Messiah: The Apocalypse of Adam." *Aufstieg und Niedergang der römischen Welt* II.25.6:4752–94. Edited by H. Temporini and W. Haase. New York: de Gruyter, 1988.

WGBH Educational Foundation. "Emergence of the Four Gospel Canon." From Jesus to Christ: The First Christians, http://www.pbs.org/wgbh/pages/frontline/shows/religion/story/emergence.html.

Whiston, William, trans. *The Works of Josephus.* Peabody, Mass.: Hendrickson, 1987.

Winckler, Hugo. *Die babylonische Kultur in ihren Beziehungen zur Unsrigen: Ein Vortrag,* 36. Leipzig: J. C. Hinrichs, 1902. Quoted in Robert Powell, *Hermetic Astrology* (2 vols.; Kinsau, West Germany: Hermetika, 1987), 1:56.

Witherington, Ben, III. "The Historical Figure of the Beloved Disciple in the Fourth Gospel." Paper presented at the annual meeting of the SBL. Washington, D.C., November 20, 2006, http://benwitherington. blogspot.com/2007/01/was-lazarus-beloved-disciple.html.

———. "The Last Man Standing." *Biblical Archaeology Review* 32, no. 2 (March/April 2006): 24–25, 76.

———. *Revelation.* Cambridge: Cambridge University Press, 2003.

Witherington, Ben, III, and Ann Witherington. *The Lazarus Effect: A Novel.* Eugene, Oreg.: Pickwick, 2008.

Yogananda, Paramahansa. *Autobiography of a Yogi.* Los Angeles: Self-Realization Fellowship, 1972.

Index of Modern Authors

Index of Subjects

Aaron: 143

Abel: 101

Abraham: 63–64, 109, 140, 161, 195, 196, 200, 201, 205

Adam: 50, 77, 80, 83, 84, 97, 99–101, 103, 112, 114, 185, 191–92, 205

aeons: 83, 84–85, 96–99, 101, 102

Ahab and Jezebel: 113, 143

Ahriman: 103, 200

Ahura Mazda: 81, 114n186, 200, 205n374

air: 47, 66, 101, 107n171, 188–89, 190

Alexander Jannaeus: 117

Alexandria: 1, 12–13, 115, 156, 164, 209, 214, 231, 242

allegory: 5–6, 55n89, 186, 195, 209, 252

Ananda (disciple of the Buddha): 128

ancient mysteries: 3, 24, 29–34, 37–46, 47, 52–53, 54, 57–60, 72, 74, 81, 90, 102, 108, 110, 207; antiquity of, 29, 105, 121; Christianity rooted in, 31–32, 38; decadence of, 30–31, 32, 33–34, 52, 85–86, 95, 102, 108; relation to anthroposophy, 33, 39, 57; secrecy in, 39–40, 59, 73–74, 122–23; suffering in, 53–54. *See also* ancient temple sleep, mystery religions

ancient temple sleep: 51–53, 55–60, 62, 63–64, 67, 68, 72, 73–74, 109, 138, 152

Andrew, brother of Peter: 61n96, 129, 240

androgyny: 78n127, 84, 88, 93, 97, 191

anonymous disciples in John: 61n96, 129, 136–37, 143. *See also* beloved disciple

Anthroposophical Society: 35, 39n71

Apollos: 129

Apostles' Creed: 177

Aquinas: 182

archai: 101, 103, 198

archons: 84, 89, 91, 98–101

Arjuna: 79–80, 128

astral body: 43–45, 48, 51–52, 103n164, 110–11, 140, 183–85, 188, 191, 194–95, 202; during temple sleep, 58–59; and human nervous system, 80; infected by the fall, 103, 112n179, 141, 150, 201, 205; like inverted tree, 79, 80; symbolized by Zophar, 151; as tree of knowledge, 78, 205; withdraws during sleep, 45–46, 48, 58

astral body of Christ: 142–43, 148, 149, 173–74, 176, 206n375; as Virgin Sophia, 172, 174; symbolized by white robe, 173

astral realms: 42n75

astrology: 195–98, 199n356

Atlantean Epoch: 78, 110, 185, 187, 192–95

Atlantis: 31n54, 93, 105, 110, 191; destruction of, 193–94, 195 *atma*: 183

atonement: 141

Augustine: 105, 124, 168–69, 172

authorities: 91, 98, 99, 181, 190.
    See also exousiai, elohim

avatars: 81, 112n179, 114n187.
    See also Melchizedek

Balaam and Balak: 199

baptism: 23–25, 27, 46–52,
    84, 209–11; by fire, 46–47;
    performed by Paul, 23–24, 46;
    performed by John the Baptist,
    47–52. *See also* Bethany beyond
    the Jordan

baptism of Jesus by John the Baptist:
    25, 112, 114, 142, 152, 177,
    203, 205, 206

beloved disciple: 54, 120, 121, 125,
    128–39, 143, 154, 168–69, 175,
    240; as author of John, 121–22,
    131–32, 145, 147; as disciple of
    the Baptist, 61n96, 138; as most
    deeply initiated pupil, 127–28,
    137–38, 154, 167; real person or
    fictitious, 118–19, 120, 128, 129.
    See also Lazarus

Benjamin: 129

Bethany beyond the Jordan: 14, 212,
    224–25

Bethany (near Jerusalem): 53, 69, 73,
    134, 135, 224

Bhagavad Gita: 79–80, 128

Biblical Archaeology Review: 22, 225,
    256, 259–60, 262n499, 264

biblical scholars, academic: 4–6; and
    loss of faith, 21–22

blood: 65, 153, 166, 195; dwelling
    place of "I Am," 44, 201

blood love: 153; through group Ego,
    201

blood of Christ: 26, 48, 50, 52, 67,
    78, 112n179, 141, 178

booth, symbolism of: 67

born again: 47

Buddha: 77, 128n215, 173n325

budhi: 183

burden of proof: 214–15, 216–19,
    220–21, 222, 262–63, 265

burning bush: 43, 112n179, 150, 201

Cain: 80, 101, 150

Carpocrates: 1, 13, 25, 156, 250

Carpocratians: 1, 11–13, 24, 227,
    236, 242

Cerinthus: 159

Christ event: 31n54, 37, 40, 47–48,
    52, 87, 193, 207. *See also* Mystery
    of Golgotha, turning point of time

Christ impulse: 37

Christ Spirit: 63, 86, 113, 152, 173,
    203, 206; descent to earth, 86,
    200, 202, 203, 204, 205n374,
    206, 207; departure from Jesus,
    158–59, 170, 172; descent into
    hell, 177–78; escaped death,
    177–78; as highest avatar, 81

Christianity as Mystical Fact: 37–39,
    54, 122, 123–24, 170, 171n319

circumstantial evidence: 17, 222,
    263. *See also* burden of proof

Clement of Alexandria: 1, 5, 11, 19,
    26, 30n52, 38–39, 54, 55n89,
    85, 105, 156, 157, 160–62, 196,
    210–11, 215, 219, 220, 221,
    227–28, 230–32, 236, 241–43,
    249–51, 252–55, 262–63

clues of a hoaxer: 219–20, 225,
    231n429, 235–37, 244–52,
    263–64. *See also* Goldsmith clue,
    Madiotes, Morton Salt

coincidences: 264–65

Conditions of Consciousness:
    179–80, 182–84, 186–90, 195.
    See also Earth Condition of
    Consciousness, Earth evolution

Index of Scriptures Cited

CPSIA information can be obtained at www.ICGtesting.com
Printed in the USA
BVOW050358300911

272343BV00003B/5/P